AN INTRODUCTION TO NEW TESTAMENT CHRISTOLOGY

BY

Raymond E. Brown, S.S.

PAULIST PRESS
New York/Mahwah

Cover design by Tim McKeen. The figure of Christ is a detail of an early Christian mosaic of Christ and the Virgin from the apse of S. Maria in Trastevere, Rome. Courtesy Scala/Art Resource, NY.

Nihil obstat
Myles M. Bourke, S.T.D., S.S.L.
Censor deputatus
Imprimatur
✠Patrick J. Sheridan, D.D.
Vicar General, Archdiocese of New York
February 7, 1994

The *nihil obstat* and *imprimatur* are official declarations that a book or pamphlet is free of doctrinal or moral error. No implication is contained therein that those who have granted the *nihil obstat* and *imprimatur* agree with the contents, opinions, or statements expressed.

Library of Congress Cataloging-in-Publication Data

Brown, Raymond Edward.
    An introduction to New Testament Christology/by Raymond E. Brown.
        p. cm.
    Includes bibliographical references and indexes.
    ISBN 0-8091-3516-7 (paper); 0-8091-0469-5 (cloth)
        1. Jesus Christ—Person and offices—Biblical teaching. 2. Bible. N.T.—Theology. 3. Bible. N.T.—Criticism, interpretation, etc.
    I. Title.
    BT198.B827   1994
    232'.09'015—dc20   94-14569
                                                                    CIP

Published by Paulist Press
997 Macarthur Blvd.
Mahwah, N.J. 07430

Printed and bound in the United States of America

To

my Fellow Priests in the Society of St. Sulpice (S.S.)

in gratitude

for support, friendship, and encouragement

FOREWORD

"Who do people say that I am?" is a question associated with Jesus as early as the first Gospel to be written. In that Gospel it produced a variety of answers (Mark 8:27–33), including one volunteered but poorly understood by Peter, his best known follower. The question has produced a variety of answers ever since, and in our own times books evaluating Jesus philosophically, theologically, or biblically may average a half dozen a year. Many of the biblical studies are of frightening complexity as scholars debate the meaning and origin of every pertinent verse or half-verse of the New Testament (henceforth NT). In this book I have no intention of engaging in the details of those technical debates or of proposing new solutions (or, a fortiori, of discussing modern christologies), for I am not writing a contribution to be read primarily by scholars. There is no attempt to cover exhaustively the abundant literature on christology, biblical or theological; bibliography will be kept to a practical minimum and confined to works in English. The book is addressed to a broad range of people interested in the Bible, whether they read it by themselves or are enrolled in study groups, college courses, or a beginning theology program. My goal is to enable all such readers to understand the issues and why there is a debate, and thus to gain the biblical background to read further and reflect with discrimination on modern proposals. Inevitably some sections of it will be more difficult than others—I think particularly of Chapter 4 and APPENDIX III with their treatment of individual passages—but, conscious of that, I have made it possible to follow the general argument of the book if one chooses to skip those difficult sections. In short and emphatically, this book is introductory.

Over the years beginning with one of my first books, *Jesus God and Man* (1967) and continuing through articles in the *New Jerome*

Biblical Commentary (1990), I have dealt with the Jesus question again and again from different angles. I am a Christian whose profession of faith contains the proclamation of Jesus as "true God and true man." Nevertheless, I recognize that this formulation of the 4th century goes beyond what is stated explicitly in the NT; and so, on the principle that there should not be a dichotomy between belief and careful biblical scholarship, I have sought to work back to the presentation of Jesus in the earliest period of Christianity. How much did he know? What self-awareness did he manifest? How did his followers reflect on him and grow in their understanding? How is what emerges from a study of Jesus in the NT related to later church formulations about him? I now bring together much of what I have written, thought, and studied in response to those questions. I have done this not by reprinting essays but by thoroughly rephrasing, expanding, and rearranging previous thoughts and combining them with new insights to constitute what I hope will serve as an intelligible introduction to the way Jesus was understood in the NT, i. e., NT christology. Teachers in both the biblical and theological fields should be able to build on it as a background book as they go on to present their own views.

Besides imparting knowledge, this study has a pastoral goal. Christian believers whose spiritual lives should be shaped by the Master, if they have not wrestled in some mature way with the identity of Jesus, are in danger of constructing a fictional Jesus and attempting to get guidance from him. Also, no matter what they have heard, they should be offered the opportunity to see that a nonliteralistic approach to the NT does not necessarily destroy or undermine classic Christian beliefs. Those who do not accept Christian claims about Jesus cannot afford to be simplistically skeptical or to dismiss those claims out of hand as if they were based on a "fundamentalist" or uncritically literalistic reading of the evidence. If non-Christians have never spent even a few hours studying Jesus' identity, they are depriving themselves of a basic insight into why the lives of so many people have been influenced by the belief that he is the Messiah of God. By its coverage may this book be of service to both groups.

Christmas 1993

TABLE OF CONTENTS

(A more detailed table of contents for the longest division of the Book, namely Part II, is supplied on pages 19–21 below, marking the beginning of that division).

ABBREVIATIONS

Ant.	The *Antiquities* of Flavius Josephus
BBM	R. E. Brown, *The Birth of the Messiah* (new updated edition; New York: Doubleday, 1993)
BBRC	R. E. Brown, *Biblical Reflections on Crises Facing the Church* (New York: Paulist, 1975)
BCBD	R. E. Brown, *The Community of the Beloved Disciple* (New York: Paulist, 1979)
BDM	R. E. Brown, *The Death of the Messiah* (2 vols.; New York: Doubleday, 1994)
BGJ	R. E. Brown, *The Gospel According to John* (2 vols.; Anchor Bible 29, 29A; Garden City, NY: Doubleday, 1966, 1970)
BJGM	R. E. Brown, *Jesus God and Man* (Milwaukee: Bruce, 1967)
BRTOQ	R. E. Brown, *Responses to 101 Questions on the Bible* (New York: Paulist, 1990)
CBQ	*Catholic Biblical Quarterly*
DBS	H. Denzinger and C. Bannwart, *Enchiridion Symbolorum*, rev. by A. Schönmetzer (32d ed.; Freiburg: Herder, 1963)—Refs. to sections
FAWA	J. A. Fitzmyer, *A Wandering Aramean* (SBL Monograph Series 25; Missoula, MT: Scholars, 1979)
FJTJ	*From Jesus to John*, ed. M. de Boer (M. de Jonge Festschrift; JSNT Supplement 84; Sheffield: JSOT, 1993)
ff.	The verses *following* the one cited
JSNT	*Journal for the Study of the New Testament*
JTS	*Journal of Theological Studies*
Matt	The Gospel According to Matthew and/or its author
ms., mss.	manuscript, manuscripts

MTC   B. M. Metzger, *A Textual Commentary on the Greek New Testament* (London/New York: United Bible Societies, 1971)

NJBC   *The New Jerome Biblical Quarterly*, eds. R. E. Brown, J. A. Fitzmyer, and R. E. Murphy (Englewood Cliffs, NJ: Prentice Hall, 1990)—Refs. to articles and sections (§).

NPNF   Collection of Nicene and Post-Nicene Fathers (in English translation)

NT   New Testament

NTS   *New Testament Studies*

OT   Old Testament

par.   parallel(s) in one or more of the other Gospels to the passage cited

PG   Patrologia Graeca-Latina (Migne)

PL   Patrologia Latina (Migne)

Q   *Quelle* or source for material shared by Matthew and Luke but absent from Mark

SBL   Society of Biblical Literature

SBT   Studies in Biblical Theology

TS   *Theological Studies*

PART I

The Meaning of Christology
and
Different Approaches to It

CHAPTER 1.
WHAT IS MEANT BY
"CHRISTOLOGY"?

Very quickly the followers of Jesus acknowledged him to be the Messiah, i.e., the "anointed" one—specifically, the expected anointed king of David's royal line.[1] The Greek for "Messiah" is *Christos*, whence "Christ." Messiah or Christ was such a common evaluation of Jesus that, whether in the combination "Jesus Christ" or by itself, "Christ" quickly became equivalent to a personal name. In its most literal sense, then, "christology" would discuss how Jesus came to be called the Messiah or Christ and what was meant by that designation. There are, however, in the NT many other evaluations of Jesus: Rabbi (Teacher), Prophet, High Priest, Savior, Master or Lord,[2] the Son, Son of Man, Son of God, and even God.[3] In a broader sense, therefore, "christology" discusses any evaluation of Jesus in respect to who he was and the role he played in the divine plan—and this is the way the term shall be used henceforth.

---

[1] APPENDIX I explains the origin of this expectation and how it developed over a thousand years.

[2] The Greek *kyrios* covers the meanings "Sir," "Master," and "Lord"; and sometimes when the evangelist, who believes that Jesus is Lord, reports a conversation, it is difficult to know whether his faith colors the title given to Jesus by someone who in the story-line has just met him. For example, John 20:28, "My Lord [*kyrios*] and My God," represents the faith that the evangelist wishes his readers to share. Granted that wish, what is meant when in 4:11 the Samaritan woman (who clearly does not understand who Jesus is) calls him *kyrios*? Should we translate it as "Sir" or "Master" or "Lord"?

[3] The issue of whether the NT calls Jesus "God" will be discussed in APPENDIX III below.

Scholars distinguish different kinds of christology. "Low christology" covers the evaluation of him in terms that do not *necessarily* include divinity, e.g., Messiah, Rabbi, Prophet, High Priest, Savior, Master. "High christology" covers the evaluation of Jesus in terms that include *an aspect of* divinity, e.g., Lord, Son of God, God.

These descriptions are phrased carefully (note the italicizations). I have put "necessarily" in the description of low christology because I am making no judgment that the NT writers who used low-christology terminology did not believe in Jesus' divinity. (Indeed, every NT writer may have believed in the divinity of Jesus, for none denies it; yet several do not use terminology or descriptions that enable us to know with precision their christological stance.) Sometimes in different passages the same writer uses of Jesus terms reflecting respectively high and low christology. For instance, Luke 1:35 and 3:22 have an angel and a heavenly voice proclaim that Jesus is the Son of God; yet Luke 7:16 does not hesitate to report that, after Jesus resuscitated the son of the widow of Nain, all glorified God saying, "A great prophet has arisen among us."

In describing high christology I have spoken of "an aspect of" divinity; for while terms listed there place Jesus in the divine sphere, neither the terms themselves nor the authors who use them necessarily convey the same understanding of divinity. There are a wide range of conceivable possibilities in understanding the degree or manner of Jesus' divinity. As to *degree*, theoretically Jesus could be seen as divine but as lesser than other divine figures who were not human, e.g., than angels who were known in the OT as "sons of God." Or Jesus could be deemed equal in divinity to "the one true God" who sent him (see John 17:3). As to *manner*, theoretically Jesus could have been a man who was deified at a point in his career—"made divine," for instance, at his baptism when the Spirit of God descended on him, or at his resurrection when God elevated him to heaven. Or he could have been divine all through his life in the sense that he was conceived as a divine being without a human father. Or he could have been a deity before he took on flesh. And even in that last possibility he could have been brought into being by God the Father as the first born of all creation (see Col 1:15), or he could have been uncreated and with the Father forever. Classical or orthodox Christian faith, articulated in the 4th century, tells us

that Jesus as Son was equal to God the Father in all things and existed from all eternity; but that articulation does not tell us how
many 1st-century NT authors, if any, had reached that precision.[4] A
description of Jesus as "Son of God," after all, would have been
applicable to him understood in any of the degrees or manners just
mentioned. Indeed, when we recognize that the books that make up
the NT were written in different places in the Mediterranean world
during a period of almost 100 years (*ca.* 50 to 125), more than likely
even the high christological terms meant different things to different
people who used them.

A basic step in any serious discussion of christology is to appreciate that Christian religious thought, since it involved the comprehension of Jesus by human beings, developed and changed, as does
other human thought. True, Christians maintain that there was divine revelation about the identity of Jesus, but that does not mean
that believers understood the revelation completely or at once. The
classic passage where Matthew reports that Simon Peter could confess that Jesus was the Messiah, the Son of the living God, because it
was revealed to him by Jesus' Father in heaven (16:16–17), also
shows clearly that Peter did not understand essential aspects of that
confession (16:22–23).

---

[4] In conventional Christian thought a conciliar formulation of dogma cannot
contradict the NT; but it may have gone beyond what was clearly articulated or visibly
understood in NT times, precisely because questions were now being asked that had
not been asked in earlier times.

CHAPTER 2.
VARIOUS APPROACHES
TO NEW TESTAMENT CHRISTOLOGY

In Parts II and III of this book I shall discuss respectively Jesus' own christology (by presenting the evidence of how he manifested and evaluated his relation to God) and the christology of NT Christians (by presenting the evidence of how those who believed in Jesus evaluated him). The observations that close the preceding chapter raise the issue of the extent to which those two christologies agree. To what extent did what his followers said and thought about him correspond to the image reflected in what he himself said and did? Conscious or unconscious answers to that question have resulted in different approaches to NT christology. A survey of those approaches[5] offers a useful entree into the basic problem of NT christology. Included will be views both scholarly and "nonscholarly,"[6] i.e., not only outlooks in circulation among scholars but

---

[5] The goal and level of this book would make it counterproductive to give more than very general classifications. One could make many subdivisions representing different nuances under each of the scholarly approaches I shall describe. In NJBC 81, §§4–9, I offered an abbreviated form of what I have written here.

[6] Nothing pejorative is intended by this descriptive classification, especially as to whether the views expressed are plausible or intelligent (scholarly views are not necessarily correct or truly intelligent). As for "nonscholars," I refer to those who are not scholars in the biblical field; often, of course, they may be well educated or even scholars in other fields. It should be noted, however, that occasionally people who would be the first to acknowledge that their own field of expertise is complicated and requires nuance will assume that discerning issues about religion, the Bible, or Jesus ought to be simple.

also outlooks current among many Christians even if not defended by publishing scholars.

(A) Nonscholarly Conservatism

This view would identify the christology of NT writings with the christology of Jesus himself. Even though the Gospels were written some 30 to 70 years after the ministry of Jesus, they are assumed to be verbatim accounts of what was said in Jesus' lifetime. Accordingly this conservatism posits that there was no significant christological development in the NT. Please note that the issue is one of *recognizing* development or difference. Another issue is whether that difference is radical and represents discontinuity. Those whom we shall describe here allow for no real difference; those who are described below as moderate conservatives allow for difference but not discontinuity.

Let me give an example. In Matt 16:13–20 Jesus acknowledges enthusiastically Peter's confession that he is the Messiah, the Son of the living God. Nonscholarly conservatism would accept that as a direct historical reminiscence from Jesus' ministry and offer it as the explanation of why later Christians called him the Son of God.[7] Again, John 8:58 and 17:5, in which Jesus speaks as a preexistent divine figure and describes the existence he had before Abraham or even before the world began, would be treated as historical statements that enabled John to write as the opening of his Gospel: "In the beginning was the Word . . . and the Word was God."[8] A simple

---

[7] To anticipate later discussion, scholars who disagree would point to the fact that in Mark 8:27–30 (held by most to be earlier) Peter's confession and Jesus' reaction are significantly different. One could suggest that there was a tradition from Jesus' ministry wherein Peter confessed Jesus as the Messiah but showed also that he had an inadequate grasp of the conflict between triumphalistic aspects in messianic expectations and Jesus' self-understanding of his role. In the light of postresurrectional christological insight Matthew would have expanded the tradition of Peter's confession to the point that it could express what was regarded as a true understanding of Jesus' Messiahship—an understanding that in fact Peter eventually proclaimed after the resurrection.

[8] Scholars who disagree would object that there is no indication of such knowledge of preexistence in Mark, Matt, or Luke.

conservatism may with rare exception be said to have been the over-all view of Christians until the 1700s, for before that not even commentators and preachers recognized the profound problems inherent in presuppositions about verbatim Gospel reporting. But this changed with the advent of the historical criticism of the NT.[9] This critique made the vast majority of scholars aware that differences existed both among NT writers and between their outlook and that of the earlier era in which Jesus lived.

Over against such changes in scholarship the "nonscholarly conservatism" of the last two centuries has continued with varying nuances. On the one hand, scholars of Protestant upbringing were the most prominent advocates of biblical criticism; and some of them used it to challenge traditional Christian beliefs, even denying the divinity of Jesus. Many churchgoing Protestant believers reacted hostilely to the scholars' views which they regarded as destructive of Christianity; and in order to protect the "fundamentals" of Christian faith[10] they rejected biblical criticism itself, not merely a radical use of it. Consequently some Protestant "nonscholarly conservatism" became consciously defensive. For the most part, on the other hand, Catholic scholars were slow to accept the more trenchant forms of biblical criticism; and some of those who were imprudently adventurous were condemned by the church authorities at Rome in the antiModernist atmosphere of the early 1900s. Because of this cautious church control, ordinary Catholics were not even aware that there could be differences between Jesus in his lifetime and Jesus as described in the NT writings. Their conservatism on this and other biblical questions was all-pervasive, but not defensive. Catho-

---

[9] It may be worth pointing out that the common use of "criticism" in reference to study of the Bible does not imply being critical or negative toward the Bible. It means submitting the Bible to the same kind of critique or detailed analysis that any other book would be subject to—for instance, recognizing differences among its authors and asking how much they knew, where they got their material, and what kind of book they intended to write. Some of the scholars who first began to apply such a critique did not believe that God had inspired the Bible, but many who believed in inspiration also came to recognize the validity and importance of this critique or criticism. God's inspiration does not change the fact that every word in the Bible was written by a human being in reference to whom such questions are appropriate.

[10] As I pointed out in BRTOQ 43, this explains the name "fundamentalism" applied to the more extreme forms of this movement.

lic Modernism with its excesses was crushed before it had gained much following, and for all practical purposes there was no liberal biblical teaching within Catholicism to defend against. However, the Roman Catholic Church began to change its position toward biblical criticism under Pope Pius XII in the 1940s and to encourage an intelligent use of it. By the 1960s official church teaching affirmed that the Gospels were not necessarily literal accounts of the words and deeds of Jesus.[11] Such an affirmation should have prepared Catholics to understand the basic christological issue that there could be a difference between Jesus' self-presentation and the affirmations made of him by the NT writers. Yet this change of teaching has not been successfully communicated to the Catholic public at large; and so nonscholarly conservatism still prevails (but also still in a nondefensive way[12]). Most churchgoing Catholics are not yet aware of any other view, even though now almost all Catholic biblical scholars (see below) have accepted that the Gospels manifest a development beyond the era of Jesus and for years have taught such a development to candidates for the priesthood or theological degrees.[13]

---

[11] I refer to the Roman Pontifical Biblical Commission's "Instruction on the Historical Truth of the Gospels" (1964), the crucial paragraphs of which are published in BBRC 111–15; see also NJBC 72, §35. The substance of this instruction was taken over into Vatican II's "Dogmatic Constitution on Divine Revelation" (*Dei Verbum* 5.19). The history of the development of Catholic biblical thought in the last 100 years is summarized in NJBC 72, §§3–9.

[12] By way of exception, a very small group of Catholics has adamantly resisted all the changes in the Church's biblical views since the 1940s, explaining them away as misinterpretations advocated by "new Modernists" and even dismissing statements made by the secretary of the Roman Pontifical Biblical Commission. They express their opinions in a few polemically partisan newspapers and magazines that have also made intemperate attacks on the Catholic hierarchy whom they regard as overly liberal!

[13] One may intelligently wonder why, if seminarians are not taught a simplistic conservatism about the NT, they do not communicate more nuanced views in their preaching. A common excuse for this failure is that anything more complex and nuanced might disturb the people—now an increasingly specious explanation when far more Catholics receive college education and might be encouraged if they found out that their church, once a danger has passed, is capable of changing its mind in face of evidence. Probably a major factor is that to communicate nuanced biblical views in a way that people will find constructive (rather than puzzling or disturbing) requires

(B) Nonscholarly Liberalism

At the opposite end of the spectrum is the view that there is no continuity between Jesus' self-evaluation and the exalted christology of the NT documents. Such liberalism dismisses NT christology as unimportant or as a distortion, and has often been closely associated with the thesis that Jesus was just an ethical instructor or social reformer who was mistakenly proclaimed to be divine by overenthusiastic or confused followers (with Paul sometimes seen as the chief instigator). We shall see below that there are scholars who hold radically liberal views (with many different nuances), but I am speaking here of those who have heard that "scholars are saying such things" and have adopted them without any significant research of their own—the "nobody believes that anymore" approach. Already in the late 18th century the influence of the English Deists and the French Encyclopedists moved some to distrust the Gospel stories of Jesus' miracles and resurrection because these stories favor Jesus' divinity. Seemingly on the basis of his own instincts, no less a figure than Thomas Jefferson produced a NT from which highly christological sections had been eliminated! In current times nonscholarly liberalism is sometimes fueled by tendentious reports of the "latest" discoveries, e.g., that the Dead Sea Scrolls show that the Jesus of the NT was only a pale imitation of the Teacher of that group, or that apocryphal Gospels discovered in Egypt show that the earliest Christians were mostly fantasists who invented incredible stories about Jesus. That such reports are rejected by the vast majority of NT scholars does little to dent the aura of sophistication in which popular christological liberalism wraps itself.

I shall now turn to scholarly approaches to NT christology that, whether right or wrong, have to be considered seriously because they have been defended with knowledgeable arguments drawn from the text of the NT. Yet the preceding paragraphs are a sobering reminder that most people answer the question of the identity of Jesus without any real struggle to gain precision about what the NT says.

---

more effort and imagination than many preachers are willing to expend. The bland is often effortless and survives even when the church teaches the contrary.

On the conservative side, as I have explained, many Protestants reflect the reaction of an earlier generation to the destructive aspects of radical biblical criticism; and most Catholics remain unaware that their church and its scholars have moved beyond views taught in catechism in the first part of the 20th century. On the liberal side, there is a tendency to invoke what the latest scholars are supposedly saying, according to reports in the media. Despite the differences among scholars I shall describe below, their efforts pay tribute to the truth that christology is so important an issue for religious adherence that one should not express judgments without seriously looking at the evidence.

(C) Scholarly Liberalism

This differs from nonscholarly liberalism in several important ways. It recognizes that the NT is shot through with christology from beginning to end and that its authors claimed far more than that Jesus was a moralizer or a social reformer. Nevertheless, as the classification "liberalism" implies, it does not accept the high christological evaluations of Jesus in the NT as standing in real continuity with his self-evaluation. In short, high christological evaluations are regarded as mistaken.[14] In advocating this position, scholarly liberals have traced the "creative" process in NT christology with careful methodology; and we owe to them some of the first detailed schemas of the development of NT thought. They stressed the possibility of tracking the growth of distinctive theological viewpoints from the

---

[14] Somewhere in between nonscholarly liberalism and scholarly liberalism is the view of those who have read scholarly liberal works (the weaknesses of which they do not subject to sufficient criticism) but whose view of Jesus is really determined more by their reaction to the suffocating fundamentalism in which they were raised. I would consider the Episcopal bishop J. S. Spong an example of this. In *Born of a Woman* (San Francisco: Harper, 1992), 36–40, he presents a Jesus who was not of divine origin, but a gifted, humble, generous, and self-giving human being whose friends certainly did not understand him as a messiah. Yet they underwent an Easter experience or internal realization that enabled them to see patterns of total dependence on God in Jesus so that his life reflected God's life. In BBM 704 I expressed this judgment: "I do not think a single NT author would recognize Spong's Jesus as the figure being proclaimed or written about."

Palestinian communities of Semitic-speaking[15] Jewish Christians, through the Syrian communities of Greek-speaking Jewish Christians, to the Greek-speaking Gentile Christians of the churches of Asia Minor and Greece, and finally to communities influenced by individual geniuses such as Paul and John. By the late 19th century, scholarship thought it had the linguistic and historical data necessary for detecting with reasonable accuracy both the individual phases of Christian development and the terminology used in each phase to describe Jesus.[16]

In addition, this was the era of great enthusiasm for comparative religion. Liberal interpreters of the NT claimed to find in Greco-Roman religious mythology the key to terminology and imagery applied to Jesus, e.g., in the myth of an older god like Zeus mating with a woman and begetting a divine son could be found the explanation of Jesus portrayed as God's Son conceived without a human father; or in the myth of the dying and rising god of vegetation, the explanation of Jesus' resurrection from the dead. A frequent claim in liberal analyses of developing christology would be that titles such as Lord and Son of God were applied to Jesus in a divine sense only in the Christian mission to Greek-speaking Gentiles—either they did not exist at an earlier Jewish-Christian stage or were used in a much humbler sense of master and Messiah (anointed king).[17] This specu-

---

[15] Usually assumed to be Aramaic-speaking, but the possibility of their being Hebrew-speaking cannot be ruled out; and some Jewish Christians might speak both languages. Aramaic was a widely used language with many very different dialects, but the Aramaic spoken in Palestine would have been about as close to Hebrew as Italian is to Spanish.

[16] A classic embodiment of the liberal method and the christology it produced was *Kyrios Christos* by W. Bousset, which appeared in German in 1913. (The publishing of an English translation in 1970 [Nashville: Abingdon] testifies to the ongoing attraction of this type of christology.) Consult NJBC 70, §§39–41. However, 20th-century discoveries actually overthrew some of the 19th-century hypotheses, as we shall see.

[17] Footnote 2 above explains how *kyrios* can mean both master and Lord. As for "Son of God," the promise of the prophet Nathan to King David that his dynasty would continue has God saying of David's son(s), "I will be his father, and he shall be my son" (II Sam 7:14). Therefore, theoretically "God's son" could have been a designation for any anointed king of the House of David and thus of the Messiah, without a sense of that figure being divine. As we now know, however, the liberal deductions based on such observations are too simple. J. A. Fitzmyer in a series of

lation gave the impression of a linear development toward a "higher christology," i.e., toward a christology which utilized titles more clearly evocative of divinity. This linear development would have moved from the Jewish world to the Hellenistic world, from an early period in the 1st century to a later period. The invented high christology was often treated as a *felix culpa* because only through such divinizing was the memory of Jesus preserved. The historical Jesus was, in fact, a preacher of stark ethical demand who challenged the religious institutions and the false ideas of his time. His ideals and insights were not lost because the community imposed on its memory of him a christology that turned him into the heavenly Son of Man, the Lord and Judge of the world—indeed, into a God. Without that aggrandizement he and his message would have been forgotten. But if in centuries past such a christological crutch was necessary to keep the memory of Jesus operative, in the judgment of the liberal scholars that crutch could now be discarded. Modern scholarship, it is claimed, can detect the real Jesus and hold onto him without the christological trappings. Different forms of scholarly liberalism have made an appearance throughout the 20th century: for example, in the early 1990s the writings of J. D. Crossan and B. Mack (p. 216 below), which use apocryphal gospels or a reconstructed Q to argue that the christological presentations of the canonical Gospels are largely fictitious.

(D) Bultmannian Existentialism

One era in which scholarly liberalism flourished antedated the First World War, a period marked by an enthusiasm for the achievements of modern technology in bringing a new and better way to live. The great war showed that humanity was more adept in learning a way to die and led to a new appreciation of the more traditional Christian emphasis on the need for salvation by God in Jesus. Spokesmen of this reaction included K. Barth in systematic theology and R. Bult-

---

articles (also NJBC 82, §§52–54) has argued convincingly that "Lord" as an exalted title goes back at least to the early Jerusalem Christian community—thus back beyond the Greek-speaking Gentile communities and not at a great distance from Jesus' own life. See footnote 117 below on "Son of God."

mann in NT study. Because Bultmann was radical in his approach to the NT, sometimes he has been erroneously described as liberal when in fact he rejected categorically the liberalism of the prewar period. Of course, he continued to accept the methodology developed by liberal scholars in classifying stages in the development of NT christology and indeed sought to refine the method more precisely. Bultmann remained almost agnostic about the relationship between NT christology and the self-evaluation of Jesus, but he did not think that christology distorted the import of Jesus. Rather, there was a functional equivalence between the NT christological proclamations and Jesus' proclamation of the kingdom of God. This functional equivalence was worked out in terms of an existentialism. Humanity needs to escape from the vicious circle of futile existence, and that can come only through the delivering action of God. Jesus came proclaiming that God was acting decisively in his own ministry and challenged people to accept this divine action. The church demanded that people accept Jesus as Messiah and Lord and by so doing was equivalently offering the same existential challenge that Jesus offered. For this reason it would be disastrous to dispense with the christology of the NT as liberals had advocated, because that would be tantamount to dispensing with the challenge that is the core of Christianity, a challenge based on what God has done for us rather than on what we can do for ourselves. Bultmann's greatest influence on christology was in the period from the 1920s to the 1950s.

(E) Scholarly (Moderate) Conservatism

In the third quarter of the 20th century there was a shift to a position more conservative than that of Bultmann in terms of a discernible continuity between the evaluation of Jesus during the ministry and the evaluation of him in NT writings. Some of the scholars listed below might be surprised to have themselves classified under conservatism; but when their positions are compared to those of liberalism and existentialism, that designation is not too inappropriate, for they posit a christology in the ministry of Jesus himself. They would be divided on whether that christology was explicit or implicit. Explicit christology would involve a self-evaluation in which Jesus employed titles or designations already known in Jewish circles. Implicit christology would relegate such titles and designations to early church usage but would attribute to Jesus himself attitudes and actions that implied an exalted status which was made explicit after his death. Among the earlier advocates of explicit christology one might list O. Cullmann, C. H. Dodd, J. Jeremias, V. Taylor, and many Roman Catholic writers in the pre-Vatican II period. Among those who tended toward implicit christology may be listed F. Hahn, R. H. Fuller, N. Perrin, and some of the postBultmannians in Germany.[18]

Explicit christology, which seemed to be fading, got new life in the late 20th century. "Son of Man" remains a title that many scholars think Jesus used of himself. "Messiah" remains a title that others may have used of him during his lifetime, whether or not he accepted the designation. The Qumran discoveries show that titles like Son of God and Lord were known in the Semitic-speaking Palestine of Jesus' time.[19] Moreover, the practice of assigning certain titles to specific post-Jesus stages in the geographical and temporal spread of Christianity is now seen to be too simple. Not all Jewish Christians had the same christology, and to a large extent Gentile Christian converts shared the view of Jesus conveyed by the Jewish missionaries who evangelized them. Thus instead of assigning low christology to Jewish Christians and high christology to Gentile Christians, one might well suspect that one group of Jewish Christians and their Gentile Christian converts manifested a lower christology than another group of Jewish Christians and their Gentile converts.[20]

This survey shows that scholarship has come to no universally accepted positions on the relationship of Jesus' christology to that of his followers, except that the extreme positions on either end of the spectrum (no difference, no continuity) have fewer and fewer advocates. Let us now turn to the texts of the NT that all have had to consider in their quest. My goal is to describe these passages rather than to force them into one of the approaches reported above.

---

[18] For more information on these scholars, see NJBC 70, §§30,57,61,63,64–70.

[19] Gospel passages pertinent to some of these titles will be discussed below in Chapter 7 under the rubric of whether Jesus affirmed that he was Messiah, Son of God, and/or Son of Man.

[20] On this point see R. E. Brown, "Not Jewish Christianity and Gentile Christianity but Types of Jewish/Gentile Christianity," CBQ 45 (1983), 74–79.

PART II

The Christology of Jesus

An attempt to discern how Jesus conceived
his relationship to God
and his place in God's plan
by reviewing Jesus' pertinent words and deeds.

DETAILED TABLE OF CONTENTS
FOR PART II

CHAPTER 3.
CAUTIONS ABOUT EXPECTATIONS AND PRESUPPOSITIONS

Although I have stated that my primary intention is to be descriptive in presenting the NT texts reflecting Jesus' attitude toward his role and what that attitude reveals about his identity, certain cautions are in order. By way of expectations, how helpful it would have been if the NT gave us a series of "I am . . . ." passages where Jesus stated a self-evaluation, e.g., I am only a prophet, or I am the Son of God, or I am God! Alas, in the first three Gospels one does not find simple examples of Jesus making "I am" statements with such a self-descriptive predicate. In John there are many "I am" statements but chiefly with a symbolic predicate: "I am the way . . . the truth . . . the life . . . the resurrection . . . the light of the world . . . the bread of life . . . the good shepherd . . . the vine." This shortage of recorded self-identifying statements by Jesus[21] may stem in part from the fact that the Gospels were written to tell people not what Jesus thought of himself but what they should think of Jesus, so that the christological statements or confessions are mostly made by others. In Matt 16:16 it is Simon Peter who says, "You are the Messiah, the Son of the living God"; in John 20:28 it is Thomas who says, "My Lord and My God." Thus, even though an inquiry may wish to be descriptive in presenting evidence about Jesus' own christology, the lack of direct statements by him on the subject

---

[21] Seeming exceptions to what I have said about the Gospels (e.g., Mark 14:61–62; John 4:25–26; 8:28; 10:36) will be discussed in Chapter 6 below.

23

forces us first[22] to survey his actions and his words on other subjects in an attempt *to discern* from them what he thought of himself and what he was doing. That involves making judgments of probability and possibility, and readers should be warned of dangers and uncertainties in such judgments.

Like most who study the NT intensively, I think that the sayings and deeds of Jesus reported in the Gospels have been influenced by hindsight after the resurrection. They have also picked up expansive interpretations in the course of being preached, as the traditions about Jesus were adapted to different audiences over a period of 30 to 70 years. At a final stage they were reorganized by the individual evangelists to fit into an overall view of Christ that each wished to present.[23] Therefore when one reads Gospel texts describing what Jesus said and did—texts that might cast light on his understanding of his role and identity—it is important to be aware that some of them reflect a later insight not yet achieved in the ministry of Jesus. Nevertheless, were I to dismiss significant texts on that score, I would be in danger of entering into a vicious circle of selecting only the texts I think historical and having them give a picture of Jesus that consciously or unconsciously I may have already decided on. I would then be slipping over from the descriptive to the highly judgmental. Therefore, it is better in an introductory book like this to treat significant texts and alert readers to what the import would be if Jesus actually said or did this, even though I may have to report that there is a good chance that a particular text reflects later insight. (In part, this cautious procedure reflects my uneasiness about the assurance with which scholars claim high accuracy in determining what Jesus did not say or do, as in media accounts that the controversial "Jesus Seminar" found approximately 82% of the words attributed to him in the Gospels to be inauthentic.[24]) That approach

---

[22] Chapters 4 and 5 below, before turning to Jesus' affirmations about himself in Chapter 6.

[23] Catholic readers should know that what I have just described is really a slight rephrasing of what the church document referred to in footnote 11 teaches as stages in the development of Gospel tradition.

[24] *Time* (Jan. 10, 1994) reported the results of this seminar study from *The Five Gospels*, eds. R. W. Funk and R. W. Hoover (New York: Macmillan, 1993). The

will help to keep the descriptive emphasis inclusive and encourage readers to think for themselves.

Thinking for oneself about Jesus is not easy, however, for we all have presuppositions that tend to color the NT picture. In AD 325 the Council of Nicaea solemnly defined the divinity of Jesus; in 451 the Council of Chalcedon solemnly defined his full humanity (in everything except sin). Since that time most Christians have affirmed that Jesus is true God and true man. But such an appreciation has never been easy to uphold evenly. God is by common understanding unlimited (omniscient, omnipotent, omnipresent, eternal, etc.); human beings are by nature limited. How then can one be divine and human at the same time? There has been a tendency to choose or favor one of these two components in Jesus' identity over the other. Let me illustrate that.

(A) Attitudes That Deny or Underplay the Divine in Jesus

Non-Christian religions, such as Judaism and Islam, on encountering the "true God, true man" dogma, have rejected the "true God" element. Beyond interreligious differences, that rejection is frequently articulated in scholarly circles in our own time, as philosophers, scientists, historians of religion, and biblical critics classify the divinity of Jesus as impossible or as popular legend. When the NT data pertinent to Jesus are judged against that background, inevitably elements that point to the supernatural or divine will be

---

seminar has taken votes on the authenticity of Jesus' sayings reported in the Gospels in this manner: red = he undoubtedly said this or something very much like it; pink = he said something like this; gray = the ideas are his even though he did not say this; black = he did not say this; it represents later or different tradition. See R. W. Funk, *Forum* 2 (#1; 1986), 54–55. In 1987 eleven Synoptic sayings wherein Jesus spoke about his future passion were all recommended to be voted black (J. R. Butts, *Forum* 3 [#3; 1987], 107ff.). In another set of votes the overwhelming majority voted that Jesus did not foretell his death in a way beyond the perceptive powers of one involved in dangerous times. A factor at the root of the issue was that most of the participants were unwilling to grant that Jesus spoke of his impending death by virtue of "superordinary" powers (M. J. Borg, *Forum* 3 [#2; 1987], 83–84). Historicity, however, should be determined not by what we think possible or likely, but by the antiquity and reliability of the evidence. As we shall see, as far back as we can trace, Jesus was known and remembered as one who had extraordinary powers.

dismissed as later accretions. Jesus could not have worked miracles, it is claimed, because miracles do not occur. Or if one allows that he might have healed people, he certainly could not have worked nature miracles such as multiplying loaves or stilling storms because they are obviously folkloric rather than truly of religious significance. Or again Jesus could not have foretold the future in any way that goes beyond intelligent guessing (see footnote 24 above). In what follows I shall give no attention to such a priori "could not have" approaches and ask simply how much evidence is there that he did or said such things.

A more subtle type of presupposition that tips the scale in favor of humanity without overtly emptying the divinity side is sometimes found among believers in Jesus. They contend that they know what it is to be human, and therefore if Jesus was truly man, he "must have" had certain experiences or developed in certain ways. When I was writing *Jesus God and Man* (BJGM 43), newspapers had recently reported these statements made by Roman Catholic theologians: "Jesus had to discover who he was. He was uncertain of his divine sonship; yet he never abandoned the quest for certainty" and "I'm sure that Jesus himself was not aware of being God." On a more popular level we are told that Jesus could not have been human without having had sexual temptations, or even without having had sexual relations with a woman companion (usually Mary Magdalene). Must he not have sinned if he was truly human? Faced with such "must have" affirmations which run a wide range, I shall follow the pedestrian route of demanding evidence in the NT—and there is not a single verse to support any of the affirmations I have just mentioned.[25] Indeed, in reference to Jesus sinning, NT affirmations directly contradict that (I Pet 2:22; Heb 4:15; John 8:46; I John 3:5).

(B) Attitudes That Limit the Humanity of Jesus

Readers who are believers in Jesus may praise my refusal to deal with "could not have" or "must have" suppositions without supporting NT evidence when those suppositions deny or depreciate

---

[25] The passage in Heb 4:15 that describes Jesus as a high priest "who in all things has been tested [*peirazein*] as we are, (but) without sin," has nothing to do with sexual temptation as the context shows. The testing is that, despite his being Son, he had to

Jesus' divinity. The refusal becomes more challenging when we look at the other side of the picture. Those who reject the divinity of Jesus have most often thought through their position and are clear about their denial. Those who have problems with the humanity of Jesus are often not even aware of their bias. Theoretically it is just as serious a deviation from Christian dogma to underplay the humanity of Jesus as to underplay his divinity;[26] but since opponents of Christianity deny the divinity, believing Christians are far more sensitive about limitations placed on the divinity than they are about limitations placed on the humanity. Realistically, it may well be that most Christians *tolerate* only as much humanity as they deem consonant with their view of the divinity. On the simplest level there are believers who transfer the picture of the glorified Jesus back into his public ministry, imagining him to have walked through Galilee with an aura about him, almost wearing a halo. They cannot visualize him as being like other men; and they are embarrassed by the Gospel vignettes of Jesus as sometimes tired, testy, indistinguishable in a crowd, treated as a fanatic and a rabble-rouser. The pervasiveness of this uneasiness becomes evident in the vociferous opposition to new translations of the Gospels that strip away the hallowed jargon of "Bible English" and have Jesus speak in an everyday manner. For example, there was protest about the irreverence of an early form of the *New American Bible* that literally and correctly rendered the contempt expressed by Jesus' *opponents* in referring to him as "that fellow"!

Let me illustrate the "could not have" or "must have" presuppositions that place limitations on Jesus' humanity. Hebrews 4:15 made a very important qualification about sin in the resemblance it finds between Jesus and other human beings: "We have a high priest not unable to sympathize with our weaknesses, but one who in all

---

learn obedience through suffering (5:8; also 2:18): In the days of his flesh he had to be brought to the point of crying out to the One who had the power to save him from death (5:7). This same anguish over suffering and death is called a testing in the accounts of Jesus' praying that the cup be taken from him in the Synoptic scene on the Mount of Olives on the night before he died.

[26] Pope Leo the Great, *Sermon 7 on the Nativity* (PL 54.216): It is as dangerous an evil to deny the truth of the human nature in Christ as to refuse to believe that his glory is equal to that of the Father.

things has been tested as we are, (yet) *without sin.*"[27] No other exception is made in Jesus' likeness to us; and so we might assume that Jesus was like us in having limited knowledge. A doctor of the church who was an undeniably orthodox defender of the oneness of person in Christ did not hesitate to state: "We have admired his goodness in that for love of us he has not refused to descend to such a low position as to bear all that belongs to our nature, included in which is ignorance."[28] Nevertheless, during the centuries a "must have" principle that is not found in Scripture took over the discussion: "One cannot deny to Christ any perfection that it was possible for him to have had." (That principle was carried to its extreme consequences in the claim of the theologians of the University of Salamanca[29] that among men Jesus must have been the greatest dialectician, philosopher, mathematician, doctor, politician, musician, orator, painter, farmer, sailor, soldier, etc.)

In terms of knowledge, since omniscience was esteemed as a perfection, the thesis gained ground that Jesus had to know all things. (One may legitimately debate, however, whether omniscience is a perfection *for human beings.*) The simplest form of argumentation supporting the thesis is that Jesus is God and God knows everything. Some with scholarly pretensions embellish the argument by stressing that the person is the subject of knowledge and there was only one person (the divine person) in Jesus. Yet the medieval schoolmen maintained that knowledge came through nature; and Jesus had two natures. In such scholastic thought God and human beings know in different ways: God's knowledge is immediate and nonconceptual; human knowledge is normally through abstraction and conceptual. Therefore, divine knowledge is not simply transferable to a human mind. Thomas Aquinas wrote:[30] "If there

---

[27] The Council of Chalcedon (DBS §301) made that same qualification: Jesus is "consubstantial with us according to humanity, similar to us in all things except sin."

[28] Cyril of Alexandria, PG 75.369. Clearly, then, "ignorance" is a permissible term and has only a limiting connotation, not a pejorative one. In modern polemics by ultraconservatives against the view that Jesus had limited knowledge, one can find the false claim that those who hold this view are claiming that Jesus was "ignorant"— a distorted rephrasing that *is* pejorative.

[29] Salmanticenses, *Cursus Theologicus*, tractatus XXI "De Incarnatione," disp. 22, dubium 2, n. 29.

[30] *Summa Theologiae* 3, q. 9, a. 1, ad 1.

had not been in the soul of Christ some other knowledge besides his divine knowledge, it would not have known anything. Divine knowledge cannot be an act of the human soul of Christ, it belongs to another nature." Thus the simplest form of the thesis that Jesus in his life functioned with a divine knowledge of all things is weak.

Yet in another approach to the problem Aquinas did posit special aids for the human nature of Jesus that would overcome limits on his knowledge: Jesus had the beatific vision (i.e., the vision of God that comes to others only after their dying in God's favor), as well as knowledge infused by God. Also a number of statements by Catholic Church authorities, none of them binding dogmatically, have favored the theory that Jesus had the beatific vision and unlimited knowledge.[31] In such an approach, if a Gospel passage suggests that Jesus did not know something or if he speaks in a way that today we know to have been inaccurate, he must have been accommodating himself to the prevalent way of thinking in his times and secretly have known better. Actually the theological climate has changed, and very prominent Roman Catholic theologians now allow for limitations in Jesus' knowledge. Some like K. Rahner, J. Galot, and J. Ratzinger do not insist on the beatific vision theory at least in its classic form. However, no matter where one stands in this theological debate, I think it important that we look at the NT evidence as it is without the "must have" element.

In opting for a descriptive approach to the NT evidence without embracing "cannot have" or "must have" presuppositions that stem from emphasizing one side of the "true God, true man" issue, I am not denying that proponents of such presuppositions have something to contribute to the overall christological picture. Objections raised by philosophers and scientists on one side and corollaries drawn by theologians on the other must be considered seriously, but they must not be allowed to determine what the NT reports. In

---

[31] See BJGM 40–41, footnotes 4,6. It is important to emphasize that there is no dogma of the church on the extent of Jesus' knowledge. As I emphasized in the NJBC 71, §§80–85, the church claims the right to interpret authoritatively what Scripture means for the life and faith of its people; but it has not entered authoritatively in historical questions such as the one we are asking: How much did Jesus know in his lifetime? The church would be concerned, however, that no answer be given to the question that denies the divinity of Jesus.

particular, even if those theologians who think that Jesus had to have unlimited knowledge (at least in religious matters) are right (which I doubt), that does not mean necessarily that people realized this in NT times or that the NT has to be read to support that. The judgment should be acknowledged as a theological conclusion rather than as a norm for discerning what NT authors conveyed about Jesus.[32] At times philosophers, scientists, theologians (and, yes, biblical critics) need to rethink religious judgments about Jesus; and biblical evidence makes its best contribution to that rethinking when presented with as few conscious presuppositions as possible. Unfortunately we can never escape unconscious presuppositions.

---

[32] On a broader level, as I pointed out incipiently in footnote 4 above, in Roman Catholic thought there is no need to torture biblical texts in order to find in NT times an awareness of church doctrines articulated in later centuries, even though those doctrines cannot be seen to contradict the NT. We should be alert to lines of development from the NT to a subsequently defined doctrine so that it is clear that the church is interpreting revelation rather than imposing extrinsic dogma; yet doctrine may stem from *later* Christians insights into what was involved in the mystery revealed in Christ.

CHAPTER 4.
WHAT CAN BE DISCERNED
ABOUT JESUS
FROM HIS WORDS CONCERNING
ISSUES
OTHER THAN THE KINGDOM
AND HIMSELF

Although I make no claim that I have detected all the Gospel material pertinent to Jesus that might cast light on how he conceived his role and understood himself, I shall make a serious effort to cover the most important and representative. Moreover, since I shall subdivide topically, readers can see what a particular type of material conveys about Jesus. We shall begin in this chapter with more general indications of his knowledge in matters secular and religious, and in the next chapter turn to deeds and sayings directly involved in the proclamation of the kingdom.[33] Frankly the latter material is more important for understanding the rest of the book, so that if readers should find discussions of Gospel texts in this chapter too difficult, they can come back to it later.

(A) What Can Be Discerned from the Knowledge That Jesus Shows of the Ordinary Affairs of Life

There are texts in the Gospels that seem to indicate that Jesus shared normal human limitations in his knowledge of the affairs of

---

[33] In these chapters I have used (with significant changes) some material from my earlier studies of how much Jesus knew in CBQ 29 (1967), 315–45 and BJGM 39–79.

life; there are other texts that attribute to him extraordinary and even superhuman knowledge about such affairs.

TEXTS INDICATING LIMITED KNOWLEDGE

#1. During the public ministry. The best example is Mark 5: 30–33. Jesus has been walking through a crowd; a woman touches his garments and is healed by his miraculous power. Perceiving that power has gone forth from him, Jesus asks who touched his garments. The disciples think that this is a foolish question when there has been so much pushing and pulling in the crowd; but the woman comes forward and confesses. The narrative seems clearly to presuppose ignorance on Jesus' part, even if that presupposition is at most incidental to the story flow. The story is approximately the same, even if toned down, in Luke 8:45–47; but Matt 9:22 leaves out the description of Jesus' question and his search.[34] In Matt, Jesus turns, sees the woman, and knows what has happened. Most likely the Marcan form is more original, and Matt is reflecting an uneasiness about the ignorance that Mark attributes to Jesus.[35]

#2. As a boy. There are two texts in Luke's infancy narrative that deserve attention. In Luke 2:46 Jesus is shown in the Temple at the age of twelve asking questions of the teachers of the Law. The next verse says that the teachers were amazed at his understanding and at the answers he gave. Jesus is evidently thought of as a precocious boy, anxious to learn. In Luke 2:52, after the above scene, Jesus is described as growing in wisdom, as well as in stature and the favor of God. This is a stereotyped formula, for a similar statement is made about Samuel in I Sam 2:26 and about John the Baptist in Luke 1:80. From a critical viewpoint these texts are difficult to use in a reconstruction of Jesus' life, for there is no scientific way of verifying this material in Luke's infancy narrative. (There is no other

---

[34] Throughout this book I shall work with the view most commonly held by scholars: The writers of Matt and Luke independently knew and used Mark, without knowing each other's work.

[35] A similar corrective attitude toward other seeming "human weaknesses" reported in the Marcan account is seen, for instance, in Matt's omitting the miracle where Jesus' attempt to heal a blind man is at first only partially successful (Mark 8: 22–26), and in Matt's toning down the gruff attitude of the disciples toward Jesus (cf. Matt 8:25 with Mark 4:38).

canonical Gospel account of Jesus as a boy; we know nothing of Luke's source.) Yet it is clear that the evangelist did not think it strange that Jesus should ask questions or grow in (ordinary) knowledge. This is an important consideration precisely because Luke's infancy narrative presents Jesus as God's Son from the first moment of his conception.

TEXTS INDICATING EXTRAORDINARY
OR SUPERHUMAN KNOWLEDGE

#3. Denial of limitations. There is a tendency in the later Gospels to suppress any suggestion that Jesus had to gain ordinary knowledge. We have already seen this of Matt under A #1 above, but it is especially true of John. If in John 6:5 Jesus asks Philip where bread can be found to feed the large crowd, the parenthetical addition in the next verse insists that Jesus was only testing Philip, for Jesus already knew what he was going to do, and thus implicitly knew that there was a lad in the crowd who have five barley loaves and two fish (6:9). Although Jesus chose some disciples of poor quality, he knew from the beginning those who would refuse to believe (John 6:64). In particular, he knew that Judas Iscariot would betray him (6:71; 13:11). All this is part of the Johannine tendency to picture Jesus without any element of human weakness or dependence.[36] Jesus can say in 10:18 in relation to his death: "No one takes my life from me; rather I lay it down of my own accord. I have the power to lay it down, and the power to take it up again." Although John insists that the Word became flesh (1:14), E. Käsemann argues that the Johannine Jesus has not undergone a kenosis, i.e., an emptying to the point of utter lowliness (as in Philip 2:6–8). In the incarnate Jesus the glory of God's own Son constantly shines forth for all who have eyes to see.[37]

#4. Capability of reading minds. All the Gospels attribute to

---

[36] John 3:22 reports that in Judea Jesus carried on a ministry of baptizing, a practice that might indicate he was under the influence of John the Baptist. In 4:2 this is carefully denied: Jesus himself did not baptize but only his disciples.

[37] APPENDIX IV will discuss Käsemann's position. There are exaggerations in it, but one must admit that taken alone the Johannine portrait of Jesus is somewhat onesided in favor of divinity. Only by balancing John with Mark do we have the scriptural basis for considering Jesus both fully divine and fully human.

Jesus the ability to know what people are thinking even though they have not expressed themselves (Mark 2:6–8 and par.; Mark 9:33–35 with Luke 9:46–47; John 2:24–25; 16:19 and 30). Such an ability is not unusual in the stories of extraordinary religious figures; and one might question whether, if historical on Jesus' part, it represented a keen perception of human nature or a superhuman knowledge. Certainly in John, and most probably in the other Gospels as well, the evangelist supposes the latter.

   #5. Knowledge at a distance. All the Gospels have incidents wherein Jesus knows what is happening elsewhere, beyond the limits of human sight:

(a) In John 1:48–49 Jesus knows (has seen) what Nathanael had been doing under the fig tree, much to Nathanael's amazement.

(b) In Mark 11:2 and par., as Jesus prepares to enter Jerusalem, he instructs the disciples to go into a nearby village; at the entrance they will find a colt tied on which no one has ever sat.[38] This story is not recounted in John, whose narrative of the entry into Jerusalem is in some respects more primitive than that of the Synoptics. In John 12:14 Jesus himself finds the animal.

(c) In Mark 14:13–14 and Luke 22:10–11 as preparation for Passover Jesus sends two of his disciples with the instruction: "Go into the city and a man carrying a water jar will meet you. Follow him and wherever he enters say to the master of the house, 'The Teacher says, "Where is my guest room where I am to eat the Passover (meal) with my disciples?" '" It should be noted that the account in Matt 26:18 has no such hint of mysterious knowledge of what is about to happen. The Matthean Jesus simply directs the disciples to go to a certain man's house to make the Passover arrangements.

(d) In Matt 17:24–27 the issue of whether Jesus pays the assigned tax, and implicitly whether his followers should pay has been raised. Jesus tells Peter to go to the Lake of Galilee and the first fish that he catches will have a shekel in its mouth; that can serve

---

[38] Matt 21:2 has two animals. One might argue that in this instance and in the one to be mentioned next Jesus had previously arranged with the necessary people what would happen, but the evangelists scarcely interpreted the event in such a rationalistic way. They saw these as instances of extraordinary knowledge.

to pay the tax for both of them. We are never told that Peter did as instructed and found the shekel, but that is implied. This story appears only in Matt, probably stemming from the peculiarly Matthean Petrine tradition (14:28–33; 16:16b–19). Its main purpose is didactic (problem of Christians' paying taxes; association of Peter and Jesus);[39] and Jesus' knowledge that the coin would be in the fish's mouth (perhaps symbolizing that God will supply what Christians need to carry out their civil duties in such circumstances) is incidental. Despite the didactic purpose, it is one of the few miracles of Jesus that closely resemble magical action, worthy of the tales of the Hellenistic miracle-workers. Many scholars would regard it as a popular tale, and both in the infancy and passion narratives Matt does seem to tap a vein of popular dramatic material that narrate extraordinary occurrences (a star signaling the birth of the King of the Jews; earthquakes at Jesus' death and resurrection; the saints coming out of the tombs and appearing in Jerusalem).

In evaluating these incidents, we encounter problems. Incidents (a) and (d) have no other verification, and (d) is extremely difficult. In incidents (b) and (c) there is another version that supposes no extraordinary knowledge. Despite these difficulties, were we to decide that the tradition of Jesus' ability to know at a distance goes back to very early tradition, we would still have to be careful about any theological assumption that would trace such knowledge to his being divine. The OT attributes this type of knowledge to many prophets, e.g., Ezekiel living in Babylon has visions of events occurring in Jerusalem. Extrasensory sight at a distance is supposed in a story about Samuel (I Sam 10:1 ff.) that is very similar to the incident of Mark 14 cited under (c).

To sum up what we have seen in the texts discussed under A, there is an ancient Gospel tradition that accepts without noticeable difficulty that Jesus had normally limited knowledge of the ordinary affairs of life; most likely the suppression of this by Matt and John is a secondary theological modification. On the other hand, probably

---

[39] For more on the purpose, see *Peter in the New Testament*, eds. R. E. Brown et al. (New York: Paulist, 1973), 101–5, a book that represents a consensus of Protestant and Catholic scholars.

as far back as one can trace the tradition, Jesus was presented as a man with more than ordinary knowledge and perception about others. In great religious and prophetic figures such superior knowledge does not exclude limitations and ignorance in other areas, and thus a combination of the two is almost to be expected in Jesus.

(B) What Can Be Discerned from the General Knowledge That Jesus Shows of Religious Matters

What was said under A would not offer difficulty to most theologians interested in the range of Jesus' knowledge, no matter what their presuppositions (see Chapter 3 above), for there are few scholars today who do not admit that Jesus had to gain experimental knowledge in ordinary affairs. Many, however, would not admit that Jesus could have been limited in his religious knowledge.[40] In this area we begin to touch on the substance of Jesus' ministry or, at least, of the Gospel accounts of that ministry, since these documents report only what is of religious import, passing over humdrum things done by Jesus that had little or no religious significance.[41] (If in A we saw examples of extraordinary knowledge about ordinary affairs, even those incidents were ultimately associated with an action that had religious significance.) Leaving till the next chapter texts that deal more directly with Jesus' grasp of his mission of proclaiming the kingdom of God, let us concentrate here on his general religious knowledge. In the use of the Scriptures and of theological concepts did Jesus manifest a knowledge far beyond that of his time, so that one would be forced to posit a supernatural source for this knowledge? Please note the phraseology of this question. In what follows I shall have to contrast the view of Jesus (as reported in the Gospels) with a modern, scientific view; and that may well sound supercilious. Emphatically I do not advocate in any unqualified way

---

[40] See, however, K. Rahner, "Dogmatic Considerations on Knowledge and Consciousness in Christ," in *Dogmatic vs. Biblical Theology* (Baltimore: Helicon, 1964), 241–67, esp. 261: "We may speak without any embarrassment of a spiritual, indeed religious development of Jesus."

[41] The same thing happened, of course, with the great figures of the OT and with Paul, and so we have simplified pictures of people whose every thought and action are centered on God or God's activity.

the superiority of a modern, scientific worldview; it is responsive to the needs of our times, but worldviews of preceding times had their own grasp of truth—sometimes a grasp that we have lost to our detriment. Yet that recognition does not answer a central question, namely, whether there was a demonstrable difference between Jesus and others of his time in general religious knowledge.

TEXTS ILLUSTRATING JESUS' KNOWLEDGE OF SCRIPTURE

The Scriptures supplied the basic religious vocabulary of Judaism; and if Jesus had extraordinary knowledge, we would expect it to be manifest here. While we shall cite below the instances in the Gospels where Jesus is said to have used Scripture, it is very difficult to be certain we are dealing with his *ipsissima verba*, i.e., his very own words. One of the prominent features in the apostolic preaching was the introduction of an OT background that would make Jesus intelligible to his fellow Jews. Such a resort to the OT was almost certainly in continuity with Jesus' own custom of citing the Scriptures, but it is not always possible to determine whether the Gospel reference to the OT stems from Jesus or from the apostolic preaching. In what follows, every modern scholar runs the risk of appearing supercilious by seeming to know more than Jesus did. There is nothing of that nature implied here: The exegesis practiced in Jesus' time had its own validity, but the issue is whether Jesus showed an extraordinary knowledge of Scripture beyond that of his time.

#1. There are instances where the citation of Scripture attributed to Jesus involves a mistake. We shall not bother with incidents where he cites Scripture and no such citation can be found in the OT, e.g., John 7:38. In such instances there is always the possibility that he is citing a book that has not been preserved for us,[42] or that he is citing a targum (Aramaic translation) or some other popular form of the biblical text.

■ In Mark 2:26 Jesus says that David entered the house of God *when*

---

[42] The canon of sacred Jewish books (that subsequently Christians came to call the OT but which was called by Jews "The Law, the Prophets, and the Writings") had not yet been fully or unanimously established, at least in the area of "The Writings." The Jews of Jesus' time, e.g., at Qumran and at Alexandria, used books as sacred that subsequent Jewish tradition did not canonize.

Abiathar was high priest and ate the loaves of the presence. The scene is found in I Sam 21:2–7; there, however, the high priest is not Abiathar but Ahimelech. Matt and Luke seem to have noticed the difficulty, for their accounts of this saying of Jesus omit any mention of the high priest (Matt 12:4; Luke 6:4).[43] Abiathar was better known than Ahimelech and more closely associated with David in later life, so that popular tradition may have easily confused the two. But if the reading is genuine, Jesus shows no awareness that he is following an inaccurate version of the story.

- In Matt 23:35 Jesus refers to all the righteous blood shed on earth from the blood of Abel to the blood of Zechariah the son of Barachiah who was murdered between the sanctuary and the altar. This identification of Zechariah seems to represent a confusion. Zechariah the son of Berachiah was a minor prophet who flourished *ca.* 520–516, but it was Zechariah the son of Jehoiada who was killed in the Temple *ca.* 825 BC (II Chron 24:20–22). If the confusion existed in the underlying Q, apparently Luke noticed the confusion, for Luke 11:51 omits "the son of Barachiah."[44]

#2. There are instances where the citation of Scripture attributed to Jesus shows no critical sense but reflects the imprecise ideas of his time:

- In Mark 12:36 and par. Jesus cites Ps 110 ("The Lord said to my Lord") and attributes this psalm to David. This is not just a general attribution, for Jesus' whole argument rests on the fact that David himself composed the psalm.[45] Almost all modern scholars,

---

[43] Some mss. of Mark also omit the italicized phrase, but the better mss. and the rules of textual criticism favor genuineness. Copyists of Mark were showing the same hesitation about including the mistake that Matt and Luke exhibited.

[44] In a modern treatment J. M. Ross, "Which Zechariah?" *Irish Biblical Studies* 9 (1987), 70–73, posits the existence of an unknown Zechariah put to death in the Temple not long before Jesus' day—a solution I regard as desperate. Lest we dismiss such confusion of OT characters as insignificant, let us remember that one of the standard Christian arguments against the sacred, revealed character of the Koran has been that Mohammed seems to have confused Miriam the sister of Moses with Miriam (Mary) the mother of Jesus. As I understand Christian thought, however, although the Bible is inspired, it is inexact to think that everything in it has been revealed; and so inexactness in a literary genre that does not require exactness is not an objection to the sacredness of the Bible.

[45] Of course, for a long time Jesus' attribution of the psalm to David was taken as incontrovertible proof that David did write the psalm, e.g., the decree of the Roman

Catholics included, think of the psalm as uttered by a proclaimer of royal oracles at the coronation or anniversary of the king. Personal authorship by David is most unlikely.

- In Matt 12:39–41 (also 16:4; Luke 11:29–32) Jesus says that the sign of Jonah the prophet will be given to the present generation. If we leave aside the question of what the sign was, Jesus' reference to the Book of Jonah is best understood if he thought of it as a historical account. Indeed, conservative scholars have used Jesus' citation to prove that Jonah is historical, despite the improbable events narrated therein (including the exaggerated width of Nineveh). Contemporary biblical scholars are almost unanimous in identifying Jonah as a parable that draws on the figure of an otherwise unknown prophet, Jonah the son of Amittai (II Kings 14:25). Nevertheless, we should not put too much emphasis on this example because we cannot be certain that Jesus treated Jonah as historical.

#3. In still other instances the citations of Scripture attributed to Jesus employ a hermeneutic that would be judged marginal today, at least by the majority of scholars for whom the basic norm is the literal sense, i. e., the sense that the original authors intended to convey by what they wrote.[46] Of course, interpretation that went beyond the literal was quite customary in Jesus' time, e.g., in the Qumran (Dead Sea Scroll) writings, in the targums (Aramaic translations that were often quite interpretative), and in the later rabbinical writings; and I have no desire to denigrate the quality of such interpretation. But here we are asking precisely whether Jesus demonstrated a knowledge of Scripture beyond that of his day. Let us look at some examples of the interpretation attributed to him.

- In John 10:33–36, in order to refute "the Jews" who accuse him of making himself God, Jesus cites Ps 82:6 which speaks of the judges as "gods." Thus he argues that the Jewish Scriptures themselves use the title "god" for human beings. There are many attempts to explain such exegesis (BGJ 1.409–11), but it seems inescapable that Jesus is glossing over a difference of meaning in the

---

Pontifical Biblical Commission of May 1, 1910 (NJBC 72, §27). For Catholic freedom in such matters now, see NJBC 72, §25.

[46] For precisions and qualifications about this, see NJBC 71, §§9–13.

word "god." The Jews have accused him of making himself God with a capital "G"; he has answered by pointing to an example where human beings are called "gods" in an applied sense. Yet, since this scene is so redolent of Johannine theology, we cannot be assured that the citation represents *ipsissima verba.*

■ If we return to Mark 12:36 and par. (see above under B #2), we find another hermeneutical problem in Jesus' insistence that the Davidic Ps 110 refers to the Messiah. He presumes that in the line "The Lord [= God] said to my Lord," the "my Lord" is the Messiah. Few modern scholars, Catholics included, would think that there was an expectation of "*the* Messiah" when Ps 110 was composed.[47] Rather at that time the psalm, which may have functioned in the coronation ceremony or liturgy, referred to any king of the Davidic line. The Pharisees were not able to refute Jesus' argument since, seemingly, they too thought that the psalm referred to the Messiah; but in what modern interpreters would regard as its literal sense, Ps 110 would not establish Jesus' point.

#4. There are Gospel passages that portray Jesus as learned in Scripture. A general admiration of the authority and depth of Jesus' teaching is reported (Matt 7:29; 22:16). In particular John 7:15 seems to relate this astonishment to his knowledge of Scripture: "How did this fellow get his education when he had no teacher?" For Jewish children a knowledge of how to read and write would have been centered on a knowledge of the Scriptures. Luke 4:17 has the tradition that Jesus could read the Bible. Also, the Gospels present Jesus as not hesitating to contradict current exegesis when such exegesis conflicted with his own interpretation of his role or of the demands of the kingdom of God. His citation of Ps 110, for instance, is to prove that the exegesis of the Pharisees is wrong: The Messiah is more than the Son of David. See also the series "You have heard it said . . . but I say to you" in Matt 5, and his employment of Scripture in answering the Pharisees on divorce (Matt 19:4) and in answering the Sadducees on the resurrection (22:31–32).

Nevertheless, the overall impact of ##1–4 involving Jesus' use

---

[47] APPENDIX I will show that the expectation of *a specific future king* of the House of David who would bring about God's purposes for Israel probably did not develop until after the Babylonian Exile.

of the Scriptures would not lead one to think of him as more than a very distinguished teacher of his times.

TEXTS ILLUSTRATING JESUS' USE
OF CONTEMPORARY RELIGIOUS CONCEPTS

Here obviously we must be selective. If we are inquiring about the knowledge of Jesus, the most useful field of study would be his attitude toward the concepts of his time that by common consent we now consider inadequate or incorrect. Did he demonstrate an awareness of this inadequacy, as might be expected if he were omniscient? Certainly he is presented in the Gospels as correcting or modifying ideas of his time that were intimately involved with his own mission (ideas about the Messiah) or with God's demand (ideas about marriage, ritual purity, brotherly [and sisterly] love). But for the moment we are concerned with Jesus' attitude toward general religious concepts that were *not* so intimately involved in his mission of proclaiming God's kingdom. As examples let us discuss demonology, the picture of the afterlife, and apocalyptic.

#5. Demonology. The Synoptic Gospels describe an extraordinary number of instances of demon possession during the ministry of Jesus. I am not questioning here the existence of the demons, or the possibility of demon possession, or even that demon possession may have been more frequent before the kingdom of God made its inroads on the kingdom of evil. Nor am I questioning the religious import of the struggle with evil involved in the expulsions of demons.[48] But some of the cases that the Synoptic Gospels describe as instances of demon possession seem to be instances of natural sickness. The symptoms described in Mark 9:17–18 seem to be those of epilepsy, while the symptoms in Mark 5:4 seem to be those of dangerous insanity. One cannot escape the impression that sometimes in relation to demon possession both the evangelists and Jesus are reflecting the inexact medico-religious understanding of their times. In the second instance Jesus drives the demons out of the insane man into a herd of swine—a destination that is in itself an

---

[48] See BRTOQ 68–69, for a discussion of how important religious truth can be expressed in a worldview different from our own—a view that from the viewpoint of science may be inferior to ours, but far richer from the viewpoint of symbolism.

example of popular ideas of demonology. The parable attributed to Jesus in the Q tradition (Matt 12:43–45; Luke 11:24–26) about the demons wandering around looking for a place to dwell is still another example of primitive ideas, akin to demons dwelling in haunted houses. Jesus occasionally corrects contemporary ideas about too close a relationship between sickness or calamity and personal sin (Luke 13:1–5; John 9:2–3), but in the general Gospel picture there is no indication that in the questions of demons and the medical causes of sickness he saw the inadequacies of the popular views of his time.[49]

#6. Afterlife. Jesus is not reported to have given detailed descriptions of the afterlife. Was this because it was not his mission to reveal such things, or because he did not know details about the afterlife? From the available biblical evidence no one can answer that question, but we should notice the materialistic images that he uses in the few instances where he does speak of the subject. In Mark 9:43ff. Jesus describes people as entering the next life with one hand, one foot, or one eye, as if in the future life people were to possess bodies such as they have on earth, including defects. Punishment is described in terms of unquenchable fire (Mark 9:48; Matt 25:41), ravenous worms (Mark 9:48), frustrated grinding of teeth and weeping (Matt 8:12; 13:42), and insatiable thirst (Luke 16:24). A great chasm separates the place of beatitude from the place of fiery punishment (Luke 16:26). In the place of beatitude people enjoy sumptuous banquets in the presence of God and the patriarchs (Matt 8:11), while the envious damned are compelled to witness (Luke 13:28). Besides the difficulty of determining whether such descriptions represent *ipsissima verba* or not, we face here the added problem of determining how much of this language Jesus meant as figurative. On the one hand, we cannot assume that all of it was meant literally, and on the other we cannot assume that Jesus shared our own sophistication on some of these questions—a sophistication from a scientific point of view that is not necessarily closer to a truth that is

---

[49] It is true that the Fourth Gospel describes no instances of demon possession, but this is scarcely a primitive trait preserved only in John. Rather John is interested in a more cosmic struggle of Jesus with evil embodied in the Prince of this World (12:31; 14:30).

best expressed symbolically. When Jesus speaks of heaven above the clouds (Mark 13:26; 14:62), how can we be sure that he knew that it was not located above the clouds? The fact that in one instance he corrected a popular view of the afterlife with which he did not agree (Mark 12:24–25 and par.: the resurrected dead will *not* marry) might suggest that he had no objection to the other popular views that colored his own language.

A related question would concern Jesus' knowledge of the immortality of the soul. Certainly most of Jesus' references to the afterlife were in terms of the resurrection of the body. Yet the picture is not simple: Passages like Mark 8:36; Matt 10:28; and Luke 23:43 are more easily explained if ideas of an undying soul were already known in Palestine—or at least of some personal presence with God on the part of the deceased before the resurrection of the body (see Philip 1:23; II Cor 5:8). Therefore, we should be careful about assumptions that Jesus showed no expectant knowledge of anything other than a resurrection of the dead which was to come at the end of time.[50]

#7. Apocalyptic. The problem just faced about the figurative language attributed to Jesus in describing the afterlife is repeated in evaluating the apocalyptic images found in Jesus' descriptions of the end of time. We hear that the sun and moon will be darkened and the stars will fall down from heaven (Mark 13:24–25 and par.); there will be wars, earthquakes, and famine (Mark 13:7–8 and par.)— in short, the phenomena that Jewish apocalyptic writings had been predicting for centuries. Of course, we do not know that such things will not happen. Yet few scholars would be willing to accept this imagery as more than a stereotyped description of catastrophe, a description that had become so standard that one could not other-

---

[50] O. Cullmann, *Immortality of the Soul or Resurrection of the Dead* (London: Epworth, 1958), has argued strongly that the NT hope is not one of immortality; a fortiori he would argue that Jesus did not preach immortality. But that may be too simple. J. Barr, *The Garden of Eden and the Hope of Immortality?* (Minneapolis: Fortress, 1993), argues that in Genesis man and woman were immortal from the beginning; and in *Old and New in Interpretation* (London: SCM, 1966), 52ff., he insists that both resurrection of the body and immortality of the soul were Gospel anticipations. See the combined expectations reflected in John 11:25–26, a passage for which unfortunately we have no Synoptic parallel.

wise describe the final divine intervention. If these apocalyptic descriptions in the Gospel go back to Jesus himself, he would surely have been conscious that he was repeating the stylized language from the Scriptures. One may always contend that Jesus was aware of giving purely symbolic descriptions; yet there is nothing in these passages to suggest that Jesus did not expect the phenomena he described.

To sum up ##5–7, in the three areas of demonology, the afterlife, and apocalyptic, Jesus seems to draw on the religious concepts of his time without indication of superior knowledge and without substantially correcting the concepts. As we shall see in the next chapter, there are other areas, especially in the proclamation of the kingdom of God, where Jesus' teaching challenged that of his times; but we do not find his uniqueness in the broad religious concepts we have been discussing in this section.

TEXTS ILLUSTRATING JESUS' KNOWLEDGE OF THE FUTURE

To a certain extent a knowledge of the future might be expected in the Gospel descriptions of Jesus since they report that he was regarded as a prophet (Mark 6:15; Luke 7:16; John 6:14).[51] It is a commonplace of modern biblical science that the prophets of the OT were primarily religious reformers involved with their own times and that they did not spend their lives gazing into the distant future. In such an understanding, Jesus as prophet would not necessarily have had foreknowledge. But we cannot judge the 1st-century estimation of a prophet from the standpoint of a modern critical understanding of OT prophecy. In postexilic Judaism (i.e., after 539 BC) prophetic foreknowledge of the future received greater stress. The Qumran *pesharim* or biblical interpretations suppose that prophets like Habakkuk were really writing about the Qumran community that did not make its appearance till hundreds of years after the prophet's time. Therefore, the evaluation of Jesus as a prophet by his contemporaries may well have involved a tradition that he knew

---

[51] It is quite plausible that Jesus was thought of as a prophet during his ministry, for the role of prophet was more spontaneously obvious than the roles implied in some of the other titles that the Gospels give Jesus (Messiah, Son of Man, etc.).

the future.[52] If Jesus had knowledge of the future, what may we discern from that about his understanding of his role in God's plan? That question sets the parameters of the investigation: We should concentrate on Jesus' knowledge of his own future or of the future of God's people that is somehow related to his identity or self-conception. If the knowledge is very detailed, it might show that he was privy to God's own knowledge; if it is less detailed, it would at least give us a clue as to what he considered his destiny.

In all the instances to be discussed below I shall begin by investigating the amount of detail involved in the future knowledge attributed to Jesus. There is a major difficulty in evaluating that because the Gospels were written after most of the events that Jesus is thought to have predicted—all were written after his death and resurrection; Matt, Luke, and John were probably written after the fall of Jerusalem. In order to indicate the fulfillment of Jesus' words, the Gospel writers could have clarified those words by adding details so that the reader would recognize their nature as prophecy.[53] Consequently, in the prophecies attributed to Jesus, one must ask how much represents his *ipsissima verba* and how much represents clarification by the evangelists in the light of the subsequent event. If we do establish that the original statements of Jesus about the future may have been vaguer than they now appear, what is the demarcation line between his having had a firm conviction about how things will turn out and real foreknowledge? Genuinely detailed foreknowledge is superhuman; unshakable conviction is not necessarily beyond human powers.

---

[52] Roman Catholics should be aware that Vatican Council I stated that Jesus did utter prophecies (DBS §3009).

[53] An older rationalist exegesis saw in these instances *vaticinia ex eventu*, i.e., passages simply created after the events by the church or by the evangelists for apologetic purposes. That approach (which, even were there no religious implications, is too simplistic in terms of biblical scholarship) has had little hearing among believers. They have judged it tantamount to making the evangelists deceptive and found it irreconcilable with an understanding of the Bible as the word of God. But the basic issue about the detail of Jesus' prophecies need not be phrased in a crudely rationalist manner. Reflecting on the respective events after they had taken place, the evangelists or their predecessors may have made more specific what had already been considered a prophecy. This would be a pedagogic step that is not deceptive or unworthy of the Scriptures considered as sacred.

#8. Foreknowledge of his own passion, crucifixion, and resurrection.[54] Because we are searching for detailed foreknowledge, we are not concerned with general predictions of suffering or death. Of concern are exact predictions about the who and the how. All the Gospels attribute to Jesus such detailed foreknowledge during his ministry. Yet we should be aware of a problem that creates a priori suspicions about the exact predictions of crucifixion and resurrection attributed to Jesus, namely, that the disciples who are supposed to have heard the predictions did not foresee the crucifixion even when it was imminent or expect the resurrection. Luke 24:19–26 is a typical account of their reaction. This failure may be attributed to the desire of the evangelists to hold up as a warning to the Gospel readers the slowness of the disciples to understand; but one may also wonder whether the original predictions, if historical, were as exact as they have now come to us. Let us consider some of the more prominent examples of these predictions.

■ Mark 8:31; 9:31; 10:33–34 and par. The Synoptic Gospels report what is regarded by most as a special group of three prophetic sayings by Jesus foretelling the passion, death, and resurrection of the Son of Man. If we concentrate on the Marcan wording, in the first prediction Jesus says that the Son of Man must suffer many things, be rejected by the elders and the chief priests and the scribes, be killed, and be raised after three days. The second prediction is less specific, for it speaks simply of action by men without identifying the exact officials. The third prediction is the most specific; not only does it mention the officials, but it says that they will condemn him and deliver him to the Gentiles to be mocked, spit upon, and scourged. (The Matthean form of the third prediction mentions crucifixion.) These three belong to that class of Son of Man sayings in which the Son of Man suffers on earth. Some scholars, like Tödt and Higgins,[55] who have devoted full-scale treatises to the Son of Man issue in the Gospels, do not consider

---

[54] I present a lengthy treatment of this material in APPENDIX VIII of BDM (2.1468–91).

[55] H. E. Tödt, *The Son of Man in the Synoptic Tradition* (Philadelphia: Westminster, 1965); A.J.B. Higgins, *Jesus and the Son of Man* (Philadelphia: Fortress, 1964). Further material on the Son of Man usage will be found in Chapter 6, C, below.

sayings of this class to be genuine words of Jesus. They point out that passages dealing with the suffering Son of Man are not found in the Q tradition of the words of Jesus shared by Matt and Luke and that therefore for such sayings we have only the authority of the Marcan tradition. Other scholars refuse to judge against the genuineness of these sayings on such general grounds; and as we shall see, suffering Son of Man sayings are found in John (probably independently of Mark). An important issue is whether the wording of the predictions is the same as the description of the events in the Marcan passion account. Even Tödt acknowledges that there are differences, and so it is not so easy to assume that the evangelist first wrote about the passion and resurrection and then went back and created the three prophecies in the light of what he had written. Is there sufficient reason then to think that the detailed prophecies may have come from Jesus himself?

Paradoxically the evidence of John both suggests that the pattern of three predictions may antedate any written Gospel and calls into question the exact wording. In John 3:14; 8:28; 12:32–34 there are three sayings of Jesus that the Son of Man must be "lifted up." In the last John makes clear that this refers to the kind of death Jesus was going to die, namely, by crucifixion when he was lifted up from the earth, but it also includes his being lifted up to God in resurrection/ascension (BGJ 1.145–46). We note that the wording in the Johannine predictions has no details; rather, it echoes the vague language of Isa 52:13: "Behold my servant . . . shall be lifted up." One might suggest that at an early level of the Jesus tradition, before the written Gospels, there was a pattern of three prophecies about the suffering and victory of the Son of Man phrased in OT language— phrased in Isa 52 language in a preJohannine tradition, and perhaps in Dan 7 language ("a son of man" brought up to God; see p. 53 below) in a preMarcan tradition. In the preJohannine development this was never made more specific by the post factum details of the passion account whereas in the preMarcan tradition that began to happen, and Mark continued the process. At least such a reconstruction is more likely than that John drew on Mark for the pattern of the three, dropped all the passion details, and added an Isaiah motif.

■ In Matt 12:39–40 Jesus offers to the Pharisees the sign of Jonah: "As Jonah was three days and three nights in the belly of the whale, so will the Son of Man be three days and three nights in the heart of the earth." This is a clear prediction of the resurrection, but comparative Synoptic studies suggest that the Matthean interpretation of the sign is a secondary addition to a more original saying, perhaps more ambiguous about the sign of Jonah. In the parallel passage, Luke 11:29–30, 32, there is another interpretation, this time in terms of Jonah's preaching: "As Jonah became a sign to the men of Nineveh, so will the Son of Man be to this generation . . . for they repented at the preaching of Jonah." (The latter clause also appears in Matt 12:41, and so Matt has elements of a twofold interpretation.) A third form of the saying in Matt 16:4 simply mentions the sign without explaining it, and this may have been the original form. In that case the two different interpretations of the sign that now appear in Matt 12 and Luke 11 may represent alternative explanations current in the early church—explanations that arose when Christians studied the career of Jonah to find in what way Jonah was a sign of Jesus, the Son of Man. This saying, then, cannot be used to establish Jesus' detailed foreknowledge of his resurrection.

■ There is a tradition that Jesus knew beforehand that Judas would betray him. John 6:70–71 attributes this foreknowledge to Jesus during the ministry. In all the Gospels the theme of forthcoming betrayal appears at the Last Supper; and in the Synoptics this is phrased in terms of the giving over of the Son of Man. In Matt 26:25 and John 13:27 Jesus knows that the betrayer is Judas. Mark 14:18–21 does not specify that;[56] but since Mark 14:10–11 has already told the readers about Judas, perhaps we are meant to suppose that Jesus knew he was the one. If this prediction is deemed genuine, one would still have to ask whether it represents supernatural foreknowledge or only a penetrating insight into Judas' character (previously John 12:6 described Judas as corrupt) and/or into the direction in which events were leading (especially in the Synoptics where the prediction is made after Judas has already made an agreement with the chief priests). From this prediction, then, one can scarcely judge the level of Jesus' foreknowledge, al-

---

[56] Neither does Luke 22:22; yet 22:48 shows that Jesus did know what Judas was planning.

though it seems likely that the evangelists would have us think that the foreknowledge was supernatural.

In summary, it is difficult to decide about Jesus' foreknowledge of his passion, crucifixion, and resurrection. Modern criticism would cast serious doubt on a detailed foreknowledge. Yet we should not undervalue the general agreement of the Gospel tradition that Jesus was convinced beforehand that, although his life would be taken from him violently (see also Luke 17:25; Mark 10:45), God would ultimately vindicate him. Such a conviction could have come from Jesus' reflection on the OT, e.g., on the career of Jeremiah and on Deutero-Isaiah's portrayal of the Servant of the Lord. (The violent death of John the Baptist may also have turned Jesus' mind in this direction.[57]) The conviction would have import christologically, for it would mean that Jesus understood what happened to him as an essential part of the divine plan for the kingdom—a theme to which I shall return later.

#9. Foreknowledge of the destruction of Jerusalem and of the Temple sanctuary. Let us begin with the forewarning of the destruction of Jerusalem in the Synoptic eschatological discourse (Mark 13 and par.). In Mark 13:2 and par. Jesus predicts that the great buildings of the Temple will be destroyed and not one stone will be left upon another. In AD 70 the Roman armies devastated Jerusalem. Jesus' words do not represent a detailed foreknowledge of what happened, for gigantic blocks of the Herodian Temple still stand in Jerusalem, e.g., in "the Wailing Wall." Mark 13:14 and Matt 24:15 have Jesus offer a sign of when this and related events will happen: "When you see the desolating abomination standing where it ought not to be." The "you" is presumably the group of disciples/apostles to whom he is speaking; the imagery is taken from Dan 9:27 and 12:11 (as Matt indicates) which use this terminology for the statue of the pagan god that *ca.* 170 BC the Syrian ruler of Palestine, Antiochus Epiphanes, had placed on the Temple altar of sacrifice. Thus

---

[57] We are hampered here by the fact that the Gospel material is not arranged in historically chronological order. In Mark 2:20 Jesus has predicted his death before any description of the death of the Baptist, but the first of the three detailed Son of Man predictions (Mark 8:31) occurs after the death of the Baptist. John (2:19–22; 3:14) would have Jesus aware of his crucifixion and resurrection even before the Baptist was arrested (3:24).

the sign could be a figurative indication that Jerusalem would be destroyed by foreigners. Luke 21:20 specifies the sign: "When you see Jerusalem surrounded by armies, know that the desolation has come near." Some scholars have judged this to be a post-70 clarification when Luke knew what the Romans had done; others have argued that Luke preserved the more original form of the prediction phrased by Jesus in language derived from OT descriptions of the fall of Jerusalem to the Babylonians in 586 BC.[58] Neither explanation would demand that Jesus had exact knowledge of the future. In his words pertinent to the destruction of the city, like Jeremiah and Ezekiel of old, Jesus would have been threatening a rebellious Jerusalem with divine punishment[59] and using traditional language to do so. The saying would not indicate that he knew precisely when[60] or how this disaster would come about.

Let us turn next to the various forms of Jesus' prediction of the destruction of the sanctuary.[61]

- Mark 14:57–58: Some were giving false testimony against him saying that, "We have heard him saying that, 'I will destroy this sanctuary made with hands, and within three days another not made with hands I will build.' " Also Mark 15:29: Those passing by were blaspheming him . . . saying, "Aha, O one destroying the sanctuary and building it in three days."

---

[58] C. H. Dodd, "The Fall of Jerusalem and the 'Abomination of Desolation,' " *Journal of Roman Studies* 37 (1947), 47–54; reprinted in his *More New Testament Studies* (Grand Rapids: Eerdmans, 1968), 69–83. If that be true, while in Mark and Matt the prototype Jesus offers for the coming disaster stems from the profanation of the Jerusalem Temple by Antiochus Epiphanes, the prototype in Luke is a more ancient devastation.

[59] Jesus was not alone among his contemporaries in this premonition. *Ca.* AD 62 Jesus son of Ananias warned of the impending destruction of the Temple (Josephus, *War* 6.5.3; ##300–9). There is also a later Jewish tradition (Babylonian Talmud, *Gittin* 56a; Midrash Rabbah on Lamentations 1:5; #31) that Rabbi Zadok began fasting about AD 30 to forestall the destruction of Jerusalem.

[60] The references to the responsibility of or effect on not only the present generation but also on their children in two different passages (Matt 27:25 and Luke 23: 28), if original, may indicate that Jesus did not expect an immediate exercise of God's judgment.

[61] In BDM 1.429–60 I have devoted a whole section (§20) to Jesus' statements about the destruction of the Jerusalem Temple sanctuary.

- Matt 26:60–61: But at last two, having come forward, said, "This person stated, 'I am able to destroy the sanctuary of God, and within three days I will build (it).' " Also Matt 27:39–40: Those passing by were blaspheming . . . saying, "O one destroying the sanctuary, and in three days building it."
- Acts 6:13–14: They set up false witnesses who said, "This man [Stephen] does not cease speaking words against this holy place and the Law; for we have heard him saying that this Jesus of Nazareth will destroy this place."
- John 2:19–21: Jesus answered them [the Jews], "Destroy this sanctuary, and in three days I will raise it up." He spoke of the sanctuary of his body.

That Jesus made a statement along these lines is very likely. For some forty years after Jesus died, the Temple sanctuary stood, visibly unaffected; during that period Christians would scarcely have created a statement that had Jesus claiming he could or would destroy it. Rather they would have attempted to discover meaning in what must have seemed like an unfulfilled prophecy. Both Mark and Acts suggest that there was an element of falsehood in the Jewish attribution of the statement to Jesus—probably in the way the statement was taken by those who scoffed at Christians, viz., to mean physical destruction by Jesus himself or his rebuilding a material sanctuary like the one destroyed. Mark would find truth in the prediction when the sanctuary to be rebuilt was understood as one not made with hands, namely, the Christian community.[62] One also had to understand that Jesus' destruction of the sanctuary made with hands was partially symbolic, namely, at his death the veil of the sanctuary was rent into two from top to bottom (Mark 15:38), signifying that the place had lost the sanctity that stemmed from the presence of God. Matthew does not regard the attribution of the saying to Jesus as false; rather the affirmation of two witnesses gives it legal status; nor does he deem it necessary to distinguish two types of

---

[62] As support for this interpretation, see I Peter 2:5: "And as living stones, be yourselves built into a spiritual house." The Marcan addition of "made with hands" and "not made with hands" (linguistically much more at home in Greek than in Aramaic) is most likely a built-in Christian corrective of the way Jesus was being misinterpreted by his enemies; notice the two adjectives are missing in the blasphemy of Jesus by the passersby.

sanctuary as Mark did. By the time Matt was written the Roman armies had physically destroyed the Jerusalem sanctuary, and so the first part of Jesus' words had a literal fulfillment. For Matt this confirms Jesus' ability (notice: "I am able") to fulfill the second part. John, acknowledging that he is giving a post factum explanation that was understood only after Jesus' death, uses the verb "raise up" rather than "rebuild"; and so he can interpret Jesus to refer to his death and resurrection. This process of various interpretations shows that the original form of the prediction, although it manifested conviction, did not show a foreknowledge of detail that could be given by God alone. Nevertheless, here Jesus is relating to his own action God's judgment on the sanctuary. If he used "I" in talking about the destruction of the sanctuary, he was going beyond OT prophetic (and contemporary Jewish) warnings about the endangered fate of Jerusalem. Thus we begin to approach the personal role of Jesus in the coming of the kingdom that will be discussed in the next chapter.

#10. Foreknowledge of the Parousia. This aspect of Jesus' foreknowledge reflects in a different way on the total problem of his identity and his role in God's plan. The instances dealt with above under #8 and #9 concerned predictions of things that actually happened; here we are concerned with the prediction of something that has not happened, and we must ask whether Jesus claimed to know when it would happen or mistakenly expected it to happen within a short time. Here under the title "Parousia" I shall group statements about the coming of the Son of Man, about the return of Jesus, and about the coming of the kingdom of God in power.[63] The divergence in these statements as to the time of the coming presents a very complicated situation that we cannot possibly hope to solve, but it will be useful to classify the different temporal aspirations that seem to be involved in them.

(a) ANTICIPATION OF A PAROUSIA IMMEDIATELY AFTER

---

[63] Such a grouping may represent an oversimplification. The coming of God's kingdom would not necessarily include the coming of the Son of Man. Some exegetes who think that the references to the future coming of the Son of Man stem from Jesus hold (implausibly, in my judgment) that Jesus expected a Son of Man other than himself.

JESUS' DEATH. The sayings treated here associate the Parousia with Jesus' victory over death.

- In John 14:3 at the Last Supper Jesus says that he is departing but will return to take his disciples along with him. The surface import is of a Parousia immediately after Jesus' death, for similar language of being taken to heaven along with Jesus is found in a Parousia passage in the oldest preserved Christian writing, I Thess 4:16–17. M.-E. Boismard[64] has argued that John 14:3 represents one of the oldest eschatological strains in John. An interpretation of a Parousia right after death might also be placed on the words of Jesus to the high priest in Mark 14:62: "You [plural] will see the Son of Man sitting at the right of the Power and coming on the clouds of heaven."[65] Mark 14:25 and Luke 23:42–43 are other passages that would be more intelligible if Jesus expected immediate victory in the kingdom after death. All this would fit in with a theory that Jesus did not know precisely what form his victory over death would take. One might conjecture that as a Jew he spoke of this victory in terms of the imagery of Dan 7 which he used to reflect on the Son of Man.[66] In fact, however, the resurrection took place after his death, and the Parousia has remained in the future. This is an approach that cannot be refuted or proved. All the statements given above are capable of other interpretations, and no one of them specifies the precise moment of the coming of the Son of Man.

(b) ANTICIPATION OF A PAROUSIA IN THE LIFETIME OF JESUS' HEARERS. An outlook that posits an interval of at least a generation between Jesus' victory over death and his Parousia gets indirect support from Jesus' references to a church or a community life; from

---

[64] In a French article on the evolution of eschatology in John in *Revue Biblique* 68 (1961), 518–23.

[65] Matt 26:64 and Luke 22:69 (each in its own phrasing) modify the verb in this saying with an adverbial phrase: "from now on." Luke omits the reference to the *coming* of the Son of Man, perhaps because the saying seemed to imply an immediate Parousia.

[66] The NT expectation would represent a modification of the literal sense of Dan 7:13–14,26–27 where *a* son of man is not an individual so much as a symbolic human figure, representing Israel or God's saints. In Daniel this son of man is depicted not as coming to people on earth but as coming to God. See pp. 91, 94 below.

his sending the disciples to Israel and beyond; from his parables depicting growth; and from his orders to baptize and to commemorate him in the eucharist, etc.

■ In Matt 10:23 Jesus instructs the Twelve to go to Israel and to preach; in the Marcan parallel (6:7,30) the scene is one of his sending them two by two into the towns around Galilee. Jesus warns them that they will meet persecution, but he assures them: "When they persecute you in one town, flee to the next; for Amen, I say to you, you will not have gone through all the towns of Israel before the Son of Man comes." Combining the Matthean and Marcan versions, A. Schweitzer put forward his famous theory that Jesus expected the Parousia before the Twelve had finished their Galilean mission. When they returned without this having happened, disappointment brought Jesus to realize that his death would be necessary to bring about God's intervention. Today few would follow Schweitzer in this interpretation. The Matthean and Marcan scenes cannot be combined. The setting of Matt 10 (e.g., references to persecution by synagogues, governors, and kings in vv. 17–18) is that of the later church; and at least in its present form 10:23 must be understood in that atmosphere and not as a reference to an expectation within the ministry of Jesus. The Syro-Palestinian church is assuring itself that, despite persecution, it will not have exhausted all possibilities of preservation before the Son of Man comes.

■ Mark 13:30 and par. "Amen, I say to you that this generation will not pass away before all these things take place." In the present context "these things" would have to include the coming of the Son of Man described in 13:26. But that context may have little value for determining the original meaning of the saying; most scholars recognize that the eschatological discourse in Mark 13 is a collection of once independent sayings. Many argue that the original reference of "these things" was to the destruction of the Temple mentioned in 13:2–4. Efforts to explain away the temporal limits of the saying by claiming that "this generation" refers to the whole human race are refuted, in my judgment, by the closely parallel saying in Mark 9:1: "Amen, I say to you, there are some of those standing here who will not taste death before they see the kingdom of God come with power." Matt 16:28 offers an interpretation of what Mark's last clause implies: "before they see the Son of Man coming in his kingdom."[67]

■ John 1:51: "Amen, amen, I say to you, you will see the sky opened and the angels of God ascending and descending upon the Son of Man." The general Johannine tendency is to reinterpret Parousia expectations in terms of realized eschatology, i.e., they were fulfilled in what Jesus did in his ministry when he came down from heaven as the Word become flesh. The saying under discussion, which comes at the beginning of the Gospel, probably refers to what will be described in the public ministry to follow. Originally, however, it may have been an independent saying that referred to what would happen after Jesus' death in which he was lifted up to the Father (BGJ 1.88–91).

■ John 21:22: "If it is my will that he [the Beloved Disciple] remain until I come, how does that concern you?" The obvious import of the saying is that Jesus will return during that Disciple's lifetime, and this is how Christians interpreted it (21:23). But since the Beloved Disciple was dying or dead by the time John 21 was written, the Johannine author of chapter 21 employs casuistry to show that Jesus' promise was not absolute.

Neither Mark 13:30 nor 9:1 was a late creation; for from the 60s on, when the apostolic generation was dying out, such statements of a quick return became a problem precisely because they were not fulfilled.[68] The same may be argued for John 21:22. These are either substantially *ipsissima verba* of Jesus or the composition of the first generation. In the latter case, one might theorize that the first generation, puzzled by the fact that Jesus did not come back immediately, consoled itself by the assurance that the Parousia would at least come while many of the generation were still alive.[69]

---

[67] In order to avoid the implication that Jesus thought the Parousia would take place while some of his hearers were alive, a number of scholars question Matt's interpretation and suggest that the saying does not refer to the Parousia, or that it is inauthentic, or that it is a secondary rewriting of Mark 13:30 and referred originally to the destruction of the Temple.

[68] The havoc that they caused at the end of the century is implicit in John 21:23 and explicit in II Pet 3:4 where scoffers use them to cast doubt on the Parousia.

[69] In Mark 9:1 "some" will not taste death before the kingdom of God comes, and in I Thess 4:13–18 there is a problem about those who die before the Parousia.

(c) ANTICIPATION SO PHRASED AS TO IMPLY AN INDEFINITELY DELAYED PAROUSIA:

▪ A Parousia Preceded by Apocalyptic Signs. The mention of such portents before the Parousia gives the impression that it is not coming too soon (see the reasoning in II Thess 2:3ff.). The eschatological discourse in Mark 13, Matt 24–25, and Luke 21 lists the signs that will precede the coming of the Son of Man, e.g., false Messiahs, persecution, war, and cosmic cataclysms. While these chapters open with the question of the destruction of the Temple, they discuss both the punishment of Jerusalem and the Parousia; and it is very difficult to interpret what the various apocalyptic signs were originally meant to precede. Many would think that such sayings did not come from Jesus but from the Palestinian church, using the language of Jewish apocalyptic and seeking to console itself when the master did not return. Yet there is also a group of sayings that specifically refer to a delay of the Parousia without invoking apocalyptic, e.g., Matt 24:48; 25:5,19.[70]

▪ A Parousia the Time of Which Cannot Be Foretold. A group of sayings insists that the disciples cannot know when the Lord is coming—his coming will be like that of a thief in the night or the unexpected return of a master (Matt 24:42–44 = Luke 12:39–40; Matt 24:50 = Luke 12:46; Matt 25:13). Luke 17:20–21 is particularly interesting in the light of the references to apocalyptic signs cited above: "The kingdom of God is not coming with signs to be observed. . . . The kingdom of God is in the midst of you." Even more famous is Mark 13:32 which implies that Jesus himself did not know when all these things would come to pass: "Of that day or the hour no one knows, not even the angels in heaven, nor the Son, but only the Father." Many scholars accept the saying as authentic.[71] Some have hesitated because it is the only place in

---

[70] We may add Luke 19:11 where Jesus corrects the belief of the disciples that the kingdom of God is to come immediately; also Luke 17:22 where Jesus speaks of an unfulfilled longing on the part of the disciples to see one of the days of the Son of Man.

[71] W. G. Kümmel, *Promise and Fulfilment* (SBT 23; Naperville: Allenson, 1957), 42, cites a list of authors who accept Mark 13:32 as belonging to the oldest tradition, even though its wording has not remained intact. Earlier P. W. Schmiedel, in *Encyclopaedia Biblica* (New York: Macmillan, 1901), vol. 2, col. 1881, listed Mark

Mark where Jesus speaks of himself absolutely as "the Son," and indeed that might be a late feature. Others have thought that the early church attributed the saying to Jesus to explain the seeming contradictions among his predictions; yet it would have run against the grain of the postresurrectional period to attribute ignorance to Jesus. Church tendencies are visible in Acts 1:7 and in certain mss. of Matt 24:36 which mention ignorance of the time but omit all reference to the Son's not knowing.

Amidst such a confusion of anticipations how can one establish the original outlook of Jesus toward the Parousia and/or the final accomplishment of God's purpose? Of course, some of the seeming contradictions may have been created by the microscopic analysis to which modern investigators subject Gospel passages. Surely, too, some confusion that now appears was caused by early Christians who reinterpreted Jesus' statements in the light of their own traditional eschatological expectations. In particular, it is not unlikely that statements that once referred to the coming of the Son of Man in judgment on Jerusalem have been reinterpreted to refer to the Parousia in glory. Yet, with all these allowances, one finds it difficult to believe that Jesus' own position was clear. The NT Epistles give independent evidence of the confusion that reigned in 1st-century thought about the Parousia;[72] and such confusion could scarcely have arisen if Jesus both knew about the indefinite delay of the Parousia and expressed himself clearly on the subject.

That leaves two alternatives. The first is that Jesus knew about the Parousia but for some mysterious reason expressed himself obscurely. That seems unreasonable; and so one is almost forced to take the other alternative: Jesus did not know when the Parousia would take place (even as Mark 13:32 affirms) and that is why his statements were obscure.[73] Some would distinguish between what Jesus taught (namely, that he did not know the time of the Parousia)

13:32 as among the five "absolutely credible" general statements of the Gospel about Jesus.

[72] Compare I Thess with II Thess; I Cor 15 with II Cor 5; I Pet 4:7 with II Pet 3:4–13.

[73] Under Pope Vigilius in 553 (DBS §419) there was a condemnation of a Nestorian proposal that Jesus Christ, true Son of God and true Son of Man, was ignorant of future things and of the day of the Last Judgment and could have known

and what he hoped for in an apocalyptic setting (namely, a Parousia soon). However, statements that refer to a Parousia within a short time are not especially apocalyptic and are clearly taught, e.g., they are preceded by "Amen, I say to you." Others would explain away by exegesis all reference to the Parousia in the promises of what will happen in the lifetime of Jesus' hearers. If we recognize the desperate character of such solutions, is it inconceivable that, since Jesus did not know when God would bring about the final victory of the kingdom, he tended to think that it would occur soon and spoke accordingly? Many theologians would propose that such knowledge was not an essential of Jesus' mission. Can they also admit that Jesus was not protected from the confusing views of time inherent in an apocalyptic outlook? Exegetes can only point out the undeniable confusion in the statements attributed to him.

* * *

This chapter has reviewed a range of the ordinary and religious knowledge manifested in the Gospel accounts of Jesus, and throughout there were signs of limitation. Those who depend on a theological a priori argument that, because Jesus was "true God of true God," he had to know all things have a difficult task in explaining such limitations. They must resort to the thesis that he hid what he knew and deliberately manifested limitations in order not to confuse or astound his hearers. That explanation limps, for his hearers are portrayed as confused and amazed in any case. Since there is at least one recorded statement where Jesus says that the Son does not

---

such things only insomuch as a deity dwelt in him as if in another individual. This error is so tied into the Nestorian theory of two persons or beings in Christ that its condemnation would really not affect the modern nonNestorian problematic. *Ca.* 600 Pope Gregory (DBS §§474–75) tended to interpret Mark 13:32 as an accommodation of God's Son to human speech. He maintained that the Son of God in his human nature knew the time of the Parousia, but this knowledge did not come from his human nature. This statement (which is not looked on as binding in faith) invokes theological distinctions that go beyond what we can determine from the exegesis of the passage. I know of no binding Catholic Church statement that would forbid the interpretation of the literal sense of Mark 13:32 in the sense presented in the text above.

know, most biblical scholars will not accept such an explanation and will query the validity of the a priori claim for omniscience.

On the other side of the picture, even in the partial range of Jesus' sayings considered thus far, there is real difficulty for those who assume that Jesus presented himself as just another human being. Under (A) we saw traditions that Jesus manifested knowledge beyond ordinary human perceptiveness, and under (B) we saw Jesus' authority in interpreting Scripture and his absolute conviction that God would punish Jerusalem and the Temple and make him victorious despite his sufferings. All this corresponds well to the repeated evaluation of him during his lifetime as a prophet, one of those specially sent by God to challenge the covenanted people. Probably most a priori approaches to Jesus from the "true man" side of the spectrum would accept "prophet" as a historical self-estimation of Jesus, but would argue that he could have been no more than that. However, in the last elements that we discussed in this chapter (B ##8–10) there were already indications that the picture may have been more complicated. Jesus saw himself as so important that rejection of him (not only of God's message) would constitute the cause for divine action against Jerusalem and the Temple. Indeed he was remembered as saying "*I* will (or am able) to destroy." Jesus claims that he is not only to be made victorious (translated by his followers, perhaps post factum, in terms of the resurrection of the Son of Man) but also to have a final role (as the coming Son of Man) when God completes what was begun during his ministry. This goes beyond the claims of OT prophets and manifests a uniqueness in Jesus' self-estimation. He is not simply one of those whom God sends but the one to bring God's plan to completion. Let us now turn to actions and sayings where that uniqueness comes to the fore and finds clearer articulation.

CHAPTER 5.
WHAT CAN BE DISCERNED
ABOUT JESUS
FROM HIS DEEDS AND WORDS
PROCLAIMING THE KINGDOM
OF GOD

Perhaps we can now sense that in Chapters 3 and 4, while seeking to identify Jesus christologically, we were often asking the wrong questions. Although we were investigating the kinds of things that *we* might think that Jesus should have known if he were more than human, we were, in fact, investigating areas that were not Jesus' primary concern. There are no Gospel indications that Jesus was interested in manifesting knowledge of a wide range of matters (secular or religious), of the future, or of heavenly realities. This dearth of evidence means that our answers had to be partial and marginal. If we turn our investigation in another direction, however, the Synoptic Gospels offer ample evidence that Jesus' primary interest was the proclamation of the kingdom of God;[74] and so the words and deeds by which he did that constitute a much better guide to his identity.

In Jewish thought there was associated with the expected coming of the Messiah (the anointed king of the House of David) the restoration of a geographical kingdom (often anticipated to reach from Egypt to Mesopotamia) in which there would be prosperity,

---

[74] The idea of God's kingdom occurs more than 100 times in the NT, some 70 of which are in the Synoptic Gospels.

peace, and justice, consequent upon the defeat of Israel's enemies.[75] Jesus proclaimed that the kingdom was at hand, but his notion of kingdom did not fit the anticipation in many ways. He spoke of the kingdom (kingship)[76] of God, not of David. The kingship that he heralded rules over both individual lives and the whole of God's people Israel (without any suggestion of geographical boundaries). While it touches people on earth, it is a kingdom of the last times and, at least implicitly, affects all creation. No earthly foreign conquerors are fought, for the enemy who resists it and must be vanquished is Satan or the devil.[77] In defeating Satan and bringing about God's rule, Jesus employed both deeds and words. We shall now examine the relation of those deeds and words to the kingdom in order to discern Jesus' understanding of himself.

(A) What Jesus' Deeds Proclaiming the Kingdom Tell Us about His Christology

Most notable among Jesus' deeds are his miracles.[78] To some it may seem a bit strange that in an attempt to discuss historically Jesus' evaluation of himself, I would examine the miracles attributed

---

[75] The picture was not simply one of material success, for the ideal monarch of the Davidic line would bring about God's values in this earthly kingdom.

[76] "Kingdom" is the traditional NT translation of the Greek *basileia*. Although primarily an activity is envisaged ("rule" or "reign"), no consistent translation is feasible; for at times there is spatial imagery (door, entering into, etc.) that would cause us to think of a place. We may say that *basileia* refers both to kingship and to the kingdom produced by that kingship. Categorizing it as a "tensive symbol" has been made popular by N. Perrin, *Jesus and the Language of the Kingdom* (Philadelphia: Fortress, 1976).

[77] The worldview in which Jesus speaks and acts supposes a demonic rule over nature (e.g., in storms) and people (possessions, sickness, death). This is illustrated in the temptations of Jesus at the beginning of the ministry where the devil shows Jesus all the kingdoms of the world and says to Jesus, "To you I will give all this authority and their glory; for it has been delivered to me, and I give it to whom I will" (Luke 4: 5–6; cf. Matt 4:8–9). The extent to which Satan (the devil, Beelzebul, the Prince of this World, demons) is specifically named and is active varies from Gospel to Gospel.

[78] I remind readers that I am not engaged here in apologetics. For instance, I shall not try to establish that Jesus' miracles really did bring the kingdom/rule of God to people—something that would probably be impossible to prove since it takes faith to relate a physical healing to God's rule in people's lives. Given Jesus' claim that his

to him. Bultmann is famous for his attitude that Jesus never worked miracles because "modern man" does not believe in miracles. If by the designation "modern" one would think of women and men living in the world today, one could make a case that more people believe in miracles than disbelieve. That becomes evident in the number of people attracted to a place or person every time something miraculous is reported. Surely, however, Bultmann's understanding of "modern" would be much more restrictive, referring to a purely scientific (and often skeptical) outlook produced by the "Enlightenment" of the last centuries. However, even some of Bultmann's adherents (e.g., Käsemann) have recognized that one cannot make this "modern" worldview the measure of history: We cannot decide that something did not happen because we do not encounter it. Rather, history must be decided on the basis of evidence. The tradition that Jesus was one who performed cures and did other extraordinary actions is as old as the tradition of his words and must be taken seriously in any historical discussion.[79] It is noteworthy that Jesus' enemies are not presented as denying that he did extraordinary deeds; rather they attributed them to evil origins, either to the

---

miracles were making present the kingdom, I am concerned with what that tells us about his self-estimation.

[79] Despite some scholars' brave assertions, there is no way to prove the claim that Q (a no-longer-existing collection of sayings) contained the oldest tradition about Jesus and that therefore he was only a wisdom teacher. A very important treatment of the historicity of Jesus' miracles may be found in the 2d volume of J. P. Meier's *A Marginal Jew* (see *Evaluative Bibliography* below). See also D. Senior in NJBC 81, §§89–117. A corrective, indeed over-corrective, response to the idea that no Gospel miracle is authentic is offered by R. Latourelle, *The Miracles of Jesus and the Theology of Miracles* (New York: Paulist, 1988), where every Gospel miracle story is accepted as historical. Some, like V. Taylor, who would consider seriously the historicity of Jesus' healings cast doubt in principle on his "nature miracles" (calming a storm, multiplying loaves, etc.). But this too reflects modern prejudice. In the Gospel worldview derived from Israel, God is the God of nature as well as of the patriarchs. There is no OT justification for rejecting nature miracles while accepting healings: Elijah both brought down fire from heaven and raised the son of the widow of Zarephath; Elisha both multiplied food and cleansed a leper. The multiplication of loaves may well be the best attested of the miracles of Jesus; it is reported in all four Gospels (and that is extremely rare for a miracle of the public ministry), probably in independent accounts by Mark and John. Indeed, it is so old that two divergent forms have developed within the Synoptic tradition and are reported by Mark and Matt.

devil (Mark 3:22–30) or in 2d-century polemic to magic (Irenaeus, *Adversus Haereses* 2.32.3–5).

In particular, one should be wary of the claim that Jesus was portrayed like the many other miracle-working teachers, Jewish and pagan, of his era. The idea that such a figure was a commonplace in the 1st century is largely a fiction. Jesus is remembered as combining teaching with miracles intimately related to his teaching, and that combination may be unique. The two most frequently cited Jewish wonder-workers are Honi (Onias), the rain-maker (or circle-drawer) of the 1st century BC, and the Galilean Hanina of the 1st century AD. Almost all that is known of these men comes from much later rabbinic literature, and by that time legendary and theological developments had aggrandized the portrayal (as pointed out by scholars such as W. L. Green and B. M. Bokser). Almost certainly in the earliest tradition they were not rabbinical teachers, and it is debatable whether they were primarily miraculous wonder-workers by their own power or men of persuasive prayer that brought God's extraordinary help.[80] The most popular pagan parallel offered for Jesus is Apollonius of Tyana (1st century AD) for whose activity we are largely dependent on a life written 200 years later by Philostratus, a life that some serious scholars regard as largely fictitious.[81] The miracles attributed to that figure, some of which may be influenced by knowledge of the stories about Jesus, have the *purpose* of causing astonishment and bringing about adulation—quite unlike the Gospel presentation of Jesus' miracles.

Indeed, the English term "miracle" is somewhat misleading in relation to Jesus' actions, for its primary connotation is something

---

[80] This is how Josephus (*Ant.* 14.2.1;##22–24) describes Honi: "a righteous man, a friend of God, who once in a dry period prayed to God to end the drought; and God, having heard his prayer, sent rain."

[81] E.g., M. Dzielska, *Apollonius of Tyana in Legend and History* (Rome: L'Erma, 1986). Sometimes Apollonius is held up as example of the Hellenistic image of a divine man (*theios anēr*), i.e., a human being supposedly gifted with godlike powers; and the Gospel or early Christian picture of Jesus is thought to be influenced by such a model. For a sharp criticism of that thesis, see B. Blackburn, *Theios Anēr and the Markan Miracle Tradition* (Tübingen: Mohr [Siebeck], 1991). He traces the picture of Jesus as a miracle-worker to the earliest levels of Christianity and an OT background.

to be astonished at (Latin verb *mirari*: "to wonder at") and puts too much emphasis on the deeds of Jesus as astounding.[82] There is no question that according to the Gospels Jesus' miracles caused people to wonder and admire, but that was a secondary effect. When there is an attempt (on the part of the devil, Herod, the Pharisees, or the people) to make it primary by asking Jesus to show off miracles, he is pictured as refusing.[83] In one of his parables, he is remembered as skeptical about whether the miraculous effectively sways those who are not otherwise persuaded: "If someone should rise from the dead, they will not be convinced" (Luke 16:31). False prophets could work prodigies that would come close to deceiving even the elect (Mark 13:22–23).

We get a better sense of Jesus' extraordinary deeds if we use the most common designation given them in the Synoptic Gospels themselves: *dynamis* ("act of power").[84] The miracle was not primarily an external proof of the coming of the kingdom (i.e., the fact that Jesus worked miracles proved that the kingdom had come), but *one of the means by which the kingdom came.* The acts of power were weapons Jesus used to reclaim people and the world from the domination of evil. When Jesus healed the sick or resuscitated[85] the

---

[82] *Miraculum* is never used in the Latin NT, and the Greek equivalent *teras* is never used alone to refer to the deeds of Jesus. This militates against the thesis of Bultmann that miracle stories were added to the Gospels to persuade people that he was equal or superior to Jewish or Greek wonder-workers. The miracles of Jesus are far closer to those in the Elijah/Elisha cycle than to the suggested pagan parallels. See R. E. Brown, "Jesus and Elisha," *Perspective* 12 (1971), 85–104.

[83] Matt 4:5–7; Luke 23:6–9; Mark 8:11–13; Matt 12:38–42; Mark 15:31–32; Mark 6:1–6.

[84] Plural: *dynameis.* John uses the terms *sēmeion* ("sign") and *ergon* ("work"). These terms are also found in the Synoptics for Jesus' miracles (e.g., Matt 12:38–39; 11:2), but infrequently and not always with the same meaning as in John. Both the Johannine terms reflect Greek OT terminology, e.g., for the miracles done by Moses leading Israel out of Egypt and through the desert (Exod 10:1; 34:10). The use of "sign" in the sense that what Jesus does signifies who he is reflects a development within Johannine theology, but that connotation is not irreconcilable with the Synoptic use of *dynameis.*

[85] I use "resuscitate" to distinguish between Jesus' restoring dead people to ordinary life and his own resurrection where he is raised up to life with God and no longer dwells in this world. Of course, resuscitations from the dead remain miraculous.

dead, he was breaking Satanic power that manifested itself in illness and death. That is why Jesus' healings were so often associated with demonic possession. He can sum up his ministry thus: "Behold I cast out demons and perform cures" (Luke 13:32), and those activities lock into the coming of the kingdom: "If it is by God's spirit that I cast out demons, then it follows that the kingdom of God has at last overtaken you" (Matt 12:28[86]). The resuscitation of the son of the widow of Nain reveals that "God has visited His people" (Luke 7:16). Some of the nature miracles reflect the same mentality. Paul tells us that all creation had been groaning in travail until the time of deliverance (Rom 8:22; see II Pet 3:12–13), and in such a worldview Satan manifested his dominion by disruptions like storms. In stilling the storm (Mark 4:37–41), Jesus stands and rebukes the wind just as he rebukes sickness and demons. To the sea he says, "Shut up," the same type of command he gives to the demon in Mark 1:25.

Yet, granted that Jesus did perform acts of power, does that tell us more about him than that he was a prophet like Elijah or Elisha who were thought to have performed many of the same miracles? Yes, precisely because in the tradition Jesus connects them with the coming of the kingdom, a definitive eschatological context absent from the prophetic miracles. Jesus by his actions clearly presents himself as changing the governance of the world and of human lives, introducing God's dominion in place of the oppressive Satanic rule. A passage like Isa 61:1–3 promised a supreme divine intervention where there would be good news for the poor, sight for the blind, consolation for the afflicted. By healing the blind, the lame, lepers, and raising the dead (and also preaching to the poor) Jesus was proclaiming that the intervention had begun.[87] The lines of demarcation between Jesus and God in this intervention are very vague. The kingdom comes both in and through Jesus. The power to do the healings and other miracles belongs to God but also to Jesus. Thus if, at the end of the preceding chapter, we saw in the general knowledge

---

[86] The wording in Luke 11:20 is slightly different: "If it is by the finger of God that I cast out demons, then the kingdom of God has come upon you," echoing Exod 8:15 (RSV 8:19).

[87] The Isaian author may have meant his description figuratively, but Jesus is fulfilling it literally.

manifested by Jesus signs of a unique self-estimation, this is strongly confirmed by the relation posited between the miracles and the coming of the kingdom. Jesus is accomplishing something no one has ever done before since Adam's sin yielded to Satan's dominion over this world.

Other deeds of Jesus, besides miracles, cast light on his self-understanding. Part of the eschatological imagery of Israel was a great banquet to be eaten by the just with God; and we know from the Parable of the Great Supper that Jesus made use of this imagery (Matt 22:1–14; Luke 14:16–24; notice that in the Matthean form the one who is put out of the supper is damned, and so clearly no ordinary banquet is meant). A firm memory from Jesus' ministry is his own meals with tax-collectors and sinners (Mark 2:15–17; Luke 7:36–50; 15:2; also 14:12–14) for which he was attacked. His fellowship and sharing table with them was an anticipation[88] of the eschatological banquet in which the gracious mercy of God was already being extended. Related to the memory of the meal involving bread and wine that Jesus ate on the night before he died (see I Cor 11:23–26) is the statement that he would not again drink of the fruit of the vine until he would drink it new in the kingdom of God or until the kingdom would come.[89] This was his last meal anticipating the heavenly banquet, and that banquet would be a continuation of what he had begun in his lifetime. It is difficult to know whether

---

[88] Notice that I have been speaking of anticipation. There is a long debate among scholars about whether Jesus' eschatology was realized (the kingdom of God is totally here at this moment) or future (the kingdom will come later). Compare for instance Luke 17:20 and Mark 9:1. Although there are absolutists on either side, it is impossible to exclude all elements of either attitude from Jesus' proclamation. The best solution is along the lines that the kingly rule of God was already making itself present in Jesus' person, proclamation, and actions, but the complete and visible manifestation of the kingdom lay in the future and would also be brought about through Jesus, the Son of Man. Parables like the mustard seed, the leaven, the seed growing by itself, the fish net, and the weeds growing among the wheat show that there is both present activity and future climax in the kingdom. In Gospel thought, after Jesus died and God raised him, God had yet something to do in and through Jesus; but already before Jesus' death sinners were called and forgiven, the sick were healed, the dead raised, and Satan's power was being broken—as both the sign and inauguration of what would be done.

[89] Mark 14:25; Matt 26:29; Luke 22:18; see also Luke 22:16.

Jesus' forgiving sins should be catalogued under his words or under his deeds, but the tradition is very strong that he claimed this power and indeed that sometimes his claim to the power produced dissent (Mark 2:5–12). Whether or not the reaction "Who can forgive sins but God alone?" was historically vocalized in Jesus' ministry, it is a perfectly logical observation. All these actions reinforce the picture of a Jesus whose self-understanding involved a unique and essential position in God's final action establishing rule or kingdom over the world.[90]

(B) What Jesus' Words Proclaiming the Kingdom Tell Us about His Christology

As we turn to Jesus' words, in the canonical writings they have been blended with his deeds and the passion, and not preserved as simply a body of sayings, such as we encounter in the apocryphal *Gospel of Thomas* and presumably in Q. This blending implicitly reflects an early Christian judgment that the proclamation is inseparably related to both who Jesus is and what he did; and indeed we shall see that his words proclaiming the kingdom have the same implications as his deeds. With his deeds as with his words, we cannot be certain of the historicity of everything attributed to Jesus. Yet the percentage that responsible scholars consider historical (e.g., J. P. Meier, NJBC 78, §§17–24) offers considerable evidence for judging Jesus' self-estimation.

We begin with Jesus' parables,[91] one of the most historically

---

[90] I am tempted to mention here Jesus' cleansing the Temple. Prophets also assailed the Temple verbally but Jesus took physical action; and this is associated by Christians with the Temple purity expected in the last times when God judges the world and there is no longer a merchant in the house of the Lord (Zech 14, especially 14:21). Yet the highly eschatological interpretation of the action may have come after Jesus' lifetime.

[91] There is an enormous literature on the parables of which I shall mention but a few of the most significant studies: Dodd, Jeremias, Perrin. See the overall summary by J. R. Donahue in NJBC 81, §§57–88. Here we are interested in the parables only to the extent that they cast light on Jesus' understanding of himself and his role. In treating the parables inevitably I am favoring the evidence in the Synoptics since John does not have parables (with the possible exception of the figurative use of the good

certain areas of his preaching. The parables of the treasure buried in the field and of the pearl of great price (Matt 13:44–46) teach that Jesus' hearers must put the acceptance of his proclamation of the kingdom over every other value. The presence of Jesus is an eschatological moment of joy like the presence of a bridegroom at the wedding banquet (Mark 2:19). Every effort must be made to prevent anyone from being lost in this final moment, as illustrated in the parables of the lost sheep and lost coin (Luke 15:3–10; Matt 18:12–13). The parable of the great supper (Matt 22:1–14; Luke 14:16–24) with the invitations sent out and either accepted or refused makes Jesus' proclamation a moment of judgment in which a definitive choice must be made. Similarly the parable of the wise and foolish virgins (Matt 25:1–13) presents an absolute demand to be ready; Jesus' proclamation is a time of decision as people face the divine coming. The parable of the dishonest steward (Luke 16:1–8) who "fixes the books" in order to have friends whom he can fall back on reflects this moment of live-or-die decision. The parabolic saying about not turning back when one puts the hand to the plow (Luke 9:62) illustrates the irrevocability of the choice. The parables of the laborers hired for the vineyard (Matt 20:1–16) and the Pharisee and publican (Luke 18:9–14) highlight the spontaneous graciousness of God in Jesus' proclamation of the kingdom, reaching out to the least likely. The parables of the unmerciful servant and the sheep and the goats (Matt 18:23–35; 25:31–46) show the strong element of final judgment based on reception or rejection of the values of the kingdom.

Beyond the parables there are demands of Jesus that throw light on how crucial was his own role in this advent of God's rule. When the demand "Follow me" is uttered by Jesus, a man cannot even take the time to bury his father (a sacred religious duty); rather "Let the dead bury the dead" (Luke 9:59–60). Being a disciple of Jesus is more important than family ties: "If any come to me and do not hate their own father and mother and wife and children and brothers and sisters, indeed, even their own life, they cannot be my disciples" (Luke 14:26; also Matt 10:37). Judgment before the angels of God

---

shepherd and the vine and the branches). I shall devote APPENDIX IV to Johannine christology.

will be based on whether one acknowledges or denies Jesus (Luke 12:8–9; see also Matt 7:21–23, 24–27). Rejecting Jesus' proclamation will bring damnation on Corazin, Bethsaida, and Capernaum (Matt 11:20–24). Losing one's life for Jesus' sake brings salvation (Luke 9:24). Entry into the kingdom depends on accepting Jesus' standards (Mark 10:15). In fact Jesus assumes that he has the power to assign his disciples roles in heaven (Matt 19:28; Luke 22:28–30). The fall of Satan from heaven is associated with the mission Jesus gives to his disciples (Luke 10:18).

If Matt's series of "You have heard it said . . . but I say to you" (5:21–22, 27–28, 33–34, 38–39, 43–44) is historically authentic, Jesus thinks he has the authority to modify and even eliminate what God said to Moses. There is very good reason to accept as authentic the saying of Jesus against divorce that is more strenuous than Moses' teaching (Mark 10:11–12; Matt 5:31–32; 19:7–9; Luke 16:18; also attested by I Cor 7:10–11). Jesus sees himself as not bound by interpretations of the law of the Sabbath rest or of ritual purity (Luke 14:1–6; 11:37–41; Mark 7:14–15).[92] One can discuss the extent to which individual stances taken by Jesus (according to the tradition) were totally outside the legitimate debatable area among the Jews of his time—many were not; but the cumulative effect is an attitude of much greater independence than that attributed to any other single teacher. The claim that the Law and the Prophets lasted until John (Matt 11:13) reinforces the notion that one greater than Moses is here.[93] Past generations wanted to see what is happening through and in Jesus and they did not; so that Jesus can tell his disciples, "Blessed are your eyes because they see, and your ears because they hear" (Matt 13:16). The "Amen" with which Jesus prefaces his statements (most unusually from the evidence of the Judaism of his times) demands obedience and acceptance even before Jesus has uttered his oracle. Those who give this obedience and acceptance to his oracles concerning the rule/kingdom of God will be accepted

---

[92] For disputes about the Sabbath see Mark 2:23–28; 3:1–6; Luke 13:10–17; 14: 1–6; John 5. The christological implications of this would be heightened if Jesus' saying that "The Son of Man is Lord even of the Sabbath" (Mark 2:28) is authentic.

[93] The newness of what Jesus has come to do is caught in the figurative saying that one cannot put new wine in old wine skins (Mark 2:22) which is set in the context of disputes over obligations of the Law.

into the kingdom. Worthy of note is that the oracles are uttered with first person authority, "I say to you,"[94] quite unlike the prophetic custom of having God speak ("The Lord says . . .": Isa 1:24; Jer 2: 12; Hosea 11:11; Amos 3:11; etc.). Why Jesus can speak with such personal authority is never explained in the Synoptic Gospels; indeed that silence over against the prophets' explanation that word of God came to them implies a very high christology wherein the authority to make demands in God's name simply resides in Jesus because of who he is.

The last point is important in judging what Jesus' deeds and words related to his proclamation of the kingdom tell us about his self-understanding. The implication of what we have seen in this chapter is that Jesus claimed to be greater than any figure that had preceded him in the salvation history of Israel—greater than the prophets and greater even than Moses. Some have tried to do justice to this superior role by calling him the eschatological prophet of the last times in and through whom God's final salvation broke through. I do not think that is an adequate description precisely because in none of the Gospels is there a moment from birth to death in which Jesus is described as receiving the prophetic vocation. Jesus is the eschatological figure through whom God's final salvation breaks through, but his relationship to the one whom Israel calls God is so uniquely close that his followers had to find titles different from the designations that had been used for previous actors in God's plan. Let us now go beyond Jesus' attitude toward the kingdom to his attitude toward himself and how he phrased it in order that we may see the relationship between that and the titles eventually used by his followers to describe him.

---

[94] Scholars have noted that the combination of "Amen, I say to you" means that Jesus pledges his person behind the truth of his proclamation. He does not report the word of God but speaks as with God's authority.

CHAPTER 6.
WHAT CAN BE DISCERNED
ABOUT JESUS
FROM HIS WORDS
CONCERNING HIMSELF

We come now to the most difficult area for the discernment of
Jesus' own christology—difficult because of the lack of evidence.
After Jesus' death Christians reflected intensely on Jesus' identity,
particularly in terms of titles that expressed their faith: Jesus is . . .
Messiah/Christ, or Lord, or Son of God, or Son of Man, or even God
(APPENDIX III). We shall discuss in Chapters 7–10 the abundant
evidence for such christology among the early Christians; here we
confine ourselves to the very limited evidence for *Jesus' application
of the titles Messiah, Son of God, and Son of Man to himself or his
acceptance of them when applied by others.*[95]

Before I begin, some cautions are in order. First, were we to
decide that Jesus did not use or accept one or the other of these titles,
that would be no decisive indication that Christians were unjustified

---

[95] I have chosen titles that are distinctive (unlike teacher, rabbi, prophet) and
thus able to indicate Jesus' conception of his own identity. The title Lord (*kyrios*)
could also be distinctive, for from early times it was a title that exalted Jesus (footnote
17 above). Nevertheless, as pointed out in footnote 2 above, *kyrios* covers "Sir,"
"Master," and "Lord," so that too often there are insoluble difficulties in a Gospel
self-designation of Jesus that uses that term—even beyond the issue of what the underlying Aramaic might imply. The title "God" would be truly distinctive; but Jesus
never uses it of himself and only once is it given affirmatively to him by someone else
in the Gospel narrative (John 20:28, discussed on pp. 188–89 below).

in applying such titles to him. God's revelation (p. 5 above) and the inspiration of the NT records that witness to that revelation guarantee for believers that the early Christian affirmations of faith understood Jesus' identity correctly, even when they went beyond his own articulation. (We shall see in subsequent chapters that early Christians most often modified the meaning of the titles in order to make them more fully applicable to Jesus.[96]) Second, whether Jesus articulated his identity in titles is not the same question as whether he was conscious of possessing the relationship to God implied in the titles. Consciousness of one's self or identity is not the same as having the precise terminology to express that awareness. Third, the issue of Jesus' self-awareness is not the same as the issue of how much knowledge he possessed. Above (pp. 31–59) I signalled extreme caution about the claim that Jesus knew all things (secular, religious, the future, etc.)—a claim that runs against much scriptural evidence and (I note for Roman Catholics) in support of which there is no clearly binding church teaching. In reference to Jesus' awareness of his own identity (note: not of his ability to phrase it), the situation is different. There is not a word in the Gospels to indicate that at any stage of his life Jesus was not aware of a unique relationship to God;[97] and although again there may not be a binding church definition that is absolutely clear, this issue is much closer to the

---

[96] Let me stress that Christians grew in their understanding of Jesus—a growth in perception that changes Jesus' identity not at all.

[97] If Jesus knew his divine identity throughout his whole recorded life, that need not have prevented growth in his comprehension of how that identity interacted with a human life where experience, the events of the ministry, and indeed his death brought increased understanding of the human situation. In BRTOQ 97–99 I warned against the inexactness of phrasing the issue of Jesus' awareness of divine identity under the heading of "Did he know he was God?" The person who opts for that phraseology generally has a Trinitarian understanding of the term "God," not fully achieved till several centuries after Jesus' time. To ask that question of Jesus as a 1st-century Jew would have been equivalent to asking him did he think he was the Almighty Father dwelling in heaven (when at the moment he was the Son on earth). I shall contend in APPENDIX III that Christians by the end of the 1st century adapted the term "God" so that it could apply to both the Father in heaven and the Son on earth, and only after that adaptation could Jesus be called God. Much older is the nonterminological issue of whether Jesus knew his divine identity.

heart of the Christian proclamation.[98] With these cautions in mind, let us proceed to our discussion of whether Jesus used certain titles to give expression to that relationship.

(A) Did Jesus Affirm That He Was the Messiah?

As I pointed out at the beginning of Chapter 1, there is no doubt that the early church confessed Jesus as the Messiah (Greek *Christos* = the expected *anointed* [king of the House of David]). Indeed, a "Christian" was one who accepted Jesus as Christ or Messiah. The fact that all four evangelists wrote believing that Jesus was the Messiah does not tell us, however, that he himself thought he was the Messiah. As part of the necessary process of finding language to express the reality of Jesus, they could have read their articulated post-resurrectional faith back into the scenes of his lifetime (see pp. 9, 24 above). In times past some have argued that all Jews expected the Messiah, and so this title had to come up in debates about Jesus in his lifetime. That argument is simply false. When I discuss the meaning and history of the title in APPENDIX I, I shall point out that in the postexilic period (539 BC on) there was a variety of expectations as to how and by whom God would intervene on behalf of Israel. If we leave aside the NT, there would be less than 30 references to the Messiah in preserved Jewish literature from 200 BC to 100 AD, with the Dead Sea Scrolls as the most abundant source. (There different Messiahs or anointed ones, including a priestly strain, are mentioned.) In the long history of the Jews written in Greek by Josephus (*Ant.*), *christos* is only used twice, both times (one of them probably added by Christians) in reference to Jesus. Indeed, in all Jewish history before AD 130 (and then dubiously), we have no evidence that any living Jew was ever referred to as the Messiah except Jesus of Nazareth. Therefore we cannot solve our question by assumptions

---

[98] See footnote 111 below for the statement of Pope Pius X. In *Gregorianum* 67 (1986), 413–28, there is a report on four affirmations of the 1985 meeting of the Roman Catholic International Theological Commission, the first of which may be abbreviated thus: The life of Jesus, lived as a perfect servant, bears witness to his awareness of his filial relation to the Father.

about what people had to think of Jesus during his lifetime or what he had to think of himself. Rather let us look at five pieces of NT evidence: three passages in the Gospels where the term Messiah is used of him, combined with two other references from which one could deduce that he was called the Messiah.

#1. Peter's confession (Mark 8:29–33; Matt 16:15–23; Luke 9:20–22). The scene is particularly important for the identity of Jesus because it is introduced by the question "Who do people say that I am [Matt: the Son of Man is]?" After inadequate answers (John the Baptist, Elijah, one of the prophets), Peter gives the answer, "You are the Messiah" (Mark); "The Messiah of God" (Luke); "You are the Messiah, the Son of the living God" (Matt). The agreement of Luke with Mark indicates that the basic confession involved only the Messiah and that Matt has added "the Son of the living God," which interprets "Messiah," in order to make intelligible the praise of Peter that will follow.

In Mark Jesus reacts by commanding the disciples "to tell no one about him." That cannot imply that Peter's confession of Jesus as the Messiah was wrong, for the heading of the Marcan Gospel (1: 1) identifies Jesus as the Messiah. Rather the silence is part of the Marcan picture of a Jesus who before the time of his condemnation to death will not accede to that identification lest the necessary element of suffering in it be overlooked.[99] When Jesus goes on to speak about the Son of Man's future suffering, Peter rebukes him; and that leads Jesus to characterize Peter as a Satan who is thinking from the human point of view rather than from God's point of view (Mark 8: 33). Surely, then, Peter has no proper grasp of what Messiah means but understands it in a way that excludes suffering. Luke reports both a command by Jesus to tell this to no one and the saying about the suffering of the Son of Man, but no praise or blame addressed to Peter.[100] At the end of the longer Matthean scene, Matt 16:20–23

---

[99] This Marcan silence or secrecy motif is often regarded as a Marcan creation and not an authentic memory from the ministry of Jesus. The standardization and the repetition of the secrecy motif may indeed be Marcan, but we cannot be certain that some memory of reticence stemming from Jesus' ministry has not been generalized (see V. Taylor, *The Gospel According to St. Mark* [London: Macmillan, 1953], 122–24).

[100] The omission of the rebuke to Peter is typically Lucan, for this Gospel almost always softens or omits material derogatory to any of the Twelve.

has approximately the same material as Mark with minor clarifications.[101] However, these verses are preceded in 16:16 by an encomium of Peter because of his confession of Jesus as the Messiah, the son of the living God: "Blessed are you, Simon Bar-Jona, for flesh and blood have not revealed this to you but my Father who is in heaven." The encomium is joined to a promise that the church will be built on the rock of Peter to whom will be given the keys of the kingdom and the power to bind and loose (16:17–19). Some look on this material that Matt has added to what he took over from Mark as a Matthean creation. However, the addition is very Semitic in tone, and a reasonable case can be made that Matt is joining two traditions about Peter's confession.[102] The first would have been the tradition he took over from Mark—a confession made by Peter during the ministry identifying Jesus as the Messiah but exhibiting a very inadequate grasp of the implications of that title. The second may have been a postresurrectional confession by Peter of Jesus as the Son of God, a comprehension that sprang from divine revelation.

There is no way to prove that the basic Marcan scene of Peter's confession (on which both Matt and Luke drew) is historical. John's parallel in 6:66–71 helps to establish a preGospel origin of Peter's confession of Jesus if one accepts the thesis of John's independence of Mark (which I favor). Yet in that parallel Peter confesses Jesus as "the Holy One of God," not as the Messiah (even if "the holy one" may be broadly equivalent to the Messiah).[103] If we were to judge that the confession itself is not implausible historically, it would suggest that Jesus' followers hailed him as the Messiah during his lifetime and that he did not deny such a designation even if he thought it involved misunderstanding.

#2. The high priest's question at the Sanhedrin trial (Mark 14: 61–62; Matt 26:63–64; Luke 22:67–69). With minor variation Mark and Matt agree that the question united two titles: "Are you the

---

[101] Namely, "to tell no one *that he was the Messiah*"; and the added "You are a stumbling block to me" addressed to Peter.

[102] See the ecumenical book *Peter* (footnote 39 above) 86–89.

[103] The Messiah confession appears on the lips of Peter's brother Andrew in John 1:41.

Messiah, the Son of the Blessed [Matt: the Son of the living God]?"
Luke, who may be following another tradition here, separates the
Messiah question from that about the Son of God (Luke 22:70).
There are problems about the historicity of the Synoptics in placing
this trial on the night before Jesus died (John 11:47–53 has a Sanhedrin session many days before) and in gathering here the basic issues
against Jesus (John has them scattered, e.g., John 10:24–25 has the
Messiah question and answer during the ministry[104]). Nevertheless,
if we leave aside the timing and the combining with "the Son of
God," the Messiah question put to Jesus in all four Gospels by those
depicted as his enemies heightens the likelihood that the Messiah
issue was raised during Jesus' lifetime. We have no idea how the
Jewish authorities (or populace in John) got the idea that Jesus
might be the Messiah—from his followers? from Jesus' own claims?
from a malevolent guess that Jesus might be so pretentious?

Jesus' answer to the Messiah question varies in the Gospels. In
Mark he answers "I am" to being the Messiah, the Son of the
Blessed. On the level of the story-line that Mark's audience (approximately in the 60s of the 1st century) is following, Mark could
scarcely supply a negative response since, as noted previously, he
had affirmed this identity for Jesus in 1:1,11. Nevertheless, when
Peter confessed Jesus to be the Messiah, the Marcan Jesus was much
less affirmative than he is now to the high priest. Presumably the
strong affirmation has been evoked by two factors: Here in a trial
destined to condemn Jesus, there is no danger of overlooking the
element of suffering; and here "the Son of the Blessed" is joined to
"Messiah" in the question (even as was "Son of God" in Matt's form
under #1 above). But if we move back from the story-line and the
time when the Gospel was written to the time of Jesus, was Jesus'
answer to being the Messiah so unambiguously affirmative? Perhaps
the responses of Jesus in the other Gospels throw light on that point.

In Matt Jesus answers the high priest's combined question
about the Messiah, Son of God thus: "That is what you say." This is
an affirmative,[105] but one that puts responsibility on the questioner

---

[104] John 7:25–27,31 assumes that everybody in Jerusalem knew about the claim
that Jesus was the Messiah.

[105] A few scholars try to argue to the contrary; but later on, in clear dependence
on Jesus' having made such an affirmation, the passersby mock him as he hangs on

for the interpretation being given to the point at issue—an interpretation about which the speaker is not enthusiastic. If one asks on
the level of the story-line why the Matthean Jesus would have been
so enthusiastic when Peter used these combined titles but is now
much more cautious when the high priest uses them, the solution is
that Peter used them as a confession uttered under divine revelation,
while the high priest uses them as a disbelieving question to find
evidence against Jesus.

Luke, who separates the question of the Messiah from the question about the Son of God, has a very ambiguous answer to the Messiah query: "If I tell you, you will not believe; and if I ask you, you
will not answer." (Luke reserves the qualified affirmative response
by Jesus, "You say that I am," for the separate Son of God query.) In
John 10 Jesus' Jewish adversaries challenge Jesus about his claimed
identity; and the two titles, Messiah and the Son of God, come up in
the same order as in the Synoptics. To the query, "If you are the
Messiah, tell us plainly," Jesus answers, "I told you, and you do not
believe" (10:24–25)—an answer very much like the answer in Luke,
so that the two Gospels may be echoing the same tradition. The
majority impression from the three Gospels other than Mark is that
on the level of the story-line, although Jesus did not deny that he
was the Messiah, he was wary when the opponents used that title
because he knew that they would not believe and did not understand
his outlook. Might that not be closer to history than Mark's simple
affirmation? Nevertheless, we must be cautious for all the evangelists
have posed the question with an eye to how Jews of their times who
did not believe in Jesus understood what Christians said about him,
and all four were supplying an answer with an eye to how Christians
confessed Jesus. One is hearing the high priest and Jesus in a narrative influenced by debates between the synagogue and the church.

#3. The Samaritan woman in John 4:25–26. She says, "I know
that a/the Messiah (the name means 'Christ') is coming; and when

---

the cross, "If you are the Son of God, come down from the cross" (Matt 27:40).
Indeed, in their mockery the chief priests and the elders report, "He said, 'I am the
Son of God' " (27:43). I shall not treat this scene on the cross (Matt and Mark 15:32)
where the chief priests mock the crucified Jesus as the Messiah, for in terms of giving
evidence about christology it is dependent on the trial scene.

that one comes, he will tell us everything." Jesus responds, "I, the one speaking to you, I am (he)." On the level of the story-line the answer makes good sense; Jesus was affirmed to be the Messiah by his followers in 1:41 without objection on his part, and now another who is moving close to believing in him makes the confession. However, very few scholars who have studied John would assume that the dialogue with the Samaritan woman is simple history; and so far as we know, the Samaritans did not expect the Messiah because they had rejected the covenant made between God and David about the continuing royal succession of David's line.[106] Thus this scene does not tell us that in his lifetime Jesus acknowledged without demurral that he was the Messiah.

#4. "The King of the Jews." All four Gospels (Mark 15:2 and par.) agree that Pilate asked Jesus if he was "the King of the Jews."[107] All four Gospels (Mark 15:26 and par.) agree that "the King of the Jews" was in the title or charge associated with the cross of Jesus. Before Pilate's question about the King of the Jews, Mark 14:61 had introduced the issue of the Messiah; and after the crucifixion charge, Mark introduces a mockery about Jesus being the Messiah (15:32). Therefore he probably wanted readers to associate the two: The Romans put Jesus to death because he claimed to be the Messiah, the King of the Jews. In Matt the probability is raised to virtual certainty because Pilate who has asked whether Jesus is "the King of the Jews" (27:11) twice indicates that he knows Jesus is called the Messiah (27: 17,22). Luke 23:2 spells out the charge that is presented to Pilate: Jesus "has said that he himself is a Messiah king." A strong case has been made for the historicity of the title on the cross: "The King of the Jews."[108] Accordingly, this title adds to the likelihood that "Messiah" was associated with Jesus during his lifetime.

---

[106] Although Samaritans came to expect the Taheb (which later Samaritan literature describes as a Moses-like figure), that expectation is hard to date.

[107] It is not clear that this question is separate evidence from the title on the cross, for the question might be a back-formation from the title, i.e., from the fact that Jesus was crucified on that charge, Christians might have assumed that Pilate asked him about it. If John has tradition independent of Mark's, the back-formation explanation is doubtful, since it is unlikely that independently both traditions proceeded to take the same step.

[108] See N. A. Dahl, *The Crucified Messiah* (Minneapolis: Augsburg, 1974), 10–36.

#5. *Early Christian Confession of Jesus as the Messiah.* I mentioned above the massive frequency of the application of "Messiah" to Jesus by his followers in postresurrection times and, in fact, seemingly at a very early period.[109] Is that plausible if no reference to Jesus as the Messiah was ever made before he died?

CONCLUSIONS. The evidence from these five points makes it extremely likely that the issue of Jesus as the Messiah did arise in his lifetime. Indeed, the evidence excludes certain theoretical possibilities about that issue. Let me italicize some judgments. I think it *most implausible that Jesus ever denied that he was the Messiah*; otherwise his followers would have said that he was executed on a *totally* false charge: He was not a king and had denied that he was one. Instead, in their preaching and writings they indicated that he was a king but not in the sense charged by his opponents. I think it *certain that some of those arraigned against him, Jews and/or Gentiles, thought that he or his followers claimed he was the Messiah* [*king*].

In fact, it is *very probable that followers of Jesus during his lifetime confessed him as the Messiah.* The counter-proposal that perhaps the Jewish opponents on their own assumed that he claimed to be the Messiah is a desperate suggestion given that #1 and #3 above attribute the use of the title to his followers or would-be followers. Moreover, if we consider #5 above, his postresurrectional followers are unlikely to have accepted with such enthusiasm something that his opponents had foisted on him. Finally, I would judge it *probable that Jesus never clearly or enthusiastically accepted the title in the sense in which both followers and opponents proposed it for him.*[110] He had no intention of doing things that many would associate with the Messiah, e.g., establishing an earthly kingdom, conquering foreign rulers, or functioning as an earthly ruler; and he thought that

---

[109] Rom 1:3–4 which implies messiahship in having Jesus descended from David according to the flesh is a prePauline formula that may go back before AD 40. See p. 114 below.

[110] There is little to support the contention that although Jesus made lucid claims to be the Messiah, they were not understood because of the obtuseness or hardness of heart of his hearers. Rather it took time after his death for the Jewish presuppositions about the Messiah to be modified and tailored to suit Jesus' career, so that believers could recognize him without reservation as the Messiah in all the phases of his life (see Chapters 7–10 below).

descent from David was not of crucial significance (Mark 12:35–37 and par.). Is it logical to suppose that Jesus never denied he was the Messiah and yet was not enthusiastic about the title as it was proposed? One can easily imagine circumstances in which it would have been perfectly logical. For example, if Jesus considered himself as God's final agent in bringing about the kingdom, he might not have denied that he was the Messiah because in the minds of many that would have signified that he was not God's final agent. On the other hand, his understanding of himself may have meant that he did not fit any previous expectation exactly and so he could not enthusiastically affirm he was the Messiah.[111] Paradoxically this attitude points to a higher christology than if he regarded himself as fitting all that was generally expected of the Messiah.

(B) Did Jesus Affirm That He Was the Son of God?

To prevent confusion, it is well to remind ourselves that calling someone "son" in relation to God is ambiguous. It need not mean divine filiation in the proper sense of having one's origin from God so that one has God's own nature, but may connote only a special relationship to God. Thus in the OT angels are called "sons of God" because they are part of the heavenly court and God's own family.[112] God treated the Davidic king as a son in the sense of exercising spe-

---

[111] For Catholics Pope Pius X (DBS §3435) condemned the Modernist proposition that Christ had not always been conscious of his messianic dignity. The theological note (evaluation) to be attached to this type of condemnation is notoriously difficult to determine. Moreover, the idea is condemned in the whole context of Modernist historicism where it served as a denial of Jesus' divinity. The present discussion of Jesus' attitude toward messianic terminology is perfectly consonant with faith in Jesus' divinity. If I had to phrase a common modern position with an eye on Pius X's statement, I would say that the Gospels always show Jesus conscious of his dignity (which involved a unique relationship to God); they are not clear as to whether he regarded "Messiah," in the sense understood by his contemporaries, adequate to express that dignity.

[112] In the wider Near Eastern religious background from which the concept of angels was most likely adapted and brought into Hebrew thought, the gods were male and female and had children who were literally "sons" (and "daughters") of Gods. But in the Bible, although some of the language and imagery may remain, angels are part of the one God's creation.

cial care for him and for the continuance of the dynasty.[113] Of the
nation of Israel, God could say through the prophet Hosea (11:1):
"Out of Egypt I called my son." In the Book of Wisdom (2:13–18)
mockers criticize the just one for considering himself a son of God,
i.e., one whom God loved and treated as if he were his own child.
Despite such uses of "son," the formal title "the son of God" never
appears in the Hebrew Bible.

In the Jewish literature antecedent to the NT it appears only
once: In what has been called a pseudo-Danielic fragment preserved
in Aramaic at Qumran (4Q246) we read "the Son of God he shall be
said to be, and the Son of the Most High they shall call him."[114] The
lack of context in this poorly preserved piece from a larger document
makes identification of the "he" difficult, although a king seems to
be in mind. Milik, dating it to ca. 25 BC, saw a reference to a Syrian
king hostile to the Jews; and D. Flusser[115] argued that the use of the
titles had an antichrist (antiGod) atmosphere of arrogance exemplified by Antiochus Epiphanes. More scholars now, however, understand the titles positively, often referring them to a future figure
on the side of God.[116] This is favored by another Qumran document
(1QSa 2:12) which speaks of God begetting the Messiah at an expected moment in the future. In particular, J. J. Collins sees a possible relationship of this "Son of God" to "one like a son of man" in
Dan 7:13–14 to whom the Ancient of Days (God) will give dominion, glory, and kingship. Nevertheless, here where we are asking historical questions, it would be methodologically unwise to make our

---

[113] Through Nathan God promised David that his son would reign after him:
"and I will be to him a father and he shall be to me a son" (II Sam 7:14). In Ps 2:7
God addresses the Davidic king as "my Son." Yet it is not clear that "the son of God"
was an official title of the king.

[114] This text was discussed and disseminated by J. T. Milik in a Harvard lecture
in 1972. J. A. Fitzmyer made the crucial lines available in NTS 20 (1973–74), 391–
94; republished in FAWA 90–94, 102–7. The text was finally published by E. Puech,
Revue Biblique 99 (1992), 98–131, and commented on by Fitzmyer, *Biblica* 74
(1993), 153–74.

[115] *Immanuel* 10 (1980), 31–37.

[116] Fitzmyer (= a king), F. García Martínez (= Melchizedek), M. Hengel (possibly = Jewish people). The Messiah is proposed by Puech and by J. J. Collins, "The
'Son of God' Text from Qumran," in FJTJ 65–82.

judgment about the use of "Son of God" for Jesus depend too much on the obscure 4Q246.

That the NT church confessed Jesus as the Son of God is admitted by all scholars, and that confession of divine sonship may well stem from the first decade of its life.[117] On the lips of Christians this title attributed to Jesus not only a special but a unique relationship to God. It is that unique relationship that concerns us when we ask, "Did Jesus call or consider himself the Son of God?"[118] (I remind readers again that this is not the same as asking "Was Jesus the Son of God?" We are asking about the way he phrased his identity.) Are Gospel passages referring to him as the Son of God genuinely from the time of Jesus' ministry? If so, did they have the exalted sonship connotation that early? Or were they at first simply affirmations that Jesus was the Messiah, the Davidic king whom God treated and protected as son?

THREE EXAMPLES OF EVIDENCE OF LESSER PROBATIVE VALUE

#1. Jesus' responses to proclamations or questions about his being the Son of God (Matt 16:16–17 and par.; Mark 14:61–62 and par.). In this chapter we have already discussed these passages under #1 and #2 above as part of the Messiah issue, because in both instances "Messiah" is attached to "Son of God" (the latter with minor variants). As I pointed out, on the level of the evangelists writing in the last third of the first century, these involve acknowledgement of Jesus as the Messiah in the sense of being the unique Son of God. Yet was the "Son of God" part of the combination added to "Mes-

---

[117] Bultmann and many scholars of the first half of the 20th century would attribute the confession of Jesus as Son of God to the Hellenistic church. The usage, however, probably can be traced back to the first generation of Christians. It appears in I Thess 1:10, the oldest preserved Christian writing (ca. AD 50). Acts 9:20 traces the title "the Son of God" back to the time of Paul's conversion (*ca.* AD 36), and the frequency of the title in Pauline writings means that it was very fixed in Pauline thought. It appears in Romans 1:3–4, which is most likely an early nonPauline confession. O. Cullmann, *The Christology of the New Testament* (London: SCM, 1959), 275–305, makes a strong case for Palestinian origin; see also M. Hengel, *The Son of God* (Philadelphia: Fortress, 1976).

[118] John as we shall see (p. 178 below) speaks of Jesus as *monogenēs,* "one of a kind," a term that can be combined with "Son."

siah" in the postresurrectional development of the tradition to help interpretation,[119] or does it go back to the time of Jesus? If the latter, during Jesus' lifetime what would such a confession have meant to Peter or to a Jewish high priest?

#2. The virginal conception and the Son of God. Independently the infancy narratives of Matt and Luke agree that Jesus is God's Son in a unique manner, for Mary conceived her child through the Holy Spirit without a male partner. Many think that this virginal conception reflects indirectly on Jesus' knowledge of his sonship, for Mary would have told Jesus of the divine paternity (if indeed he even had to be informed). The absence of infancy narratives in Mark (and John) suggests that the addition of them to the Gospel picture is relatively late (even if they contain earlier material). We have no information about the source from which Matt and Luke drew the material they present in the infancy narratives;[120] nor can we consider the two infancy narratives as totally historical since in major details they disagree both with what is narrated in the subsequent ministry and even with each other.[121] (Yet the manner of conception and the identity of Jesus as God's Son are the most important facts on which the two infancy narratives do agree.) The portrayal of Jesus and of Mary during the public ministry never recalls a single detail

---

[119] We remember that in the parallels to the first passage (Peter's confession) Luke 9:20 lacked "Son of God" and John 6:69 had "Holy One of God"; in the parallels to the second passage (interrogation by the chief priest) Luke and John made "Son of God" a separate issue from Messiah. Matt 14:33 has an added confession: The disciples in the boat say, "Truly, you are Son of God," after Jesus has walked on the water and calmed the wind. The complete absence of this confession in the Marcan parallel (6:51–52) suggests that Matt has supplied a postresurrectional articulation of what Mark implies: The reason why Jesus could do such things, as Christians came to recognize, was his status as God's Son.

[120] For the period of the public ministry those who walked with Jesus as disciples are plausibly the source of tradition about what he did and said. Certainly they were not present during the time of his infancy. Joseph seems to have died before Jesus began his ministry, and the last information about Mary in the NT is that she was in Jerusalem (presumably having come from Galilee for the pilgrimage feast) with the followers of Jesus before Pentecost (Acts 1:14). The NT offers no evidence that she lived on with the Jerusalem Christian community once it was formed after Pentecost, and there is no early claim that she was the source from which either evangelist got infancy information.

[121] BBM 32–37, 576–77.

from the infancy narratives. Therefore, historically we have no way of discerning Jesus' self-knowledge gained from the manner of his conception.[122]

#3.   *The affirmation of Jesus' divine sonship at the baptism and transfiguration.* In the Synoptic Gospels God, speaking from heaven, identifies Jesus as "my beloved Son" both at the baptism[123] and at the transfiguration.[124] The difficulty of establishing scientifically the historical character of a theophany (where God appears or speaks to people from heaven) is enormous. Another obstacle to using this testimony in our quest stems from the intent of the narrative. In Mark, although apparently both the vision and the voice are directed to Jesus, the hypothesis that the scene tells Jesus who he is has been rejected today by most scholars. For instance, E. Haenchen writes: "The account [Mark] does not wish to describe an inner experience of Jesus, for that would be something far from the evangelist's mind."[125] The purpose of the Marcan scene is pedagogical: The voice of God at the baptism speaks *for the sake of readers* to tell them at the outset who Jesus is.[126] (That it is not meant for those

---

[122] A possible exception would be Luke 2:49 where at age twelve Jesus speaks to his "father" (2:48) and mother in terms of God being "my Father." But this scene is peculiar to Luke and difficult to invoke in historical discussion.

[123] Mark 1:11; Matt 3:17; Luke 3:22. In John 1:34 John the Baptist (through revelation from God) bears witness that Jesus is "the Son of God"; however that reading is textually dubious and the alternative reading "the chosen one of God" may be more original. See footnote 178 below on the Suffering Servant background.

[124] Mark 9:7; Matt 17:5; Luke 9:35 (without "beloved"). John recounts no transfiguration.

[125] *Der Weg Jesu* (Berlin: Töpelmann, 1966), 61. In 1967 in BJGM 85 I pointed out that Haenchen rightly characterized the thesis that the baptism represented the call of Jesus as springing from the Protestant Liberalism at the beginning of the century (e.g., J. Weiss), and that it was embarrassing to find popular Catholic writers suddenly discovering and espousing it on the assumption that it represented the latest in biblical exegesis. The argument that Matt must imply a revelation to Jesus since Jesus is the one who sees the Spirit of God descend is refuted not only by the fact that the voice speaks of him in the third person ("This is my beloved Son": Matt 3:17), but by 3:13–15 where Jesus shows himself aware of his dignity *before* the baptism. The Lucan voice is addressed to Jesus (3:22: "You are my beloved Son"), but 2:49 shows that he was aware of his filial identity long before.

[126] The issue in Matt and Luke is slightly different. Readers have already been told in the infancy narratives through angelic revelation that Jesus is God's Son. (In

present at the scene is evident from the fact that throughout the Marcan Gospel before the death of Jesus no human being shows knowledge that he is the Son of God.) The transfiguration reminds the readers that the disciples have not understood who Jesus is and would not understand even if he revealed himself clearly. We cannot treat these interventions of the heavenly voice simply as historical events that would necessitate Jesus' being able to express his identity as the Son of God.

TWO EXAMPLES OF EVIDENCE OF GREATER PROBATIVE VALUE

#4. Jesus' references to God as Father. To support the contention that Jesus referred to himself as the unique Son of God, it has been customary to argue that Jesus spoke of God as "my Father" and that he never joined himself to others in speaking of "our Father." The argument is not without problems. *First*, the expression "my Father" never appears in Mark and appears only four times in Luke. Frequent usage is a Matthean feature, and for not a single one of the Matthean usages of "my Father" is there a Synoptic parallel. It is instructive, for instance, to compare Matt 12:50 ("the will of my Father") to Mark 3:35 and Luke 8:21 ("the will [or word] of God"), and to compare Matt 26:29 ("my Father's kingdom") to Mark 14:25 ("kingdom of God"). Clearly in these instances it is likely that Matt has introduced "Father" in passages that originally lacked the designation.

Second, if the Matthean Jesus speaks of "my Father," he also speaks frequently to his disciples of "your Father."[127] In Matt 7:21, for instance, Jesus speaks of the will of "my Father"; in 18:14 (better textual witnesses) he speaks of the will of "your Father." What right has the exegete prima facie to assume that "my Father" implies a more intimate relationship to God than "your Father"?[128]

Luke they have also been told this through Jesus' own words spoken when he was twelve.) Now God confirms this by speaking aloud.

[127] A whole group of passages in the Sermon on the Mount teaches the disciples to think of God as their Father in a very special way (Matt 5:16,45,48, etc.).

[128] A possible modification is that implicitly Jesus is the one who gives others the right to speak of God in this way.

Third, J. Jeremias[129] has argued that Jesus' custom of addressing God as "Abba" ("Father") in prayer is distinctive; the Aramaic address (*'abbā'*) is a caritative (= "Daddy") and implies intimate, family relationship. Thus Jesus claimed a special, familiar relationship to God as his Father beyond the general relationship postulated in contemporary Judaism. Other scholars have challenged Jeremias, and certainly qualifications are needed.[130] We have a number of examples of Jews addressing God as "Father" or "My Father" as they prayed in Greek (*III Maccabees* 5:7; 6:3[4]; Wis 14:3; Sir 23:1); and now there is an example of a Dead Sea Scroll prayer-psalm addressing God in Hebrew as "My Father" (4Q372: *'ăbî*). In the Greek of the Gospels various expressions are used by Jesus to address God as "My Father" and "Father" (*pater mou, pater, patēr*), and we cannot simply assume that all represent Aramaic *'abbā'*. Indeed, in the Gospels the only example of the Aramaic term transliterated into Greek (*abba*) is Mark 14:36.[131] In attested Aramaic for the period 200 BC– AD 200 *'ăbî* is normal for a child's address, "My father"; and only in literature to be dated after AD 200 does *'abbā'* replace it. Therefore the "Daddy" interpretation for Jesus' usage should be dropped.[132] However, when all the qualifications are made, if we acknowledge that historically Jesus did address God in Aramaic as *'abbā'*, then we need also to acknowledge the unusual character of that. Even afterwards *'abbā'* is not used of God in the often Aramaized Hebrew of the Mishna, and appears only once as an address to God in the early Aramaic translations of the Bible (targums). As Fitzmyer phrases it: "There is no evidence in the literature of pre-Christian or first-century Palestinian Judaism that *'abbā'* was used in any sense

---

[129] His most concise treatment is "Abba," in *The Central Message of the New Testament* (London: SCM, 1965), 9–30; see also R. Hammerton-Kelly, *Concilium* 143 (3; 1981), 95–102.

[130] The current state of the discussion has been presented with precision by J. A. Fitzmyer, "Abba and Jesus' Relation to God," in *À cause de l'évangile* (Mélanges J. Dupont; Lectio Divina 123; Paris: Cerf, 1985), 1.15–38.

[131] Luke 22:42, the parallel to Mark 14:36, uses *pater*; on that basis, most plausibly the Greek *pater* in Luke 11:2 ("Father" as contrasted with "Our Father" in Matt's Lord's Prayer) translates an underlying *'abbā'*.

[132] J. Barr, " 'Abbā Isn't Daddy," JTS NS 39 (1988), 28–47.

as a personal address for God by an individual."[133] Thus there is a distinctiveness to Jesus' usage. Nevertheless, Jesus offered to share this relationship with his followers: He taught them to pray to God as "Father" (Luke 11:2, the original form of the address in the Lord's Prayer), and they carried the custom of using "*Abba*" even into the Greek-speaking world (Gal 4:6; Rom 8:15).

Fourth, even in John where the relationship to God of Jesus as Son (*huios*) is kept distinct from the relationship of Christian believers as children (*tekna*),[134] "Father" language addressed to God is not clearly distinctive. In John 20:17 the risen Jesus says: "I am ascending to my Father and your Father." Drawing on the analogy of similar phrasing in Ruth 1:16, we understand that Jesus means "my Father who is now your Father" (footnote 245 below). Through the postresurrectional gift of the Spirit, God becomes the Father of those who believe in Jesus.

From all this evidence of Jesus' using "Father" language for God, at least this conclusion can be drawn: *If Jesus presented himself as the first of many to stand in a new and special relationship to God as Father, that priority implies that his sonship was in some way superior to the sonship of all who would follow him.*

#5. Jesus' references to himself as Son. Possibilities of a stronger conclusion emerge when we turn from the passages where Jesus speaks of God as Father to the passages where he speaks of himself as Son, but here too we must proceed with caution. There is absolutely no doubt that the Jesus of the Fourth Gospel claims to be God's Son[135] who alone has seen and heard God and who has come to earth to reveal God to human beings. He even describes himself as God's "only Son" (John 3:16). The high status of that Son is exemplified in statements like "The Father and I are one" (10:30);

---

[133] "Abba" 28. On 29–30 he challenges two passages proposed by G. Vermes, *Jesus the Jew* (Philadelphia: Fortress, 1981), 210–11, one of which (in the Mishna) is uncertain and the other of which is from the much later Babylonian Talmud.

[134] Of course this is scarcely a distinction made in Jesus' spoken Aramaic; and it is not a distinction kept throughout the NT, e.g., Gal 4:5; Rom 8:15 uses an abstract noun related to *huios* for the adopted "sonship" of Christians.

[135] *Huios* ("son") by itself or with the genitive "of God" is applied to Jesus in John over 30 times.

"Whoever has seen me has seen the Father" (14:9). To what extent can we attribute such clear Son-of-God christology to the ministry of Jesus? The Fourth Gospel was written to manifest that Jesus is the Son of God (20:31); in the evangelist's plan, although the words of the Johannine Jesus may be rooted in the words of Jesus of the ministry, they are suffused with the glory of the risen Jesus. Moreover, in APPENDIX IV we shall see that John's christology gained clarity through hindsight as the Johannine community was challenged about Jesus by the synagogue. Therefore use of John to determine scientifically how Jesus spoke of himself during his lifetime is very difficult.

Nevertheless, the Johannine practice of having Jesus refer to himself as "Son" is not without parallels in the other Gospels, and it is to three instances in the Synoptic accounts of the ministry where Jesus seems to speak of himself absolutely as "the Son" of God that we must now give careful attention.

First, in the Q tradition of Jesus' sayings there is a famous passage shared by Matt 11:27 and Luke 10:22: "No one knows the Son except the Father, and no one knows the Father except the Son and anyone to whom the Son chooses to reveal Him"—the so-called "Johannine logion."[136] This saying has many Semitic features and could well reflect an original saying of Jesus. J. Jeremias has made the attractive suggestion that the original was parabolic in style inasmuch as Jesus drew on the maxim that a father and son know each other intimately and so a son is the best one to reveal the innermost thoughts of the father.[137] This saying, then, does not prove clearly

---

[136] The fact that the relationship in this passage is between a Father who needs to be revealed and a Son makes most unlikely that this is a reference to the Son of Man rather than to the Son of God. The "Johannine" designation springs from the fact that the logion resembles the thought and style of the Fourth Gospel. Had it been preserved at first as an isolated saying unattached to any Gospel, scribes would surely have attached it to John. The fact that it is found in Q warns us against thinking that Johannine language and christology is entirely a Johannine creation; rather it is a massive (and independent) development of themes that are also attested in the Synoptic tradition.

[137] "Abba" (footnote 129 above) 23–25. In this interpretation the definite article before "Son" is the definite article of parabolic style indicating a generic situation, as in "*The* sower went out to sow seed." English tends to use an indefinite article in such a situation, but the definite form is good Aramaic.

that Jesus described himself as "the Son" in an absolute sense (although that is not excluded since many of the parables have allegorical features as well, and Jesus could be playing on his being "the Son").

Second, in Mark 13:32 Jesus says: "Of that day or the hour no one knows, not even the angels in heaven, nor the Son, but only the Father." It is curious that the very passage that speaks of Jesus absolutely as the Son (of God) is the most famous passage in the Gospels for indicating that Jesus' knowledge was limited! We discussed this passage above (p. 56) and saw that it is not without difficulty. Although some think that the early church could have added the exalted designation of Jesus as "the Son" to compensate for recognizing that his knowledge was limited,[138] probability favors this designation of Jesus for himself as original.

Third, the parable of the tenants in the vineyard (Mark 12:1–12), although it may have undergone developments, contains a basic, simple comparison that probably goes back to Jesus. In that parable, after treating harshly servants sent to obtain the rent, the tenants kill the son of the owner. There is no hint that the son is ultimately vindicated, as might be expected were the death of the son a postresurrectional development in the parable. The son stands in a line of martyred and rejected prophets, but has an identity that goes beyond theirs. Mark 12:6 and Luke 20:13 (but not Matt 21:37) describe this son as *agapētos*, "uniquely beloved."

These three Synoptic passages make it *likely that Jesus spoke and thought of himself as "the Son," implying a very special relationship to God that is part of his identity and status.*[139] Yet he never indisputably uses of himself the title "the Son of God."

(C) Did Jesus Affirm That He Was the Son of Man?

There is massive modern disagreement about whether this was a title in Jesus' time, what it may have meant, and whether Jesus used it of himself. It may be a consolation to know that there are

---

[138] As J. P. Meier has pointed out (NJBC 78, §35), however, a simpler solution would have been to suppress reference to his limited knowledge.

[139] I have not added Matt 28:19 where the risen Jesus tells the eleven disciples, "Going therefore, make disciples of all nations, baptizing them in the name of the

traces of ancient puzzlement in the words addressed to Jesus in John 12:34, "How can you say that the Son of Man must be lifted up? Just who is the Son of Man?"

The Gospel usage of this title for Jesus presents statistics that are dramatically different from the statistics discussed in relation to "the Messiah" and "the Son of God." The acceptance or usage of those titles during Jesus' lifetime is difficult to discern even from the surface evidence of the Gospels, in part because of their infrequency; but "the Son of Man" appears some 80 times in the Gospels and in all but 2 partially debatable instances (Mark 2:10; John 12:34) clearly as self-designations by Jesus. It has been estimated that these constitute some 51 sayings,[140] 14 of which are in Mark and 10 in the Sayings-Source (Q). Outside the Gospels the phrase occurs only 4 times, viz., Heb 2:6; Rev 1:13; 14:14; Acts 7:56; and only in the last of these (which is a Lucan borrowing from the Gospel usage) does it have the definite article as in the Gospels. The debate whether the historical Jesus used this title of himself or whether it is a product of early church reflection retrojected into Jesus' ministry has raged throughout the last hundred years. If one takes the latter view, one faces two major difficulties: Why was this title so massively retrojected, being placed on Jesus' lips on a scale far outdistancing the retrojection of "the Messiah," "the Son of God," and "the Lord"? And if this title was first fashioned by the early church, why has it left almost no traces in nonGospel NT literature, something not true of the other titles?

Nevertheless, there are curious features about this title in the Gospel usage.[141] No person addresses Jesus by this title, and Jesus

---

Father and of the Son and of the Holy Spirit," a passage found nowhere else. Since other evidence points to a simpler baptismal formula "in the name of Jesus," we probably have here a liturgical formula used at the end of the 1st century in Matt's church when Christians, under the guidance of the Holy Spirit, had come to a fuller understanding of the divine agency in salvation. According to this theory, the risen Jesus did utter an evangelizing command, but the Matthean wording of the command reflects Christian experience of the evangelizing task.

[140] J. Jeremias, *Zeitschrift für die Neutestamentliche Wissenschaft* 58 (1967), 159–64.

[141] These observations are drawn from J. D. Kingsbury, *The Christology of Mark* (Philadelphia: Fortress, 1984), 166–79. He contends (174–75) that unlike "Son of God" or titles that focus inwardly on Jesus' identity, "Son of Man" focuses out-

never explains its meaning. When the question comes up as to who Jesus is, despite his many uses of "the Son of Man," it is never a suggested identification of him. (And it is not used of him by the early Christians in their confessions of praise or their creeds.) Exaltation as the Son of Man with the power to judge is what Jesus affirms most clearly in his trial before the Jewish authorities on the night before he dies. Nevertheless, although Jesus is mocked on the cross about all the other details of the trial (the destruction of the sanctuary, the Messiah, the Son of God), there is no reference to his identification of himself as the Son of Man. Given these difficulties, let us now survey very briefly some issues that enter into the debate about the historicity of Jesus' use of the title.[142]

When and how did "the Son of Man" become a title? Since *ho huios tou anthrōpou*, the usual Gospel phrase, is unknown in secular Greek and makes as little sense in Greek as "the son of man" would make as a title in English conversation, the origins of the usage must lie in a Semitic context. The divine voice that speaks to Ezekiel addresses him over ninety times as "son of man" (= "O human being"), a term that highlights the contrast between the heavenly message and the mortal recipient. More pertinently, "one like a son of man" in the Aramaic of Dan 7:13 enters the discussion, but the designation there simply means one like a human being.[143] Because

---

wardly on Jesus' relation to the world. In the present instance it focuses on what through God's initiative will be given to Jesus by way of status and what he will do—factors that complement and manifest what he is. Thus I would judge that the title had both an outer and inner dimension.

[142] For a good survey of the overly abundant literature on this question, see J. R. Donahue, CBQ 48 (1986), 484–98; also M. Casey, JSNT 42 (1991), 17–43. Casey's own views are marked with a confidence that he can detect which Son of Man sayings in the Gospels are original by reconstructing the underlying Aramaic (for which, however, he depends on post-1st-century targums). After Jesus' time, he contends, there was a secondary development of the concept and of sayings in the light of Dan 7 and the parousia of Jesus.

[143] O.J.F. Seitz, "The Future Coming of the Son of Man," *Studia Evangelica VI* (Texte und Untersuchungen 112; Berlin: Akademie, 1973), 478–94, has pointed to Ps 80 as complementing the picture of Dan 7. If the latter relates one like a son of man to the holy ones of the Most High, Ps 80:15–16, in a prayer to God, relates a son of man to the vine of Israel: "Take care of this vine, and protect what your right hand has planted, a son of man whom you yourself made strong." The plea continues in 80:18: "May your help be with the man of your right hand, with the son of man whom

there is little else in canonical Scripture pertinent to this figure, it became fashionable for a while to appeal to comparative religious evidence and to posit the existence in the Near East of a widely accepted picture of a heavenly man (often thought to be of Iranian origin) as background for what the NT meant by calling Jesus "the Son of Man." When that approach was rejected for lack of evidence, a strong vein of scholarship (e.g., in the years 1965–90: B. Lindars, N. Perrin, G. Vermes) came to deny that there existed in Judaism any expectation of a specific figure known as the Son of Man or the Heavenly Man. Yet through appeal to Jewish apocrypha (rather than comparative nonJewish religion), another vein of scholarship that now seems to be reviving has argued that there was a 1st-century Jewish expectation that God would make victorious and enthrone over Israel's enemies a specific human figure who would be the instrument of divine judgment—a figure who could be appropriately designated "the Son of Man" because he embodied or exemplified the destiny of all righteous human beings. To respect the uncertainty of the scholarly situation, I have decided to answer the question of the plausibility of Jesus' use of "the Son of Man" within each of these two approaches, namely, if there was a specific Jewish concept of "the Son of Man," and if there was not. I shall apply each approach to a text that is especially significant for the christological topic of this book, Mark 14:61–62 and par., where the high priest has asked whether Jesus admits being the Messiah, the Son of the Blessed/God and Jesus responds in terms of the Son of Man being seen seated at the right of the Power and coming on the clouds of heaven.

#1. *If There Was a Jewish Concept of the Son of Man.* In apocalyptic Jewish circles whose voice is echoed in the noncanonical literature of the 2d and 1st centuries BC and 1st cent. AD, there may have developed a strong image of a heavenly Son of Man through reflection on Dan 7[144]—an image not widely attested outside those

---

you yourself made strong." Seitz argues that, since this psalm deals with the elevation of an earthly being, it may have constituted the primary background of Mark 14:62.

[144] While the supporting evidence has been known for a long time, there have been problems of dating and interpretation. The second half of the 20th century has refined scholars' appreciation of the pseudepigrapha, especially as the study of the Dead Sea Scroll material found at Qumran (NJBC 67, §§79–117) has reinforced our

circles and hence leaving relatively sparse traces, but an image that could well have appealed to Jesus and his early Christian followers because of their own strong apocalyptic bent.

It has long been recognized that the "Parables" (Similitudes) section of the Jewish apocryphal writing *I Enoch* (37–71) contributed to the Son of Man issue. Yet the absence of this section from the many fragments of *I Enoch* found at Qumran seemed at first to favor regarding the Parables section as a Christian composition and insertion into *I Enoch* and therefore a writing that reflected rather than explained NT usage.[145] Lately, however, the arguments for pre-Christian or nonChristian Jewish composition of the Parables section have been recognized as having greater force; and proposals have emerged for why the Qumran sectarians might not have agreed with the theology of this section of *I Enoch* and so not have preserved it. Collins[146] proposes a date *ca.* AD 50 for composition. The references to the Ancient (Head) of Days in *I Enoch* 46:1 and 47:3 indicate that the author used Dan 7:9–10,13–14, and support the likelihood that his portrayal of the Son of Man arose from reflection on Daniel. Indeed the language of Enoch leaves open the possibility that we are seeing the emergence of a set figure from the vaguer Danielic picture. In *I Enoch* 46 Danielic imprecision is represented at first with the reference to one "whose face had the appearance of a human being," but then upon questioning he is explained to be "the Son of Man who has righteousness." Although he is like one of the holy angels, he has a higher rank than that of the angels.[147] The Son of Man is one whose name was named in the presence of the

---

grasp of the wide range of contemporary Judaism. In what follows I am indebted for insights to J. J. Collins, "The Son of Man in First-Century Judaism," NTS 38 (1992), 448–66.

[145] See the report on the discussion by D. W. Suter, *Religious Studies Review* 7 (1981), 217–21.

[146] In "Son of God" (footnote 116 above) he argues that a pre-70 AD date can scarcely be denied because of the influence of the Parables on Matt 19:28; 25:31 and the absence of a reference to the fall of Jerusalem.

[147] Part of the difficulty of imaging the Son of Man in *I Enoch* is the seeming identification of him with the exalted, celestial Enoch in 71:5,11–17, especially 71:14. For many that has meant that the Son of Man in *I Enoch* is more a role than a specific figure. To counteract the Enoch identification R. H. Charles deliberately changed the translation, and some have argued that this passage was a secondary addition to the

Lord of Spirits before the sun and the stars were created (48:2–3). He is described as "the Elect One" (the chosen servant of Isa 42:1?), for the two titles are juxtaposed in *I Enoch* 62:1,5. Indeed 48:10 and 52:4 seem to identify him as the Messiah of the Lord. The Son of Man is shown seated on the throne of glory in 62:5, presumably by deduction that one of the thrones in Dan 7:9 was meant for him (Collins)—an enthronement which could suggest that already in Jewish circles Dan 7 was being joined to Ps 110:1 ("sit at my right") as is reflected in Mark 14:62. In *I Enoch* the Son of Man has a judging role. Previously there were in Dan 7:13–14 hints of judgment, for "one like a son of man" was brought into the heavenly court where the books are opened that will decide the fate of the great kingdoms represented by the beasts (7:10c). Nevertheless, we were not told specifically in Daniel what participation this one like a son of man would have when upon the coming of the Ancient of Days judgment is pronounced (7:22).[148] The imagery of Isaiah (11:1–4) that describes the spirit given to the Davidic king to enable him to judge righteously may be echoed in *I Enoch* 62:2 where the spirit of righteousness is poured out on the chosen one to enable him to kill sinners. In *I Enoch* 63:11; 69:27,29 the wicked are brought before the Son of Man to be shamed, while the name of the Son of Man is

---

Parables. Collins ("Son of Man" 455–57) argues that in 71:14 Enoch is not identified with the Son of Man but is addressed as a human being who is exalted to share the likeness of the heavenly Son of Man. In 70:1 Enoch's name is lifted up alive to the presence of the Son of Man, an imagery that seems to distinguish between the two.

[148] Sometimes Dan 7 is presented simply as the enthronement of this representative human figure (an ascension to heaven with the clouds) with no indications of future activity related to those on earth, in which case the combination of enthronement and parousia in Mark 14:62 would be a major innovation. However, G. R. Beasley Murray, "Jesus and Apocalyptic" in *L'Apocalypse johannique et l'Apocalypse dans le Nouveau Testament*, ed. J. Lambrecht (Gembloux: Duculot, 1980), 425–26, makes the point that the scene involves the participation of this human figure in the theophany of the Ancient of Days, and a theophany always involves an intervention in human affairs on earth. He quotes K. Müller that nowhere in the OT or early Jewish and talmudic literature do "clouds" ever play a role when the concern is to express the activity of heavenly beings among one another entirely in the realm of transcendence. Only when they step out of hidden transcendence are clouds brought into play, and so there would be an implication in Dan 7 that the human figure has yet a role in which he will descend to exercise authority.

revealed to the blessed. Collins ("Son of Man") contends that the Parables of *I Enoch* "show how the Danielic text inspired visions of a heavenly savior figure in first century Judaism."[149]

Reflection on Dan 7 and the Son of Man appears after *I Enoch* at the end of the 1st cent. in *IV Ezra* (*II Esdras*) 13, another Jewish apocalypse, composed originally in Hebrew or Aramaic. Daniel (7:1-28) saw four monstrous beasts representing the great kingdoms of Near Eastern history whose power was replaced by the authority that God gave to one like a son of man who came with the clouds of heaven. When Ezra sees a monstrous eagle, he is told (12:11) that it is "the fourth kingdom that appeared in a vision to your brother Daniel." In 13:3 one "in the form of a man" comes up from the sea and flies with the clouds of heaven. This superhuman figure destroys the forces of evil with flaming breath from his mouth and gathers a peaceful and joyous multitude. In his commentary M. Stone[150] writes: "The man is interpreted as the Messiah, precreated and prepared in advance, who will deliver creation and direct those who are left." He maintains that the dream vision itself, independent of the interpretation, may have come from a pre-Ezra source; that source would have drawn from Dan 7 even as did the author of *IV Ezra*.

All this evidence suggests that in apocalyptic Jewish circles of the 1st cent. AD the portrayal in Dan 7 had given rise to the picture

---

[149] As I point out (with bibliographical references) in BDM 1.511, if the author of *I Enoch* specified the Danielic picture to portray a heavenly enthroned human figure as judge, namely the Son of Man, other Jewish writings offer catalysts that could have moved his thought in that direction. Ezekiel the Tragedian (before 150 BC) has God, with crown and scepter, bring Moses to the heavenly throne to be seated there, crowned, and enabled to survey the heavens. The celestial Melchizedek figure at Qumran contributes to the portrait of an enthroned figure who would come to judge, and a hymnic fragment of the War Scroll has one who had prowess as a teacher and in rendering legal judgment exalted to a seat in the heavens and reckoned with gods in the holy congregation. Seemingly ascent to the heavens was an important part of the 1st-cent. Palestinian background.

[150] *Fourth Ezra* (Hermeneia; Minneapolis: Fortress, 1990), 397. The term "my son" is used in some versions for the man figure in 13:37,52, even as it was used for the Messiah in 7:28. Other versions read "my servant" as in 13:32, which may echo Isaian servant language. We saw that in the Parables of *I Enoch* the Son of Man had both servant and messianic identification.

of a messianic human figure of heavenly preexistent origin who is glorified by God and made a judge.[151] Against that background Jesus, if he was familiar with apocalyptic thought, could have used "Son of Man" terminology.[152] He need not have read the Parables of *I Enoch*, but only have been aware of some of the burgeoning reflection on Dan 7 that gave or would give rise to the presentation of the Son of Man in the Parables and of the man in *IV Ezra*. Indeed, the setting supplied for Jesus' self-reference to the Son of Man during his trial in Mark 14:61–62 would make good sense. The high priest has asked if Jesus is the Messiah, the Son of the Blessed. Jesus would be using the "Son of Man" role to interpret the Messiah issue, explaining in what sense he was responding affirmatively to that designation proposed by the high priest.[153] Jesus' claim to such an apocalyptic Son of Man role would also explain the high priest's indignant charge of blasphemy, if blasphemy be understood as arrogant pretensions infringing on divine prerogatives.

#2. If There Was No Jewish Concept of the Son of Man. Although I find the evidence and speculation advanced under #1 attractive, probably the majority view among scholars is that Jesus or

---

[151] Beyond the apocrypha, if Justin (*Dialogue* 32.1) reports Jewish views correctly, the identification of Daniel's "one like a son of man" with the King Messiah was accepted by the mid-2d cent. AD.

[152] Scholars generally distinguish three types of Son of Man sayings found on the lips of Jesus in the Gospels: (1) those that refer to the earthly activity of the Son of Man (eating, dwelling, saving the lost); (2) those that refer to the suffering of the Son of Man; (3) those that refer to the future glory and parousia of the Son of Man in judgment. Remarks here pertain particularly to the third type.

[153] Above (p. 81) I discussed the Qumran "Son of God" fragment (4Q246) and J. J. Collins's contention that "Son of God" there is to be related to the use of "son of man" in Dan 7. If he is right and there was in apocalyptic Judaism an interpretative chain binding together the Davidic Messiah expectation (in reflection on II Sam 7:11–16), the Danielic "son of man" who was to be taken up to heaven, and the royal one whom God called "son" and made to sit at the right of the throne (Ps 2:7; 110:1), then there may have been more connection than hitherto diagnosed between the titles in the high priest's question (the Messiah, the Son of the Blessed/God) and Jesus' response in terms of "the Son of Man." Nevertheless, the whole interpretative chain, with Dan 7 as the linchpin, is highly speculative. Moreover, were it true, we would still be uncertain whether phrasing the christological dialogue at Jesus' trial in terms of one title as a response to a question about the others came from Jesus or his early followers.

his followers were responsible for the specification of the Son of Man concept, since there was no established Jewish portrait or expectation of that figure. There are different theories as to how Christians developed the concept.

Some who want to attribute that development to the early church would argue that Jesus used a Semitic expression equivalent to the Son of Man but not as a title. G. Vermes points to evidence from the Aramaic targums where "son of man" serves as a circumlocution for "I"; but J. A. Fitzmyer has insisted, quite correctly, that all the evidence advanced is later than the NT and does not establish proof for this usage in Jesus' time. True, the phrase can mean "someone"; and B. Lindars[154] has argued that in some nine sayings of Jesus that appear to be authentic, "son of man" is used to mean "a man such as I" or "a man in my position." However, when one looks at Mark 8:31 or 8:38, which would be among these sayings, it is hard to see how they make sense thus translated. Accordingly, if Jesus used the expression "the Son of Man," it would seem to have been in the titular sense. The suggestion that Jesus used this title to refer to a future figure who would come to judge but that this figure was not Jesus himself has lost much of its following. Granted Jesus' conception of the role he himself was playing in making present the rule of God, his anticipation of another unidentified human figure to bring the work to a conclusion seems unlikely.

The writings of N. Perrin[155] treat the Gospel presentations of the Son of Man as derived from Christian midrashic (i.e., interpretative) reflection on Dan 7, employing Ps 110:1 to herald Jesus as the exalted Lord, and Zech 12:10 ("looking upon him whom they have pierced") to develop the notion of the Son of Man coming from heaven to be seen below. Of course, these are OT passages that appear in the NT and were clearly in the NT arsenal for interpreting Jesus. But two points should be made in reference to Perrin's thesis.

First, it is truly likely that the Gospel picture is developed beyond any single OT or known intertestamental passage or expectation, and that this development probably took place through the

---

[154] *Jesus Son of Man* (Grand Rapids: Eerdmans, 1983), 25–29.

[155] Gathered in *A Modern Pilgrimage in New Testament Christology* (Philadelphia: Fortress, 1974).

interpretative combination of several passages. Yet any affirmation that all this development *must have* come from early Christians and none of it came from Jesus reflects one of the peculiar prejudices of modern scholarship. A Jesus who did not reflect on the OT and use the interpretative techniques of his time is an unrealistic projection who surely never existed. *The perception that OT or intertestamental passages were interpreted to give a christological insight does not assign a date to the process.* To prove that this could not have been done by Jesus, at least inchoatively, is surely no less difficult to prove than that it was done by him. Hidden behind an attribution to the early church is often the assumption that Jesus had no christology even by way of reflecting on the Scriptures to discern in what antici- pated way he fitted into God's plan. Can one really think that credible?

Second, Perrin speaks of a *pesher* technique. He means a read- ing of OT Scriptures and the interpretative application of them to the present situation, as illustrated by Dead Sea Scroll biblical com- mentaries called the pesher on Habakkuk, the pesher on the Psalms, etc. Obviously something like the interpretative technique em- ployed in those commentaries would have been used by Jesus and/ or by Christians in developing the image of the Son of Man. Yet a pesher is a line-by-line commentary on an OT book where the controlling factor has to be revelation through that sacred writing. It is highly significant than none of the twenty-seven books of the NT is a pesher or line-by-line commentary on the OT. Rather the Gos- pels are in a sense commentaries on Jesus. The hermeneutical focus has changed. While OT passages are applied to Jesus, the idea is not primarily that the OT makes sense of the present situation, but that the present situation makes sense of the OT: The control is supplied by Jesus, not by the Scriptures. I mention this because I do not think that the christological interpretation of the Son of Man came simply from the interpretation of OT texts; the christology existed from a perception of Jesus (or from Jesus' perception of himself) and found voice and color in phrases from OT passages that were now seen to have a deeper meaning than hitherto recognized.

In sum, I would contend that in this second approach (in which there was no established Jewish concept of the Son of Man) *nothing rules out the following possibilities:* Jesus reached a firm conviction that if he were rejected and put to death as the prophets of old had been, God would bring about the divine kingdom by vindicating him against those who regarded him as a false spokesman and who rejected as diabolical the power over evil and sin that God had given him. In reflection on Dan 7 and other OT passages (Ps 110:1; perhaps Ps 80:18) Jesus might have expanded the symbolic concept of "one like a son of man" to whom God would give glory and dominion. It became "the Son of Man," the specific human figure whom God glorifies and through whom God manifests the final triumph; and Jesus used it of himself seen as the instrument of God's plan. Early Christians, taking their clue from Jesus' own language, developed the idea further, applied it to different aspects of his life, and used it frequently to describe Jesus' self-understanding.[156] But part of the reason that it appears in the Gospels in a way "the Messiah" and "the Son of God" do not is precisely because this description was remembered to have come from Jesus in a very affirmative manner.

As we reflect on the historicity of Mark 14:62 in this approach, Jesus could have spoken of "the Son of Man" as his understanding of his role in God's plan precisely when he was faced with hostile challenges reflecting the expectations of his contemporaries. Inevitably the Christian record would have crossed the *t*'s and dotted the *i*'s of the scriptural background of his words. Even though *all* of Mark 14:61–62 and par. is phrased in the Christian language of the 60s (language *not* unrelated to the issues of AD 30/33), there is reason to believe that in 14:62 we may be close to the mindset and style of Jesus himself.[157] Above (pp. 49–52) we saw that there was also a

---

[156] U. Luz, "The Son of Man in Matthew: Heavenly Judge or Human Christ," JSNT 48 (1992), 3–21, shows how Matt developed the application of the title and suggests how in the 2d century there were further Christian developments. In Luz's view "the traditional word-shell 'son of the man' was filled with new christologies."

[157] The difficulty of what Jesus would have meant by telling the high priest and the Sanhedrin members "*You will see* the Son of Man sitting at the right of the power and coming on the clouds of heaven," may favor authenticity. (See p. 53 above on the difficulty of this text.) If Christians produced such a statement post factum, presumably they would have clarified it.

likelihood that Jesus spoke about the future destruction and rebuilding of the sanctuary.[158] Each of these future statements about God's
plan has a threatening element of judgment plus an element in
which Jesus, vindicated by God, would have a part in bringing
God's plan to its culmination. The threatening element would be
quite understandable against the background of the history of the
prophets.

* * *

We come now to the close of Part II of this book: our investigation of the presentation of Jesus in the Gospels to discern how
Jesus himself conceived his relationship to God and his place in
God's plan. The long Chapter 4, considering the evidence pertinent
to this question from Jesus' general knowledge of both ordinary and
religious matters, produced meager results. Apparently neither Jesus
nor the evangelists were concerned to offer their respective hearers/
readers an overall picture of Jesus' knowledge that might help to
define or clarify his status. Yet there were traditions that attributed
to him knowledge and authority characteristic of a prophet, indeed
of a prophetic figure who brings God's plan to completion.

Chapter 5 investigated what can be discerned about Jesus from
material more central to his interests: the proclamation that through
his *deeds* and in his *words* God's kingly rule was making itself felt.
In the interests of the kingship of God he acted against evil with a
power that went far beyond the range of ordinary experience. From
the beginning of Jesus' ministry to the end he exhibited unshakable
confidence that he could authoritatively interpret the demands that
God's kingship puts on those who acknowledge it. Although when
Jesus spoke of the next life or of the signs of the last times, he seems
to have repeated the descriptions current in his time, when he spoke
of God's kingly rule, he spoke with originality. This was his metier,
and here he brooked no opposition. He could and did declare sins
forgiven, modify the Law of Moses, violate the Sabbath ordinances,

---

[158] Like the difficulty mentioned in the preceding footnote, the problem of understanding how the rebuilding would be fulfilled constitutes an argument for authenticity. Post factum one tends to fashion clearer "prophecies."

offend against the proprieties (eat with tax collectors and sinners), make stringent demands (forbid divorce; challenge to celibacy and to leave family ties), defy common sense (encouragement to turn the other cheek)—in short, teach as no teacher of his time taught. Among the holy men of Israel (Jeremiah, Elijah, particular rabbis) one may find parallels to Jesus as regards individual attitudes, sayings, or deeds; but the total picture of Jesus breaks the mold. His conviction about the ultimate success of his mission (perhaps accompanied by a lack of knowledge about just how that victory would be achieved) resembles to some extent the conviction of the OT prophets. But no prophet broke with the hallowed past in so radical a way and with so much assurance as did Jesus. Moreover, the certainty with which Jesus spoke and acted implies a consciousness of a unique relationship to God. The Gospel traditions agree in depicting him as a man who thinks he can act and speak for God. The superior authority and power manifested by Jesus and acknowledged by many who encountered him supposed more than that he was the final prophet of the last times through whom God's salvation breaks through. His implied relationship to God was more than that of an agent; God was acting not only through him but in him.

Chapter 6 sought in Jesus' words about himself a way of designating this unique relationship between Jesus and God; it investigated his attitude towards designations stemming from the theological heritage of Judaism (Messiah, Son of God, Son of Man) that might have befitted a unique figure in God's plan. Seemingly, although some among friends and foes thought that he was or claimed to be the Messiah (i.e., God's anointed king from the House of David who would bring about the kingdom), Jesus never clearly or enthusiastically embraced that title—his words and deeds implied that he was that final agent, but his conception of the kingdom and his role in it departed in many ways from what was generally expected of the Messiah. Even though the data for the Jewish use of the title "the Son of God" and for Jesus' own use of it during his public ministry are sparse, there is respectable evidence that he pictured himself in a filial relationship to God whom he called Father, sometimes portraying himself as the Son. Those who accepted Jesus' proclamation of the kingdom would become God's sons or children, but his sonship was prior and foundational. As for "the Son of Man," whether or not that title designated an expected figure in Judaism, it is likely that Daniel's apocalyptic portrayal of "one like a son of man" whom God exalts, makes victorious, and endows with ultimate power and kingship to be universally manifested in a context of judgment entered into Jesus' understanding of how his mission from God would terminate. Thus one might propose that an emphatic filial relationship to God as the Son and apocalyptic exaltation were components that would have to modify "Messiah" in order for Jesus to give a less qualified response to the issue of whether that title befitted him.

In Chapter 2 of the book when I pointed to "moderate conservatism" as perhaps the most agreed upon scholarly approach to christology, I explained that those who accepted it were divided between an "explicit" and an "implicit" evaluation of Jesus' christology. Either Jesus evaluated himself with titles or designations already known in Jewish circles, or such titles and designations belonged to the postresurrectional period as early Christians tried to find language to do justice to Jesus' attitudes and actions. What I have surveyed in Part II points almost to an in-between position: Jesus encountered and even used certain titles and designations but often in an incipient form whereby they needed to be combined to do justice to his conception of God's plan. The explicitation by early Christians, then, would not have involved using the titles for the first time, but honing and reinterpreting the titles to make them more capable of being used individually to describe Jesus without distorting him. The continuity between the christology of Jesus and the christology of the church[159] would have involved more than finding language to describe what was implicit in Jesus' words and deeds— it would have also consisted in the ongoing refining of christological terminology that he had begun to refine. It is to how early Christians did such refining that we now turn.

---

[159] In my judgment continuity is a very important issue. See also B. F. Meyer, *The Aims of Jesus* (London: SCM, 1979) for an approach to the historical Jesus that shares this interest.

PART III

The Christologies of
New Testament Christians

An attempt to discern how the New Testament

writers evaluated Jesus

by the way they described various moments

in his career.

PREFACE TO THE DISCUSSION

The developing sequence from the way in which Jesus presented himself during his lifetime to the way in which those who believed in him presented him afterwards is more complex than such a sequence would be for any other figure. In the case of others one might find an adequate explanation for development in logical, psychological, and other familiar diagnosable factors;[160] but in the tradition about Jesus a unique factor massively intervened that goes beyond human diagnosis, namely, the resurrection. In the publicly received tradition of Israel (i.e., what a later generation would dub canonical) no one had hitherto been raised from the dead to eternal life,[161] and so this claim of faith about Jesus had an enormous import. Besides heralding a victory over death, God's raising of Jesus to glory vindicated both the origin and the truth of the authority/ power that he had claimed and manifested. His followers who saw the risen Jesus realized that he was even more than they had understood during his public ministry. The resurrection, therefore, makes it very difficult to explain away as romanticized creation the more explicit christology attested after the resurrection.

Theoretically and ideally, a presentation of NT christology

---

[160] To name a few of these: the theological expectations of his followers; their status in relation to fellow Jews and pressures placed on them; the influence that came from contact with Gentiles.

[161] Others had been resuscitated (see footnote 85 above) and some were said to have ascended to glory without dying (Enoch, Elijah). Yet there were apocryphal tales about famous figures that went beyond what was accepted in the canonical tradition, and some of those may have come closer to claiming what the NT claims of Jesus, e.g., the ascension of Moses.

should be able to take for granted the reality of the resurrection, since what is being studied are the records of those who both believed in and proclaimed the resurrection. Yet realistically, an introductory christology book such as this will be read by students who have heard that some scholars deny the reality of the resurrection; they may be suspicious, therefore, of the honesty of a presentation that omits all discussion of the issue. I shall try to do justice to both approaches by including a discussion of the reality of the resurrection but placing it in APPENDIX II below, so that it does not interrupt the treatment of christology proper.

We continue, then, by moving on from Part II where we were considering the evidence for Jesus' evaluation of himself to Part III where we consider how after the resurrection Christians of the NT period evaluated him. There are several different ways in which we could proceed.[162] If this were a more advanced and detailed analysis of NT christology, we could take one by one individual NT authors and study the christology of each, e.g., of Matt, of Luke-Acts, of John, of Paul. I shall give a taste of that approach in APPENDIX IV by discussing some features of Johannine christology, because it is so unique among the Gospels. Overall, however, I think that in this introductory work such a specialized approach would not be wise.[163] The task of relating the individual christologies would still remain, and readers might emerge with too compartmentalized an understanding of thought about Christ. It is more useful to get a sense across-the-board of how Christians were evaluating Jesus during various periods in the first century.

Another approach would be to work with the individual titles applied to Jesus in the NT, as many books on christology have done. In the last chapter we saw that perhaps some titles were used during

---

[162] One of the strengths of the 1983 Pontifical Biblical Commission's statement on christology is that it discusses a variety of approaches with the strengths and limitations of each. See J. A. Fitzmyer, *Scripture and Christology: A Statement of the Biblical Commission with a Commentary* (New York: Paulist, 1986). A good deal of NT christological information arranged according to the questions people often ask is found in BRTOQ §§38–81.

[163] Books following this approach are often not easily readable; pedagogically more satisfactory is E. Richard, *Jesus One and Many: The Christological Concept of New Testament Authors* (Wilmington: Glazier, 1988).

Jesus' lifetime either by Jesus himself or by others speaking about him. One could track the further development of these titles after his death and resurrection, as well as the introduction of other titles. Again I shall give a taste of that approach, this time in APPENDIX III, by tracing the usage of the title "God" for Jesus—a title that according to the available evidence he did not use of himself and is not attested of him during the early decades of Christianity, but began to be used with increasing frequency toward the last third of the 1st century into the 2d century. That tracing is an especially fruitful enterprise because "true God of true God" became the classic description of Jesus' divinity. It did not seem wise, however, to concentrate here on other titles and attempt to trace them through the NT; for such an approach is very technical and probably too difficult for many beginners who might be reached by this book.[164] Moreover, as explained in Chapter 2 (under C), learned liberal scholars of the late 19th and early 20th century developed a rather precise geographical-linguistic "graph" on which they thought they could plot the developments in the use of titles for Jesus, assigning them respectively to an Aramaic-speaking, Palestinian-Jewish Christianity; a Greek-speaking, Diaspora-Jewish Christianity; a Greek-speaking, Gentile Christianity; etc. For reasons given in that chapter many scholars are no longer confident we can work with such precision, and in particular we are less certain in judging which designations Jews in Palestine could not have used for Jesus.

In this introductory volume another approach is more interesting and profitable in my judgment[165]—one that does not ignore the way Jesus was designated (hence titles), but is less subjective since it concentrates on NT passages as they now stand without speculating whether they should be associated with the various types of communities just described. Drawing on the whole NT, we shall study how evaluations of Jesus were associated with different aspects of Jesus' career. For those aspects I employ the term *"christological moment,"* meaning a scene in the life of Jesus that became the vehicle for

---

[164] This judgment may be confirmed when readers study APPENDIX III, for many may find the treatment of the title "God" there too difficult.

[165] I develop here with much greater detail the outline presentation in NJBC 81, §§12–23.

giving expression to NT christology (e.g., Jesus' conception, youth, baptism, death, resurrection, second coming). Discussion of a "moment" is not meant to include the issue of whether revelation historically took place at or in the respective scene—for instance, was there revelation about Jesus' identity when he was baptized, and if so, to whom?—but only the extent to which the NT writers communicated christology to their readers in describing that moment.

An element of chronology will be brought into the discussion by arranging the material according to the probable time sequence of the NT evidence pertaining to the respective moment. The first preserved Christian document is I Thessalonians written *ca.* 50, i.e., two decades into Christian history. Yet we have access to Christian thought of the preceding decades of the 30s and 40s in several ways. In his letters of the 50s Paul has formulas stemming from an earlier period, sometimes from the 30s. Some Gospel material was shaped long before the first written Gospel (namely, Mark, presumably in the 60s); and we have a probable entree to that earlier period of Gospel formation when, for instance, Mark and John independently agree.[166] The sermons attributed to Peter and Paul in Acts were composed by Luke in the 80s, but they contain some christological expressions that are not found elsewhere in Luke and have the air of being primitive. Even if these expressions are not genuinely ancient but result from Lucan archaizing (i.e., imagining on the basis of information[167] how early Christians spoke and thought), these expressions may help to confirm early thought detectable by other means. If one begins with the reconstructed pre-50 material and then moves through the extant NT writings in the likely order of their composition, one can trace a peculiar pattern of christological moments that seems to move "backwards" in terms of Jesus' career. The earlier evidence interpreted christologically scenes at the end of Jesus' life; the later evidence interpreted christologically scenes at the begin-

---

[166] Although a number of prominent scholars think John was entirely dependent on Mark, most still maintain that John in large part preserves a tradition similar to but *independent* of the Marcan tradition which is the basis of the Synoptics. See D. M. Smith, *John among the Gospels* (Minneapolis: Fortress, 1992), especially chapter 6; BDM 1.75–93.

[167] It is virtually impossible to study Acts and think that Luke had no information whatsoever about the past.

ning of his life. This is not illogical: The resurrection seen as God's intervention brought Jesus' followers to authentic faith in who he was, and only in the light of that faith did they turn to interpret the earlier aspects of his life.[168]

That observation may be useful but requires caution on several scores. First, our evidence for christological usage (even for the pre-50 period) is drawn from the writings that have been preserved. Christian thought about Jesus was certainly broader and more variegated than what we find in the few preserved writings. If we arrange the thought according to the likely chronological order of the documents, we must be reminded that development of thought is rarely linear and that at any given moment different views surely coexisted. Second, when liberal scholars in the early 20th century sought to trace a pattern such as the one given below, they did so with the supposition that developments *created* a christological meaning that never existed during Jesus' life. It is far safer to work with the self-understanding of the NT writers who thought that they were vocalizing and appreciating a reality that was already there. Thus in the chapters that follow I shall present a development during the 1st century that involves a growing Christian understanding about the identity of Jesus, not the creation ex nihilo of a new identity.

---

[168] For further treatment of this approach and responses to some scholarly objections, see BBM 709–12.

CHAPTER 7.
CHRISTOLOGIES EXPRESSED IN TERMS OF JESUS' SECOND COMING OR RESURRECTION

In the present chapter I shall discuss christologies centered on two "christological moments," namely the second coming (parousia) and the resurrection—christologies attested in the period of preaching between the 30s and 50 before preserved Christian writings first appeared.

(A) Second-Coming (Parousia) Christology

This is a christology that looks to the future. An expectation of the parousia or the return appearance of Jesus from heaven was strong throughout the NT period. We are concerned here, however, only with statements that *attach a christological evaluation of Jesus' identity* to this moment of his second coming. The antiquity of these statements is plausible but not certain.

The first item of evidence is a christological statement in Peter's second sermon in Acts that does not resemble typical Lucan christology. In Acts 3:19–21 Peter posits an interval of repentance before the parousia. That event will involve God's sending the appointed Messiah, Jesus, "whom heaven must welcome until the time for establishing all that God spoke by the mouth of the holy prophets." This can be read to mean that only when Jesus comes back will he be the Messiah. A strong strain in Jewish expectation of the Messiah would have this anointed Davidic king setting up a monarchy centered on Jerusalem, where the Gentiles would come to worship. The Messiah would then bring victory, peace, and prosperity to Israel on earth. In fact, Jesus did none of that. Yet the Jewish anticipations could be kept intact and still applied to Jesus if one hoped that when he came back he would do everything that Judaism expected from the Messiah. Then, having completed the establishment of the kingdom of God, Jesus would be the Messiah foretold by the prophets.[169]

A future christological interpretation is possible also for the prayer *Maranatha*, "Our Lord, come!", preserved in transliterated Aramaic in I Cor 16:22, and in Greek translation in Rev 22:20.[170] When we have liturgical formulas preserved in two languages, like the "*Abba, Patēr*" of Jesus' prayer in Mark 14:36 (both words meaning "Father") and the "*nai, amēn*" of Rev 1:7 (both meaning "yes, so be it" as a response), probabilities are that the formula arose among Aramaic-speaking Christians and was preserved among Greek-speaking Christians who accompanied it with an equivalent in their own language. (Eventually among Greek speakers this equivalent would replace the Aramaic.) Although Aramaic-speaking Christianity lasted long beyond the 30s and 40s, in order for such a formula as *Maranatha* to have been preserved in Aramaic in I Corinthians written *ca.* 55, it plausibly dates back to Paul's first experiences with Christians in the 30s. If that Aramaic word were of recent vintage, why would he have bothered teaching it to the Greek speakers at Corinth? The prayer may originally have implied that when Jesus came, he would then be Lord ruling the earth; thus it would have attached a christological value to the moment of the parousia.

"Future Son-of-Man Sayings," i.e., passages that speak of the Son of Man returning from heaven in the future in order to judge

---

[169] I am not suggesting that the psalmists or the prophets like Isaiah had a clear foreknowledge of *the* Messiah and foretold in detail what this figure of the distant future would do. Rather their words were reflected on and reinterpreted in the post-exilic period to shape the expectation of the great future Messiah. *Throughout this discussion an understanding of the development of messianism such as I have outlined in* APPENDIX I *is presupposed.*

[170] See J. A. Fitzmyer, NJBC 82, §53.

the world or raise the dead are found in all the Gospels, as well as in postulated preGospel sources. Many scholars maintain that they were the earliest Son-of-Man usage to take shape in the tradition;[171] and we saw above (pp. 98–100) the possibility that they stemmed from Jesus' own self-reflection on Dan 7. The original connotation may have been that when Jesus would come back, he would fulfill the Danielic description of a "son of man" (human being) to whom the Ancient of Days would give all power and judgment.

Attaching the identity of Jesus to the future second coming (namely, he will be Messiah or Lord or Son of Man) probably enjoyed a relatively short eminence in Christian thought, for the passages discussed above may be our only NT instances of this christology.[172] I suggest that the reason for such brevity of recorded emphasis is theological. Christianity is a religion of hope, and what God has yet to do in and through Jesus remains an important component of its theological outlook. Nevertheless, the substance of the Christian proclamation to the world is what God *has done* in Jesus. If the gospel or good news is put on the scales, that aspect outweighs insistence on what God *will do*. "Who, in faith's eye, Jesus already is" outweighs in the balance "Who, in hope's anticipation, Jesus will be."

(B) Resurrection Christology

This is a christology that places emphasis on the present, namely, on who Jesus *is*, with the resurrection as the "moment" that gives expression to that reality. In our considerations we are still looking at christological evidence from the period before preserved Christian writing, and in that pre-50 period there is more abundant evidence for resurrection christology than there was for second-

---

[171] On these sayings, see J. Meier, NJBC 78, §§38–41.

[172] Expectation of the second coming is attested throughout the whole NT and is an enduring part of Christian faith, but here I am speaking only of making the parousia a christologically defining moment. For more on parousia or future christology, see J.A.T. Robinson, JTS NS 7 (1956), 177–89; reprinted in his *Twelve New Testament Studies* (SBT 34; Naperville, IL: Allenson, 1962), 134–53; Fuller, *Foundations* 143–47, 184–85; R. F. Zehnle, *Peter's Pentecost Discourse* (SBL Monograph Series 15; Nashville, 1970), 57–59, 92–93.

coming christology. Not only is it the dominant christology of the sermons attributed to Peter and Paul in Acts, but also it is found in the Pauline Epistles in some statements that have a likelihood of prePauline origin. Jesus is Messiah, Lord, and Son of God in the Father's presence in heaven, and he has achieved this status by being raised up or exalted.

Let us begin with christological references to the resurrection in Acts. In 2:32,36 we hear Peter proclaim, "This Jesus God raised up. . . . God has made him both Lord and Messiah, this Jesus whom you crucified." Acts 5:31 has Peter announcing, "God exalted him at His right hand as Leader and Savior." It is Paul who speaks in 13: 32-33: "That which God promised to the Fathers, He has fulfilled for us their children by raising Jesus, as it is written in Ps 2: 'You are my son; today I have begotten you.' " The latter passage echoes a psalm related to the coronation of the kings of Judah. The prophet Nathan promised that David's offspring would be treated as God's own son, so that when a king was crowned, in a sense he became God's son. The resurrection of Jesus, considered as his enthronement in heaven, could be spoken of as his royal coronation and thus, in the Davidic context, as the moment of his being begotten as God's Son.[173]

---

[173] Influenced by the infancy narratives in Matt and Luke (to be discussed below), when Christians hear of the begetting or birth of the Messiah, they tend to think of the annunciation to Mary and the birth at Bethlehem. But probably the earliest use of birth language for Jesus as the Messiah involved his death (birth pangs) and his resurrection. That is reflected in John 16:19-22 where, at the Last Supper on the night before he dies, Jesus compares the context of his departure and return to the sorrowing travail of a woman in birthpangs and her later joy when a child is born. It is also behind the imagery of Rev 12:1-5 where a woman clothed with the sun, with the moon under her feet, and a crown of twelve stars (= Israel; see Gen 37:9-10) is in labor till she brings forth her child who is to rule the nations (= psalm language for the messianic king) who is immediately caught up to God and the heavenly throne. This cannot concern Bethlehem, for it would omit Jesus' whole life on earth. Rather it describes the agony of the crucifixion and death that brings about the birth of the Messiah through resurrection and being taken up to God. (In Jewish thought "the birthpangs of the Messiah" are not his pains but the sufferings of Israel that precede God's sending the Messiah.) The understanding of resurrection as the birth of the Messiah also has left its mark on the NT theology of baptism in terms of the Christian being baptized (by immersion under water) into Jesus' death and coming forth (from the water) as a new creature, born again or from above.

As for the prePauline evidence, at the beginning of Romans
(1:3-4) Paul quotes to the Christians at Rome a formulation of the
gospel proclamation that he expects them to recognize. The Roman
community was not founded by Paul but probably by missionaries
from Jerusalem arriving there in the early 40s.[174] Presumably the
formulation, then, reflects the thought of that period. In it Paul describes Jesus Christ: "Born of the seed of David according to the
flesh; designated Son of God in power according to the Holy Spirit
[Spirit of Holiness[175]] as of resurrection from the dead." Here, although by natural birth Jesus is the Messiah descended from David,
by resurrection he is the Son of God through the Holy Spirit in
power. Again, most scholars acknowledge that there is a prePauline
hymn quoted in Phil 2:6-11; indeed, some would argue that the
hymn was originally composed in Aramaic and may go back to Palestine of the late 30s.[176] Within that hymn Phil 2:8-9 affirms: "[Je-
sus] became obedient unto death, even death on the cross. Therefore
God has exalted him and bestowed on him the name [i.e., 'Lord']
that is above every name." In OT thought knowing the name of a
person is tantamount to knowing the person's identity, whence the
importance of the revelation to Moses of God's name in Exod 3:14.
Thus, the exaltation of Jesus after death identifies him as Lord.

As reflected in some of the texts considered above, the resurrection was originally contrasted with a public ministry of lowliness, so
that through the resurrection in some sense Jesus became greater
than he had been in the ministry. This is what scholars mean by a
"two-step" christology. It is embodied in the various formulas[177]
in which God, at the resurrection, makes Jesus Lord and Messiah,
begets/designates Jesus as the divine Son, or gives Jesus an
exalted name.

---

[174] See R. E. Brown and J. P. Meier, *Antioch and Rome* (New York: Paulist,
1983), esp. 97–104.

[175] The Hebraized Greek way of describing the Holy Spirit (a noun in a genitive
relationship rather than an adjective) is not normal Pauline language and is one of the
indications that this formulation was not Paul's own but presumably was in use
at Rome.

[176] See J. A. Fitzmyer, CBQ 50 (1988), 470–83.

[177] Note that the issue is the christology of the individual formulas, not the
christology of the NT works in which they are preserved.

Resurrection christology would have required a greater change in the Jewish expectations of the Messiah than did second-coming christology, for now the victory, peace, prosperity, and divine worship are all transferred to heaven from the earth of Jewish expectation. To those with the eyes of faith Jesus is Lord reigning in heaven. If we remember that Acts has given us an expression of parousia christology as well as expressions of resurrection christology, a continuity can be established thus: the reigning Messiah whom believers see in heaven with the eyes of faith now, others will see with their own eyes at the parousia when he comes down from heaven.

One can make a reasonable case that all the examples of resurrection christology cited here reflect pre-50 formulations. When we move to the post-50 period of preserved Christian writing, Luke and Paul, despite their reporting these passages, have gone beyond them in their personal christology. Neither holds a two-step christology; neither believes that through the resurrection Jesus received an identity as Messiah or Son of God that he did not already have. The origins of two-step christology may lie in the fact that through the resurrection the first disciples learned aspects of Jesus that they had not known clearly before—an insight translated into terms of *Jesus' becoming* (being made, being begotten, etc.). The NT writers who repeat these formulations apparently would think of them as equivalent to *Jesus' being revealed as*, i.e., his manifesting an identity as Messiah, Son of God, Son of Man, Lord, etc. that he already had during his lifetime but was obscure to those who saw him physically. That observation leads us to the next form of christology which dominates the Gospels written in the period approximately from the 60s to 100.

CHAPTER 8.
CHRISTOLOGIES EXPRESSED
IN TERMS
OF JESUS' PUBLIC MINISTRY

All the Gospels present a Jesus who was clearly Messiah, Son of Man, and Son of God (and sometimes specifically Lord) during his public ministry. Gospel readers immediately know this because they are made party to a revelation connected to the baptism of Jesus where God speaks from heaven and calls him "My beloved Son" (Mark 1:11; Matt 3:17; Luke 3:22[178]). In the two-step resurrection christology discussed at the end of the preceding chapter, the ministry of Jesus from the baptism to the cross could without difficulty be presented as one of lowliness (Phil 2:7 speaks of Jesus in "the form of a servant") since exaltation came only with resurrection. In ministry christology, however, where exalted status and lowly service coexist, there is inevitable tension.

Let us consider one way in which that tension was handled by the evangelists. A resurrection christology passage, such as Acts 13: 33, can apply Ps 2:7 to Jesus without qualification: "You are my

---

[178] The situation in John 1:33–34 is complicated. John the Baptist says that he received a revelation pertinent to Jesus whom he would recognize on the occasion of the descent of the Spirit (thus, at the baptism); and as a result of that revelation he testifies to Jesus' identity. As explained in footnote 123 above, in most mss. of John that testimony is phrased as "This is the Son of God," but some witnesses read "This is the Chosen One of God," which may be the original reading. It echoes the description of the Servant of the Lord in the Greek of Isa 42:1: "Jacob my boy/servant . . . Israel my chosen one," a description that is also echoed in the Synoptic depiction of the baptismal revelation.

son; today I have begotten you." The Synoptic baptismal designation, "My *beloved* son; *with you I am well pleased*," has modified Ps 2:7 by combining it with words (italicized) from the description of the Servant in Isa 42:1. By this combination the evangelists indicate that to understand Jesus as the messianic king during his public ministry one must recognize that he was simultaneously both the Messiah/Son and the Servant who did not cry out (Isa 42:2) and was pierced for our offenses, bearing the guilt of all (Isa 53). Since it is not clear that in preChristian Judaism the ideas of the Messiah and the Suffering Servant had been joined, Jews who did not accept Christian claims might well point out that a Messiah whose life terminated in suffering was a drastic change of the concept of the expected anointed Davidic king. Christians would reply that Jesus threw light on the whole of the Scriptures and showed how once separate passages should be combined.

Beyond this common approach, in describing the ministry of Jesus individual NT writings treat differently the tension between the exalted Messiah/Son image and the lowly Servant; and this difference contributes greatly to the distinctiveness of each of the four Gospels.

Mark preserves the greatest amount of lowliness by describing a precrucifixion ministry in which no human being recognizes or acknowledges Jesus' divine Sonship. Thus the christological identity of Jesus is a "secret" known to the readers (who are told at the baptism) and to the demons (who have supernatural knowledge; Mark 1:24; 3:11; 5:7) but not to those who encounter him or even to those who follow him as he preaches and heals. Mark 8:27–33 shows how little even Peter, the most prominent disciple, has understood Jesus. He has come to recognize that Jesus is the Messiah, but his understanding of messiahship would not allow Jesus to suffer. He is like the blind man of 8:22–26: Jesus has laid hands on the man, and he has come to partial sight (people look like trees); but it will take further action by Jesus before he sees clearly. If Mark's readers or hearers wonder why Jesus does not reveal his christological identity clearly to his disciples, the scene of the transfiguration in Mark 9:2–8 supplies an answer. There Jesus is transfigured before them and the glory that has been hidden throughout the ministry shines forth brightly. God's voice that the readers heard at the baptism speaks again from heaven, proclaiming, "This is my beloved Son." Yet still the disciples do not understand, for in Mark's outlook only through suffering and the cross can either they (or future followers) comprehend the full identity of Jesus. It is quite deliberate, then, that in Mark only after Jesus' death do we finally have a believing acknowledgment of him as Son of God (15:39).

If Mark's form of the tension between a ministry of lowliness and a high christological identity is most visibly preserved in the effect Jesus has on his followers, more subtly it is manifested in Jesus himself. As we saw in Part II it is possible for the Marcan Jesus not to know things. Even though he is God's beloved Son, he admits that only the Father and not the Son knows when future things affecting the fate of the world will come to pass (13:32). And although Jesus can be very certain about his own fate, predicting that the Son of Man will suffer and be killed (8:31; 9:31; 10:33–34) and challenging James and John to drink the cup he will drink (10:38), when the time comes, the Son asks the Father to let the hour of suffering and crucifixion pass and to remove the cup from him. It is almost as if Jesus cannot be fully the Messiah till he has gone through the experience of the cross and cried out, "My God, my God, why have you forsaken me?" (15:34). In this Mark is not far from Hebrews (5:8): "Despite his being Son, he learned obedience from the things he suffered." Mark's is not a two-step christology where Jesus gains a new and higher identity after death and resurrection; but seemingly the full identity of Son/Servant, already present at the baptism, is neither experienced or manifested until the cross.

Matt resolves some of the tension in the account of the public ministry taken over from Mark by allowing the exalted status of Jesus to break through the lowliness so that on certain occasions his disciples recognize who he is. The postresurrectional formulations of Jesus' identity that Mark allows only the demons to vocalize during the ministry are now vocalized by Jesus' followers. Comparing Mark 6:47–52 and Matt 14:23–33, the scene of the walking on the water, is instructive. In both Jesus comes walking across the sea to the disciples who are buffeted in their boat by the wind; the disciples are terrified thinking it is a ghost; Jesus urges them to have no fear, gets into the boat, and causes the wind to cease. Mark reports that they were absolutely astounded, for they did not understand and their hearts were hardened. Matt reports that they worshiped him, saying "Truly you are God's Son." Why the difference? Mark's readers know why Jesus can do this, for they heard at the baptism that he is the Son of God; Mark also expects the readers to realize that after the resurrection the disciples came to that faith as they looked back on the story—otherwise there would be no "Gospel of Jesus Christ, the Son of God" (Mark 1:1). But he shows that during the ministry and before the cross the disciples had no way of understanding such a truth. Matt, with more insistent pedagogy, reads the postresurrectional christological faith of the disciples directly into the scene, making certain that the readers understand what Mark expects them to understand. A similar phenomenon can be observed in the two accounts of Peter's confession at Caesarea Philippi (Mark 8:27–33; Matt 16:13–23). Neither evangelist disguises that Peter's understanding of Jesus' messiahship, although vocally correct, is wrong in its presuppositions and implications because it rejects suffering—indeed so wrong that it is Satanic and reflects only human, not divine thought. But once more Mark leaves it to the readers to suppose that after Peter saw the risen Lord in Galilee (as he was instructed to do in 16:7), he received insight from God and came to a full faith in Jesus as the Messiah, the Son of God. Matt spells that out both by including in Peter's confession the postresurrectional component (not simply the Marcan "You are the Messiah," but "You are the Messiah, *the Son of the living God*") and by having Jesus praise this as going beyond human thought ("flesh and blood has not revealed this") because it came from the Father in heaven. This inclusion of postresurrectional "answers" to the ambiguities of the ministry was one of the factors that won for Matt the appreciation of the later church as the best catechetical tool for communicating the whole picture of Jesus and so made it the most used and best known Gospel.

The way in which Matt portrays a Jesus whose divine sonship can be seen by his disciples (at least at moments of faith) affects the Matthean account of the actions both of Jesus and of his disciples. On the way to heal the daughter of Jairus, when Jesus is touched by the woman with a hemorrhage, the Marcan Jesus (5:30–31) can ask, "Who touched my garments?" and be rebuked by his disciples for asking a foolish question, given the fact that he is the midst of a crowd. The healing power has gone out from the Marcan Jesus, and he does not know whom it has affected. Seemingly neither the limitation of Jesus' knowledge nor the rudeness of the disciples is tolerable within Matt's picture, for there (9:22), without any question and therefore without any reaction by the disciples, Jesus turns and heals the woman whose thoughts he already knows. When the Marcan Jesus has fallen asleep in a boat during a storm, the disciples can wake him with a rebuke, "Teacher, do you not care if we perish?" (4:38). This becomes a prayer in Matt's account (8:25): "Lord, save us; we are perishing." The withering effect of the cursing of the fig tree by the Marcan Jesus does not become apparent until the next day (11:20–21), whereas the tree withers immediately when the Matthean Jesus curses it (21:19–20). The Marcan Jesus can lay hands on a blind man with the result that the man sees only partially, so that Jesus has to lay on hands once more before the man sees clearly (8:22–26). Although Mark intends this parabolically to illustrate the difficulty of bringing the disciples to see with eyes of faith, the story could be read to imply a defect in Jesus' miraculous power. Matt's christology will not allow such an implication, and so he omits the two-stage healing of the blind man.[179]

Luke. We have seen that Matt has brought postresurrectional christology into the account he took over from Mark by allowing the disciples during the public ministry to vocalize a high faith comprehension of Jesus and that this has affected the way Matt presents Jesus and the disciples' relation to him. The situation in Luke is more complicated because the author has a second book (Acts) in which Peter and others can vocalize postresurrectional christology, and so he does not need to bring formulations of that christology into his Gospel. (By comparison, we may say that Matthew has written his "Acts of the Apostles" by superimposition on the Gospel narrative.) Consequently Luke does not increase the intensity of Marcan christological confession during the ministry in the way Matt does; yet Luke is even more sensitive than Matt in refusing to

---

[179] Matt preserves from Mark what precedes this story (16:5–12 = Mark 8:14–21) and what follows it (16:13–20 = Mark 8:27–30); and so his omission of Mark 8:22–26 is deliberate.

portray the human limitations of Jesus or irreverence toward him on the part of disciples. For example, the confession by the Lucan Peter (9:20–22) that Jesus is "the Messiah of God" does not differ substantially from that of the Marcan Peter, "You are the Messiah," and is not so christologically strong as the Matthean Peter's "You are the Messiah, the Son of the living God." (In Acts [2:36; 3:14–15; 5:31], after all, the Lucan Peter will be given the opportunity to confess Jesus as Lord, Messiah, Holy and Righteous One, Author of life, Leader, and Savior, and [4:12] as having the only name under heaven by which we must be saved.) But Luke does not report what both Mark and Matthew recount, namely, that so serious was Peter's misunderstanding of messiahship, Jesus compared him to Satan.

Luke, like Mark, does not have the disciples confess Jesus as Son of God during the public ministry, but does refer to Jesus as the Lord,[180] so that readers remain conscious of Jesus' high christological identity. Luke will not report details too descriptive of Jesus' lowliness such as those found in Mark's and Matt's passion account. For instance, Luke does not take over from Mark that in Gethsemane, with his soul sorrowful unto death, Jesus was distraught, troubled, and falling to the earth on his face, and that on the cross he screamed with a loud cry: "My God, my God, why have you forsaken me?" Nor during the passion will Luke report the disgraceful particulars of the disciples' behavior recounted by Mark and Matt: that Jesus foretold that they would lose their faith and be scattered; that Jesus found them sleeping three times and rebuked Peter; and that they all fled.[181] The noble Lucan Jesus who is at peace with God and himself (23:46) has disciples who remain with him in his trials (22:28).

John. If we imagine scales on which the Synoptic Gospels balance Jesus' lowliness as Servant and his exalted identity as Messiah/Son, the weight on the exalted side increases as one moves from Mark through Luke (the Gospel without Acts) to Matt. Neverthe-

---

[180] Some of the third-person references (Luke 10:1; 13:15; 17:6) are less ambiguous as to the higher sense of *kyrios*; see footnote 2 above.

[181] Luke knew, as Acts shows, that eventually these disciples became the great preachers of the Christian faith and that some laid down their life for Jesus. This relativized for him the importance of their temporary failure to the point where it could be overlooked.

less, the lowliness aspect is never lost sight of. With John the weight is so increased and the scales so tipped on the side of exalted identity that human weaknesses virtually disappear. (While my concern here is John's ministry christology, this portrayal of Jesus is heavily affected by John's theology of preexistence to be discussed in the next chapter.) Matt and Luke still need a transfiguration to remind readers and the disciples of Jesus' glory that is for the most part hidden—for one brief moment it is made manifest. In John the glory of Jesus is manifested to his disciples in his first miraculous sign (2:11), so that a transfiguration would be otiose. Yes, the Word has become flesh; but this is not a self-emptying and taking on the form of a servant to the extent described in Philip 2:7. Rather in the Johannine becoming flesh, "we have seen his glory, the glory of an only Son coming from the Father."[182] If in Philip 2:8–9 after Jesus' death on the cross, God exalts him and gives him the name which is above every other name, in John Jesus has that name during his life on earth and uses its power to protect those whom the Father has assigned to him (17:6,12; see p. 139 below). As for having the disciples recognize Jesus' identity, we saw that in Luke's Gospel no human being professes Jesus as Son of God, in Mark the first one to do so is the Roman centurion after Jesus dies, and in Matt the disciples or Peter use this confession at highly significant moments in the middle of the ministry. In John, at the very beginning of the Gospel, in the first several days of the disciples' encounter with Jesus, they confess him as Messiah, King of Israel and Son of God (1:41,49).[183] Over and over Jesus speaks of himself as the Son and publicly claims unity with the Father (10:30,38; 14:9), so that even his opponents understand him to be stating that he is equal to God (5:18; 10:33; 19:7). They regard this as arrogant pretense ("making himself" equal to God), but the Johannine Jesus "makes" nothing of himself. He simply *is* the Son and the Father has turned over all things to

---

[182] Nevertheless, an important restriction put on the glory that the Johannine Jesus shows forth during his lifetime on earth is that it is not the same as the glory that he had with the Father before the world began (John 17:5).

[183] In response they were told they shall see greater things, namely, the angels of God ascending and descending on the Son of Man (John 1:50–51). The Son of Man who has come from heaven in glory embodies the greater revelation yet to be appreciated by the disciples.

him, so that whoever refuses to honor the Son refuses to honor the Father (5:19–23). The poetic opening of the Gospel describes the Word who was God in the beginning (1:1) and who became flesh as Jesus (1:14); the ending of the Gospel has one of Jesus' disciples, Thomas, confessing him as "My Lord and my God" (20:28). AP-PENDIX III will show that some of the most prominent NT passages that call Jesus "God" are found in the Gospel and Epistles of John.

This exalted christology, the highest among the Gospels and, indeed, perhaps the highest in the NT,[184] affects John's description of the way Jesus acts during the ministry. The Johannine Jesus knows all things, so that when he asks a disciple a simple question, "Where shall we buy bread for these people to eat?", the evangelist stops to reassure the readers that Jesus asked this, not because he did not know, but in order to test the disciple's reaction (6:5–6). In the middle of the ministry at the very first mention of Judas Iscariot, Jesus indicates that when he chose the Twelve, he knew that one of them was a devil who would betray him (6:70–71). Because Jesus is one with the Father, there is an awkwardness in having him petition God as if there were any suspense as to whether the request would be granted. Thus, when Jesus approaches the burial place of Laza-rus, he takes a stance as if to pray about the deceased; but the words are scarcely a petition: "Father, I thank you because you heard me. Of course, I know that you always hear me; but I say this because of the crowd standing around, that they may believe that you sent me" (11:41–42). In the passion account the Johannine Jesus is not in any sense a victim but is in complete control: "I lay down my life . . . no one has taken it from me. Rather, I lay it down of my own accord: I have power to lay it down, and I have power to take it up again" (10:17–18). The Marcan Jesus, when his soul is sorrowful, prays to the Father that this hour might pass from him (Mark 14:35); but the Johannine Jesus, when his soul is distressed, muses to himself, "And what should I say? Father, save me from this hour?" He pronounces

---

[184] As I have stated earlier, all the Gospels and, in my judgment, all the NT books where the issue arises, treat Jesus as divine even if divinity is expressed in different ways. Important in judging "the highest christology" are the clarity and un-ambiguity of a particular book's articulation of his divinity. APPENDIX IV will offer suggestions about factors that may have led to the Johannine articulation.

that he will not pray thus because his whole goal has been to come to this hour; rather he says, "Father, glorify your name" (John 12: 27–28). Jesus gives Judas permission to go off to betray him (13:27–30). When he says "I am," the party of Roman soldiers and Jewish police that have come to arrest him fall backwards to the ground (18:6). The disciples of the Johannine Jesus do not flee as he is arrested; he arranges for them to be let go so that it may be seen that he has not lost any of them (18:8–9). This Jesus does not die alone and abandoned; not only is the Father always with him (16:32), but at the foot of the cross stand his mother and the beloved disciple (19: 25–27)—symbols of a believing community that he has gathered. Therefore, knowing that he has accomplished all that the Father has given him to do and has completed the Scripture, he can decide "It is finished" and give over his spirit (19:28–30). Obviously, as last words, this is a far cry from the "My God, my God, why have you forsaken me?" of Mark and Matt.

These examples suffice to show that despite the four evangelists' agreement that during his ministry Jesus was already Messiah and Son of God, the way in which they balance that with a picture of him as rejected and misunderstood varies so that very different Gospel pictures of Jesus emerge. For those who accept the later church confession of Jesus as true God and true man, the different picture in each Gospel, while supporting overall that confession, gives its peculiar insight into one or the other side of that mystery: Mark, for instance, more insight into Jesus as true man; John, more insight into Jesus as true God. No one Gospel would enable us to see the whole picture, and only when the four are kept in tension among themselves has the church come to appreciate who Jesus is.

Although we have discussed the public ministry of Jesus, the largest part of the Gospel accounts, our survey of the "moments" used in the NT to vocalize an appreciation of Jesus is not over. The oldest Gospel, Mark, has told us that Jesus was the Messiah and Son of God from the very beginning of his public ministry (and thus not simply that he became or was made God's Son through the resurrection or will be the Messiah when he comes again). That affirmation, however, leaves open questions. Was Jesus the Son of God before being baptized by John? Were God's words on that occasion, "You are my beloved Son; with you I am well pleased" (Mark 1:11) a formula adopting Jesus as the divine Son? I see no reason to suspect that in Mark's view Jesus became the Son of God at the baptism, but his total silence about Jesus before the baptism leaves an ambiguity that the other three evangelists chose to remove. All three start their Gospels before the baptism and use preministry "moments" to indicate Jesus' identity. We now turn to that phase of NT christology.

CHAPTER 9.
CHRISTOLOGIES EXPRESSED
IN PREMINISTRY TERMS

We may treat Christian reflections on the identity of Jesus before he began his public ministry under three headings: (A) Family-circle or boyhood christology centered on Jesus as a youth; (B) Conception christology centered on the conception/birth of Jesus; (C) Preexistence christology centered on what preceded Jesus' human life. (Actually the picture is more varied, since both A and C can be subdivided.) Their common thrust is to show that the identity of Jesus manifested during his public ministry continues an identity that he had earlier. Nevertheless, when examined critically these preministry christologies are remarkably independent of each other. John's Gospel, for instance, which is a leading exponent of preexistence christology (or, more exactly, precreation christology) betrays no awareness at all of the infancy stories of Matt and Luke in which conception christology is vocalized, and vice versa. And within the same subdivision, even though Luke and Matt have common motifs about the conception of Jesus as God's Son, the stories in which those motifs find expression are quite different. What we shall see in this chapter, then, demonstrates the abundance and variety of early Christian reflection on the identity of Jesus.

(A) Family-circle or Boyhood Christology

One might think that the first logical step in reflecting on Jesus' identity before he was baptized and thus before he began his public ministry would be to report what he was like as a young man living with his family or, earlier, what he was like as a boy growing up. Yet that whole period leaves very little traces in the canonical Gospels. Matt, for instance, who begins his infancy story with Jesus in the womb of his mother, jumps from what happened to Jesus at about age two (Herod's pursuit of the child, the flight into Egypt, and the transfer of the family from Bethlehem to Nazareth) to the scene of his baptism. The slender evidence for the type of christology under discussion here consists of a Lucan story of Jesus at age twelve, a Johannine account of a miracle that Jesus does in the presence of his mother and brothers, and an apocryphal boyhood gospel about miracles performed by Jesus beginning at age five.

Of these the best known is the story of Jesus when he was left behind in the Jerusalem Temple, narrated in Luke 2:41–51. Although Luke makes this incident sequential to the story of the conception and birth where Jesus' identity as God's Son has been already revealed, it probably once stood by itself. (Note that the parents who have sought Jesus sorrowing are annoyed at his having stayed behind and do not understand when he speaks to them about his Father.) This is the first time in Luke that Jesus speaks, and his words reveal his identity. Mary has spoken of "your father [Joseph] and I"; but implicitly correcting Mary's reference to "father," Jesus makes it clear that the prime claim on his life is exercised by his heavenly Father, his true Father. Jesus informs his mother that natural parentage has no authoritative claim on him: She and Joseph should have recognized that he would be in his Father's house (or about his Father's business—the elliptical phrase has several connotations). If at the baptism the voice of God from heaven will identify Jesus as "My beloved Son," already in his boyhood Jesus has affirmed that identity.[185]

The story in John 2:1–11 is more complicated. In the sequence

---

[185] When such a story was brought into canonical Luke with its account of the public ministry of Jesus, it created a logical difficulty. If Jesus as a boy spoke openly of his divine sonship, how is it that he was unknown when he began his ministry (4:22–24) and that he did not speak openly of this identity throughout the ministry? The ending of the story in Luke 2:50–51 attempts to cover that difficulty, because it suggests that, except for this one instance in the Temple, Jesus was obedient to the parents who did not understand him and so did not go on proclaiming his identity in an open manner when he was growing up.

in which John has introduced it, Jesus has already been baptized and gathered disciples. Yet the miracle takes place in Cana, a Galilean town near Nazareth[186] before he goes to Capernaum (2:12) which will be the central place of the ministry. Moreover, his mother is a central figure in the story, and his "brothers" are present.[187] At least, then, the story involves a transition from family circle to ministry. More likely, in my judgment, this miracle story once belonged to a genre where Jesus performed miracles within his family circle even before the baptism (see next paragraph). His mother's expectation that he could do something to alleviate the shortage of wine for the friends or relatives at the wedding implies that he has done miraculous things before; and in itself the changing of water to an abundant amount of the best wine resembles the apocryphal stories of Jesus' boyhood where he performs miracles for family convenience. Jesus' response to his mother distinguishing between her concern (one of convenience) and his concern (the hour to manifest his glory) is functionally the same as his response to his mother in the Lucan Temple story just discussed. The reader will discover that "the hour" embodies what the Father has given him to do, and that the glory that he begins to manifest at Cana (2:11) is related to the glory that he had with the Father before the world began (17:5). Thus in both the Lucan and Johannine stories, before the ministry fully begins, in resistance to family concerns, Jesus is staking out his role and the relationship to God as Father that is part of his identity.

Probably family-circle or boyhood christology developed in popular circles rather than in the public preaching responsible for shaping much Gospel tradition. That suspicion is fueled by the existence of the late-2d-century, extracanonical *Infancy Gospel of Thomas* (*IGT*) where Jesus performs a series of miracles beginning

---

[186] In the Synoptic Gospels during his ministry Jesus does not work miracles in his home Galilean region (e.g., Mark 6:5); and so the localization of this Johannine miracle at Cana is another argument for an original temporal setting before the public ministry.

[187] In Mark 3:21,31–35 the beginning of his ministry marks his departure from home and his distancing himself from his relatives, specifically from his mother and brothers. The fact that in the Cana story Jesus seems still to be attached to that circle suggests this may originally have been a preministry story.

at age 5.[188] Some of these are convenience miracles, e.g., miraculously supplying water that his mother needs and lengthening a wooden plank his father needs. If John's Cana story originally was related to such a tradition, as I suggested above, it becomes intelligible why his mother expects him to be able to do something about the shortage of wine. In another direction *IGT* is basically asserting in a popular, imaginative way that the miraculous power that Jesus possessed during his public ministry was possessed already by Jesus from his earliest days. He heals a boy with a wounded foot, multiplies wheat, and resuscitates a recently dead little child. Because of the childlike character of some of the miracles, e.g., making birds out of clay and having them fly away, the christological import of this gospel is often overlooked. When the boy Jesus does that miracle, a "certain Jew" objects to his working with clay on the Sabbath, even as the Pharisees will object during the public ministry (cf. John 9:6,16). And just as the adult Jesus will react to the Sabbath protest, so the boy Jesus shows himself unmoved by the objection, implying that he is not bound by the Sabbath and thus hinting at his authority.

If one arranges these three examples of family-circle christology in the order of Jesus' respective age in each and thus moves from the *IGT* through Luke 2:41–51 to John 2:1–11, one receives a firm answer in both words and deeds that Jesus was God's Son, not only before he was baptized by John but even from the first moment of his conscious behavior.

(B) Conception Christology

In the introductory chapter of their Gospels both Matt and Luke relate Jesus' human identity as descendant of David to the fact that his legal father, Joseph, was of the House of David (Matt 1:20; Luke 1:27). They both relate his divine identity to his having been conceived of Mary through the Holy Spirit without a human father (Matt 1:20; Luke 1:35). Yet the Lucan and Matthean infancy stories are very different, and they must have been composed indepen-

---

[188] The last story in the series is a form of the Lucan narrative of Jesus in the Temple at age 12.

dently of each other. Therefore most likely these common points
about the conception come from a shared tradition antedating both
Gospels.

Matt (1:21,23; 2:15) phrases the divine identity in terms of the
one who will save his people from their sins, Emmanuel (God with
us), and God's Son. At the very end of the Gospel, Matt 28:20 will
return to the Emmanuel identity as the risen Jesus says, "I am with
you all days until the end of the age." Thus implicitly Matt is telling
us that at and through his conception Jesus already had an identity
that would be more widely manifested after the resurrection.

The Lucan phrasing of the divine identity of Jesus as "Son of
God" is particularly interesting if we remember Rom 1:3–4, which
we discussed on p. 114 above as an example of resurrection christology. There, using an older formula, Paul identified Jesus as descended from David according to the flesh but designated Son of
God in power according to the Holy Spirit through resurrection
from the dead. Thus in Jesus' twofold identity, Son of David and
Son of God, human descent through birth is associated with the first,
and "Holy Spirit" and "power" are associated with the second. Luke
seems to have been familiar with this type of language; for in his
expression of ministry christology, after God's voice has said from
heaven, "You are my beloved *Son*," we are told that "Jesus returned
to Galilee in the *power* of the *Spirit*" (Luke 4:14). In the Lucan account of the conception of Jesus, the angel Gabriel first tells Mary
that the child she is to conceive and bear will be Son of David. The
words in 1:32–33, "He will be great and will be called the Son of the
Most High, and the Lord God will give to him the throne of David
his father; he will be king of the house of Jacob forever; there will be
no end to his kingdom," are simply a rephrasing of the oracle of
Nathan to David in II Samuel 7:9–16[189] that lies at the basis of all
messianic hope (APPENDIX I, A). There God spoke through Nathan:
"I will make for you a great name . . . I will raise up your son after
you . . . I will establish the throne of his kingdom forever, so that I
will be for him a father, and he will be to a son . . . Thus your house
and your kingdom shall stand firm before me forever. Your throne

---

[189] We find another rephrasing of this oracle in the Dead Sea Scroll literature;
see also pp. 80–81 above and BBM 311.

is eternally established." If OT language supplies the first half of the twofold identity of the Lucan Jesus, the language of early Christian preaching (e.g., Romans) supplies the second half of the identity.[190] In response to Mary's, "How shall this be?", the angel Gabriel explains how Mary will become the mother of the Son of God (1:34–35): "The *Holy Spirit* will come upon you; the *power* of the Most High will overshadow you; and so the child to be born will be called holy, *Son of God*."

When we line up the passages using the language of Spirit/power in relation to divine sonship, it is associated with the resurrection in the prePauline formula in Romans, with the baptism in Luke's opening of the ministry, and now with the conception in Luke's infancy story. In the Romans formula the twofold identity appears to be sequential: Son of David through birth, then Son of God through resurrection.[191] In Luke's conception christology the two sonships are simultaneous. In the plan of Luke's whole work, the christological message is both artistic and insistent. Jesus' identity as God's Son is proclaimed by an angel at his conception, by Jesus himself the first time he speaks (2:49), by God at the baptism (3:22), and by Paul after the resurrection (Acts 13:32–33).

We saw above in Chapter 8 under ministry christology that, by comparison with Mark, the other two Synoptists allowed the exalted identity of Jesus as God's Son to outweigh his lowliness. This choice makes greater sense once we realize that these two evangelists have informed their readers that there was never a moment on earth when Jesus did not have this divine identity. Indeed, conception christology affects the way that both Matt and Luke narrate the whole story of Jesus following the birth. Since they will draw upon Mark where Jesus is religiously unknown even in Nazareth at the beginning of his ministry, each has to wrestle with the problem of those who received the revelation of his identity earlier. These would have included the magi who received revelation from the appearance of a

---

[190] We may suspect that Luke's readers who had already been evangelized would have recognized in Gabriel's words to Mary the same gospel that was preached to them about Jesus.

[191] Despite his use of the early formula, Paul himself would not have thought of the divine identity as sequential to the human (as we shall see below under C).

star in Matt 2:1–2, and the shepherds who received revelation from an angel in Luke 2:10–12; and both these groups are carefully removed from the scene immediately after they have honored the child (Matt 2:12; Luke 2:20). Luke 2:25–38 has also Simeon and Anna who are supernaturally moved to recognize Jesus' identity when he is brought to the Temple, but they are both aged and so would not have lived to see Jesus grow up. Joseph (Matt) and Mary (Luke) are the main recipients of christological revelation at Jesus' conception. The absence of Joseph during the public ministry (including the failure to mention a father in the list of Jesus' family in Mark 6:3) suggests that he also had died. Thus Mary remains as the sole figure from the infancy narrative who is active as Jesus begins his ministry.

Since Mark reports no preministry christology and may have known little of Jesus' origins, he can portray Mary among Jesus' relatives who do not understand or appreciate what he is doing in his new career (3:21,31; 6:4). But Matt and Luke know that Mary conceived Jesus through the Holy Spirit and can scarcely acquiesce to such a picture. Matt, who preserves the passage that respectively precedes and follows Mark 3:21, carefully omits that verse which has Jesus' relatives think he is besides himself; and Matt 13:57 omits from Mark 6:4 that Jesus was without honor among his own relatives. Luke's infancy picture of Mary is far more elaborate than Matt's. Mary not only conceived through the Holy Spirit but also was the first one to whom the gospel message of Jesus' twofold identity was proclaimed. To this she gave the basic response expected of a Christian ("Be it done to me according to your word"), and so became the first disciple. Harmoniously with such a positive presentation, the body of the Lucan Gospel not only omits the unfavorable Marcan passages omitted by Matt, but reinterprets the only scene where Mary appears during the Synoptic account of the public ministry. When she and Jesus' "brothers" come looking for him, they are no longer contrasted with the family of disciples as in Mark 3:31–35; rather the mother and brothers are praised as "those who hear the word of God and do it" (Luke 8:19–21). Moreover in Acts 1:14 Luke takes care to show that after the ascension of the Lord the mother and brothers, along with the Twelve and the women, were still faithful, awaiting the coming of the Spirit.

(C) Preexistence Christology

Thus far the "moments" discussed as vehicles for vocalizing the Christian understanding of Jesus were moments within his earthly career. But certain NT passages indicate that early Christians believed God's Son to have had a prehistory before that career. In what follows it is not always easy to distinguish between a precise notion of the preexistence of the divine Son and a plan of preparation in God's "mind" for the coming of the Son.

Preexistence in the Moses and Abraham Periods. Some passages that associate Jesus with OT events need be no more than a comparison. For instance, John 3:14 uses desert-wandering imagery for Jesus: "Just as Moses lifted up the serpent in the wilderness, so must the Son of Man be lifted up." Other passages may be meant more literally. For instance, Paul's phrasing is striking in I Cor 10:4: "Our fathers [= ancestors]" who accompanied Moses in the desert-wandering all drank the same spiritual drink: "They drank from the spiritual rock that was following them, and the rock was Christ."[192] Matt 1:2 starts the story of the birth or genesis of Jesus with Abraham's begetting Isaac, so that Jesus seems already to have been present in the story of Abraham.[193] In John 8:56 Jesus says: "Abraham rejoiced to see my day; he saw it and rejoiced." When "the Jews" object that this is impossible, granted that Jesus is less than fifty years of age, Jesus insists "Before Abraham came to be, I am" (8:58).

Preexistence in the Adam Period. The Lucan genealogy (3:38) identifies Jesus as Son of Adam, Son of God. It is difficult to know whether the second is to be taken more literally than the first, as many interpreters assume. In any case other texts suggest that early Christians somehow associated Jesus with Adam.[194] The parallel be-

---

[192] E. E. Ellis, "*Christos* in 1 Corinthians 10.4,9," FJTJ 168–73, on the analogy of I Cor 8:6 ("Jesus Christ, through whom all things are") argues for a wisdom background and precreational preexistence in 10:4.

[193] Less clearly a reference to the preexistence of Jesus in patriarchal times is Gal 3:16, where Paul contends that Jesus is the descendant or seed of Abraham.

[194] See C. M. Pate, *Adam Christology as the Exegetical & Theological Substructure of 2 Corinthians 4:7–5:21* (Lanham, MD: University Press of America, 1991). In this introductory book I shall not discuss the myth of the original man (*Urmensch*) that some with comparative religious interests would introduce from an Iranian background.

tween Jesus and Adam in Rom 5:12–17 does not in itself indicate the preexistence of Jesus in the Adamic period. The most important evidence would be the prePauline hymn of Philip 2:6–11 depending on how that hymn is interpreted.[195] (Some scholars refuse to see any note of preexistence in the hymn; others interpret it as explained here; most interpret it as explained in the next subsection.) The hymn may imply that originally there were two figures, Christ Jesus and Adam, coexistent and parallel, in the image (likeness) of God (for Adam, see Gen 1:27). One (Adam) did not accept the status of a servant inherent in *being* human but grasped at being equal to God and failed, thus being reduced to an unhappy state (Gen 3:5,15–19). The other (Christ Jesus) did not grasp at being equal to God but emptied himself voluntarily, not only by accepting the status of a servant (that is inherent in being human) but by going farther and becoming obedient to death on a cross. Therefore he was raised by God to equality by being given the divine name "Lord."

Precreational Preexistence. Incarnation means that at his human conception the Son of God did not come into existence;[196] rather he was a previously existing agent in the divine sphere who took on flesh in the womb of Mary. Technically incarnation does not tell us whether this agent was created (as were the angels who exist in the divine sphere) or existed with God before any creation. A fortiori, it does not tell us whether the agent was God or equal to God. Having issued that caution, I shall treat here possible NT references to incarnation alongside texts that imply precreational preexistence because many scholars, influenced by the Prologue to

---

[195] See also G. Howard, "Phil 2:6–11 and the Human Christ," CBQ 40 (1978), 368–87.

[196] We do not know how Matt and Luke understood the conception of Jesus through the Holy Spirit without a human father. For them was that the becoming of God's Son? The "therefore" in Luke 1:35 ("The Holy Spirit will come upon you, and the power of the Most High will overshadow you; *therefore* the one to be born will be called holy, Son of God") could be interpreted to point in that direction. One may not simply assume that Matt or Luke thought in a Johannine incarnation pattern. Although some scholars think Luke knew John's Gospel, that is far from certain; and John never mentions the conception of Jesus. Ignatius of Antioch (*ca.* 110) is the first one known to have put together conception and incarnation christology, for he refers to both Jesus as God's Word and the birth from a virgin (*Magnesians* 8:2; *Smyrnaeans* 1:1).

John's Gospel where the Word who becomes flesh does exist before creation, join the two ideas.

In the discussion of the Adamic period above, we saw one possible understanding of the prePauline hymn in Philip 2:6–11. In that interpretation neither Adam or Jesus was yet equal to God, whence the temptation to *grasp at* equality, with Jesus refusing and Adam yielding. More scholars, however, would understand Philip 2:6–7 to mean that Jesus did not consider being equal to God something to be *clung to*. In this interpretation, unlike Adam who, as a creature, was not equal to God but sought to be, Jesus was already equal to God but was willing to empty himself to accept the form of a servant by *becoming* a human being.[197] Those who support this interpretation argue correctly that a more normal understanding of the Greek in Philip 2:7–8 would have the Son becoming a human being. Also in its favor is II Cor 8:9 which speaks of the Lord Jesus Christ "who, although being rich, became poor for your sake."

Obviously if the Son became human, he must have preexisted; but for how long? That is not clear from either the Philippians or the II Corinthians passage. In reference to the Philippians passage some would claim that Jesus' being equal to God has to include eternal preexistence. But equality in status and glory seems to be the main focus of the hymn, and one may wonder whether the wording can be pushed to include equality in every aspect. Another hymn in the Pauline corpus (Col 1:15–20, which may have antedated the letter) presents Jesus as having very high status without positing precreational preexistence. After 1:15 calls Jesus the image of the invisible God, it speaks of him as the firstborn of all creation in and through whom all things were created (cf. Sirach 24:9). The parallel description in the hymn (1:18) portrays him as the firstborn from the dead through whom God reconciled all things to Himself. "Firstborn from the dead" means that the Son himself died and was the first one to rise, so that through him others could rise from death. Does

---

[197] Two issues are involved. The first is how to translate *harpagmos* (a desired acquisition): something to be grasped at, or something already possessed to be held on to. The second is how to translate *genomenos* in the phrase that is appositive to "taking (or accepting) the form of a servant," namely, does it mean "being" or "becoming" in the likeness of human beings.

"firstborn of all creation" similarly imply that the Son was created first and then through him others? If so, this would be a preexistence dating back to the moment of creation. I Cor 8:6 speaks of everything existing through Jesus Christ but again leaves unsettled the idea of creational or precreational preexistence.

Hebrews (4:14–15; 5:8) describes a Christ who was God's Son but tested in everything as we are (yet without sin) and who had to learn obedience through suffering. The author of Heb 10:5–10 clearly thought of an incarnation, for he describes the sentiments of Christ as he came into the world and entered a body God has prepared for him. What status did God's Son have before coming into the world? Heb 1:5ff. makes it clear that the Son is greater than any angel. Heb 1:2 says that through the Son God created the world.[198] Was the Son himself created? The same passage speaks of God having appointed or placed him as heir of all things; that could carry a connotation of making him Son, or could describe giving an already existing Son a role in creation. The latter is favored by the language used in 1:3 where the Son is described as a reflection of the glory of God, bearing the stamp of God's being, and upholding the universe by his power;[199] and by the address to the Son as to God in 1:8 (see APPENDIX III, p. 186 below). Thus it is likely that Hebrews envisions a divine Son who preexisted creation, participated in the creation of everything else, and became incarnate as Jesus Christ.

The Johannine Gospel offers lucid examples of precreational christology.[200] The opening verses (1:1–2) of the hymn that serves as a Prologue makes clear that not only through the Word (who is the Son; see 1:18) were all things created but also the Word existed in God's presence before creation. If in Gen 1:1 "In the beginning" means in the beginning of creation, in John 1:1 "In the beginning" means before anything was created. That in John's mind the preexistence of Jesus as God's Son is not merely hymnic figurative lan-

---

[198] Heb 2:7–8 adds that God has put everything in subjection to the Son (who for a little while was less than the angels), and that nothing has been left outside his control.

[199] See the comparable language in Wis 7:25–27.

[200] This is only part of the larger Johannine christological picture. APPENDIX III will make the point that John clearly called Jesus God (20:28). APPENDIX IV will suggest some facts that may have catalyzed Johannine christological development.

guage or poetic license is clear from 17:5 where the Johannine Jesus speaks literally and consciously of having had a glorified existence with the Father before the world began (see also 16:28; 3:13; 5:19; 8:26,58).

A particular facet of Johannine precreational christology appears in the use of "I am" by Jesus. The corresponding Greek *egō eimi* can be simply a phrase of common speech, equivalent to "It is I" or "I am the one." However, it also has a solemn and sacral use in the OT, the NT, Gnosticism, and pagan Greek religious writings.[201] Of most importance for our quest is John's absolute use of "I am" with no predicate, which I shall distinguish by capitalizing. Thus, 8:24: "Unless you come to believe that I AM, you will die in your sins"; 8:28: "When you lift up the Son of Man, then you will know that I AM"; 8:58: "Before Abraham even came into existence, I AM"; 13:19: "When it does happen, you may believe that I AM."[202]

There is a natural tendency to feel that these statements are incomplete; for instance, in John 8:25 "the Jews" respond by asking, "Well, then, who are you?" Since this usage goes far beyond ordinary parlance, all recognize that the absolute I AM has a special revelatory function in John. The most common explanation is to associate this Johannine use with "I AM" employed as a divine

---

[201] For the spectrum of usage, both general and Johannine, see BGJ 1.533–38.

[202] I would add two other texts. The first is 6:20 where the disciples in the boat are frightened because they see someone coming to them on the water, and Jesus assures them, "I AM; do not be afraid." The second is 18:5: The soldiers and police who have come to the garden across the Kidron to arrest Jesus announce that they are seeking Jesus of Nazareth, and he answers, "I AM." Some would tell us that the first means simply, "It is I, i.e., someone whom you know, and not a supernatural being or a ghost." And they would tell us that the second means simply, "I am he, i.e., the one you are looking for." A better solution is to recognize a play on the expression "I AM" as having a twofold meaning: While it has a simpler story-line import (as just exemplified), it also has a higher connotation. In the first example the sacral comes from the context that involves Jesus' walking on the water and a dangerous storm from which they are immediately brought to land; in the second example it comes from those who, hearing Jesus' response, fall back to the ground. Both, then, would be instances of a theophany or divine appearance of one who, like the God of Israel, is master of storms and the sea and at the mention of whose name every knee must bend.

name in the OT and rabbinic Judaism.[203] The OT offers excellent examples of the use of "I am," including impressive examples of the absolute use. Let us begin with the statement, "I am Yahweh/God," since the absolute use of "I AM" in the OT is a variant of it. In Hebrew the statement contains simply the pronoun "I" and the predicate "Yahweh" or "God" without a connecting verb. This formula is revelatory in a limited way, expressing divine authority and giving reassurance and a reason for trust (Gen 26:24; 28:13; Exod 6:6; 20:2,5; Lev 18:5; Ezek 20:5). In particular, where God promises, "You shall know that I am Yahweh" (Exod 6:7; cf. 7:5), we come close to John 8:24,28 cited above. The most important use of the OT formula "I am Yahweh" stresses the unicity of God: I am Yahweh (or I am He) and there is no other, e.g., in Deutero-Isaiah, as well as in Hosea 13:4 and Joel 2:27. The Hebrew for "I Yahweh" or "I He" is translated in the Greek OT simply as "I am" (*egō eimi*); and since the predicate is not expressed, that translation puts added emphasis on existence.

There is even evidence that the use of *egō eimi* in the Greek of Deutero-Isaiah came to be understood not only as a statement of divine unicity and existence, but also as a divine name. The Hebrew of Isa 43:25 reads, "I, I am He who blots out your transgressions." The Greek translates the first part of this statement by using *egō eimi* twice. This can mean, "I am He, I am He who blots out your transgressions"; but it can also be interpreted, "I am 'I AM' who blots out your transgressions," a translation that makes *egō eimi* a name. Isa 51:12 is similar. The Hebrew of Isa 52:6 states, "My people shall know my name; in that day (they shall know) that I am He who speaks"; but the Greek can be read, "that *egō eimi* is the one who speaks," so that "I AM" becomes the divine name to be known in the day of the Lord.

---

[203] Although some scholars have suggested a background of the Johannine formula in pagan religious usage (in the Isis magical formulas, the Hermetic corpus, the Mandean writings, and the Mithraic liturgy), it remains difficult to find parallels to this *absolute* use. For instance, the magic texts that read simply "I am" are not examples of an absolute use, since a name is to be supplied by the user of the text.

Against this background the absolute use of "I AM" by the Johannine Jesus becomes quite intelligible; he is speaking in the same manner in which Yahweh speaks in Deutero-Isaiah.[204] For instance, in John 8:28 Jesus promises that when the Son of Man is lifted up (in return to the Father), "then you will know *egō eimi*"; in Isa 43: 10 Yahweh has chosen Israel, "that you may know and believe me and understand *egō eimi*." The absolute Johannine use of "I AM" has the effect of portraying Jesus as divine with (pre)existence as his identity, even as the Greek OT understood the God of Israel.[205]

John did not invent this usage for Jesus, for there are examples that *verge* on the absolute use of *egō eimi* in the Synoptics even though one can argue that a predicate is assumed. For instance, in Matt 14:27 (Mark 6:50): As Jesus comes walking across the water, he says to the disciples in the boat, "*Egō eimi*; do not be afraid." This is the same use we saw in John 6:20 (footnote 202). That in this scene Matthew intends more than a simple "It is I" is suggested by the profession of faith elicited from the disciples (Matt 14:33), "Truly, you are God's Son!" Or again, when speaking of the signs of the last days, Jesus warns, "Many will come in my name, saying *egō eimi*" (Mark 13:6; Luke 21:8). The context does not clearly suggest a predicate (even though Matt 24:5 supplies one: "I am the Messiah"); and the juxtaposition of *egō eimi* and "my name" brings us close to Johannine usage. Thus, John's absolute use of "I AM," rather than a creation from nothing, may be an elaboration of a

---

[204] There are many Johannine references to the divine name that Jesus bears. In his ministry Jesus made known and revealed the Father's name to his disciples (17: 6,26). He came in the Father's name (5:43) and did his works in the Father's name (10:25); indeed, he says that the Father has given him the name (17:11,12). The great sin is to refuse to believe in the name of God's only Son (3:18). In Acts and Paul (e.g., Philip 2:9–11) the name given to Jesus at which every knee should bend is *kyrios* or "Lord"—the term used in LXX to translate "YHWH" or "Adonai." It is possible that John thinks of *egō eimi* as the divine name given to Jesus.

[205] If we understand "Yahweh" as derived from a causative form (see F. M. Cross, Jr., *Harvard Theological Review* 55 [1962], 225–59), the Hebrew of Exod 3:14 reads, " 'I am who cause to be' sent me to you," or perhaps more originally in the third person, "He who causes to be." But the Greek reads, "I am the Existing One," using a participle of the verb "to be."

usage in early tradition that has left some traces in the Synoptic Gospels as well.[206]

The Pauline and Hebrews passages discussed at the beginning of this subsection C show similarly that precreational christology involving an incarnation was not a Johannine aberration or creation from nothing but, at most, a clarification within a Gospel framework of ideas that circulated elsewhere among early Christians. (That is an important fact to keep in mind in light of the tendency of some to argue that the "true God of true God" portrayal of Jesus at the council of Nicaea stems only from John.) The implications of incarnation in John, however, seem to go beyond other NT works. From John's portrayal of Jesus one may doubt that John would say with Philippians that there was an emptying in the incarnation, or with Hebrews that the Son had to learn obedience. The Johannine Jesus is too much one with the Father for the latter affirmation.

Among the *Gospels* only John openly supposes an incarnation in which the divine Word becomes flesh and dwells among us as Jesus Christ (see footnote 196 above). Under ministry christology we saw that, much more than the Synoptics, John lets Jesus' exalted status dominate the picture of his earthly career. Clearly the Johannine concept of the incarnation is a major factor in that change of emphasis. When the other Gospels speak of the coming of the Son of Man, they are referring to the parousia at the end of time; while not excluding that, John puts primary emphasis on the coming of the Son of Man from God in the incarnation. If in other NT thought the supreme act of God's love in Jesus was the self-giving involved in the crucifixion (Rom 5:8), in John 3:16–21 God's supreme act of love and giving is sending the Son into the world as a light to those whose deeds are wrought in God. If other Christians are waiting for the Son of Man to come back to preside at judgment and give the reward of eternal life, the incarnational coming of the Johannine Son of Man constitutes judgment, as people decide for the light that

---

[206] Other examples might include the use in Luke 24:36 (some textual witnesses) where, after the resurrection, Jesus appears to his disciples and says, "*Egō eimi*; do not be afraid." Once again this may simply mean, "It is I" (see 24:39); but the post-resurrectional context suggests a revelation of the Lordship of Jesus. A less plausible candidate is the use of "*Egō eimi*" in Jesus' answer to the high priest in Mark 14:61–62.

has come into the world or for darkness. He brings God's own eternal life to those who believe, making them God's children—in the story flow seemingly even before the crucifixion/resurrection.[207] What the other Gospels tend to put at the end of the public ministry as Jesus comes close to crucifixion and resurrection, John tends to put first when the Son of God who has come from heaven begins to speak, e.g., cleansing the Temple; prediction of sanctuary destruction; and the issue of his being the Messiah, the Son of God (all in John 1–2). One gets the impression that John has a knowledge of the type of Gospel presentation found in the Synoptics (not necessarily the individual Gospels) and regards it as elementary. He retells the Jesus story from the viewpoint of the incarnation, almost making the words of Jesus in 1:50b his theme, "You will see greater things than that." Almost every scene of the Gospel becomes a vehicle for manifesting the glory of Jesus, "glory as of an only Son from the Father" (1:14).

---

[207] We cannot be sure how consistently John had worked out this issue. John 7: 39 says that as yet there was no Spirit because Jesus had not been glorified, but 4:10 seems to offer the Samaritan woman living water here and now. In later theology this tension would lead to a debate whether human beings were redeemed already by the incarnation, and even to speculation whether that would have been sufficient had Jesus not died on the cross.

CHAPTER 10.
GENERAL OBSERVATIONS
ON THESE CHRISTOLOGIES

Thus far I have been treating (under the rubric of the "moments" used to vocalize them) the christologies *of the NT*. Obviously, however, christological reflection did not cease with writing of the books that the church accepted as the NT.[208] For instance, when in the 2d to the 4th centuries the Christian proclamation was heard by those trained in formal Greek philosophical thinking, inevitably there arose questions about the phrasing of christology that had not been raised in the 1st century; and in fidelity to NT directions the church rejected certain proposals as inadequate. Let me concentrate on the statements of christology at Nicaea (true God of

---

[208] The theological axiom that revelation ceased with the death of the apostles is complex. It vocalizes the insight that the revelation of God in the Son was unfolded through apostolic preaching, so that not simply what Jesus said or did, but also the way he was interpreted by those sent through the Holy Spirit to proclaim him constituted the divine revelation in Jesus Christ. Since the Son is God, once God had given the Son, the divine self-revelation to creatures was exhaustive. Theologically the unfolding of the identity of Jesus in the NT constitutes the revelation of what we need to believe to be saved (John 20:31: "These things have been written so that you may believe that Jesus is the Messiah, the Son of God, and believing may have life in his name"). God's people did not and do not need another revealer. Yet the full implications of that completed revelation in Jesus Christ were not grasped in the 1st century or in any century since; that will come only when we see him face to face (see I John 3:1–2). The further comprehension of that revelation enshrined in official church teaching represented by a council like Nicaea has been necessary so that the NT revelation not be lost or misunderstood. This development is not found "in" the NT but stems from interpreting NT revelation in a direction indicated by the NT.

true God) and at Chalcedon (true God and true man) both as a way to complete the NT survey just given and as an entree into analyzing its fundamental direction.

No NT passage states precisely that the Son coexisted from all eternity with the Father. No earlier NT "moment" is found than "In the beginning was the Word" of John 1:1. In the 4th century Arius was content with that phrasing but interpreted it to mean that the Word had a beginning before the creation of the world. Jesus was truly the divine Son of God as the Scriptures affirmed; but since fathers exist before sons, only the heavenly Father, not the Son, is eternal and without origin.

In reply Athanasius maintained that in having the Word become and in making a temporal difference between Father and Son Arius was moving contrary to the NT (which resisted temporal limitation in the identity of Jesus). And so Athanasius led the Council of Nicaea to condemn Arius by insisting that the Word or divine Son had no beginning. The council used formulas such as begotten not made; there never was a time when he was not; true God of true God, coeternal with Father. The fact that such specifications were not found in the NT did not embarrass Athanasius, for he recognized that Arius was raising a question not specifically asked in NT times and which therefore could not be answered by quoting the NT. The all-important issue for Athanasius was whether the necessary postbiblical specification was loyal to the direction of the NT: "If the expressions are not in so many words in the Scriptures, yet they contain the sense of the Scriptures."[209]

If readers have understood these last three chapters, they should be able to see how the Nicene affirmations are truly in the direction of the NT and represent the last step in attaching to christological "moments" the identity of Jesus. We began with parousia or second-coming christology, i.e., statements that indicate that Jesus will be the Messiah or Lord when he comes again. Although found only in passages that may reflect the earliest days of Christian preaching, that christology was and remains true. The formulation is problematic only if, by way of limitation, it signals that Jesus has not had this

---

[209] "Letters concerning the Decrees of the Council of Nicaea" 5.18–21; NPNF series 2, 4.161–64—specifically 5.21; 164.

identity before the parousia, so that only then will he *become* Messiah and Lord. Resurrection christology avoids such a misunderstanding by insisting that Jesus is already Messiah, Lord, and Son of God through and at the resurrection. Again, although found in passages that reflect early Christian preaching, that christology was and remains true. The formulation is problematic only when, by way of restriction, Christians might think that he did not have that identity before the resurrection and *became* divine when he was exalted to God's right hand. Ministry christology prevents such a misunderstanding by having God at the baptism indicate that Jesus is "My beloved Son," so that all that Jesus did and said in his public ministry stemmed from the Son of God.

This christology that Jesus was God's Son at the baptism when his public life began—a christology that is found in every Gospel and, in a sense, enabled Gospel writing—was and remains true. The formulation is problematic only when, by way of restriction, Christians might think that he did not have that identity before the baptism, so that at that moment he *became* God's Son and was adopted to a totally new status by the divine proclamation, "This is my beloved Son." Among the Gospels only Mark leaves itself open to such a misunderstanding. Matt and Luke (who used Mark) and John prevent it by their various species of preministry christology. In an example of family-circle christology Luke reports that as a boy of age twelve Jesus already spoke of God as Father. Matt and Luke in different infancy stories affirm that already by conception in the womb of Mary Jesus was not only Son of David but also "God with us" and God's Son. That was and is true. The formulations of conception christology are problematic only when, by way of restriction, Christians might think that God's Son *became* or began his existence when divine power overshadowed Mary and the Holy Spirit came upon her, so that she conceived without human intervention. Without showing cognizance of the problem, various other NT writings prevent such a misunderstanding by portraying Jesus as present at certain key moments in the OT history of God's people (the times of Moses and Abraham), or as the one through whom all things were created, or as an entity with God who entered flesh (incarnation), or as the Word spoken by God before the act of creation—the various forms of preexistence christology. All these formulations were and remain true. They are problematic only when someone like Arius raises a question that their formulators apparently never thought of: Even if it was before creation, did the Word have a beginning? Was the relation between Father and Son such that the Father was from all eternity but the Son *became*, albeit before time? Nicaea did indeed move in the direction of the NT when it rejected this final attempt to phrase Jesus' identity in the language of becoming. True to John's usage of verbs, Nicaea implicitly chose the terminology of "is/was" for Jesus over that of "become/became."[210]

Why was there a tendency to interpret (wrongly) biblical affirmations about Jesus as if they were formulas of becoming? I suspect that the root of the problem lay in the idea of the Messiah, the anointed king of the House of David raised up by God for Israel (APPENDIX I), which was such a fundamental part of the Christian understanding of Jesus that, through the Greek translation *christos*, "Christ" was made part of his name. The language of becoming fits kings. One may be born heir to the throne, but at a certain *moment* such a figure must be crowned and *become* king. Once Jesus was identified as the Messiah, there would be the question, unconscious perhaps, about when he became Messiah. In fact, however, what Christians could legitimately proclaim is the moment in his career when through God's revelation they could, would, or did recognize him as Messiah. The various christologies I have described are true in that sense, but inevitably they tended to be misunderstood as statements about the coronation or becoming of the Messiah. This was fostered because resurrection could be understood as enthronement in heaven, and OT language of kingship was used to describe that and other "moments." We saw the coronation Ps 2 used for both the resurrection and the baptism, and the monarchical-succession promise to David in II Samuel 7 used in the Lucan annunciation of the conception.

As I pointed out, each "moment" that was used to rephrase christology moved Christian thought farther and farther from Jewish expectations of the Messiah. In the instance of the future second

---

[210] After all, he is the Son of the One whose most sacred OT name (Yahweh) has been understood to mean "He who is."

coming there was a relatively easy retention of Jewish anticipations about the (first and only) appearance of the Messiah. A more difficult adaptation of those anticipations to the idea of a spiritual reign of the Messiah in heaven was necessitated by resurrection christology. A violent reinterpretation of Jewish anticipations of a royal Messiah in order to fit the suffering Christ was part of ministry christology. Once Christian formulations about Jesus began to depart more obviously from possibilities of his having "become," the presentation of Jesus as Messiah grew more and more unacceptable to Jews. Already in the 2d century it was clear that Jews denied that Isa 7:14 could be interpreted as anticipating a virginal conception; and in unpleasant polemics the idea that Jesus had no human father (conception christology) was translated into Jewish legends of his illegitimacy. The claim that he had the divine name was seen as proof that, adept in black magic, he had learned the secret of God's name and its accompanying power. In John's Gospel where a preexistent Son (and hence Messiah) is proclaimed, Jewish opposition to Jesus is vociferous. For "the Jews" the Johannine Jesus is unwarrantedly making himself equal to God (5:18; 10:33; 19:7). And the formulation of Nicaea "true God of true God" has been consistently seen by Jewish thinkers as incompatible with "The Lord our God is one." Paradoxically, then, as Christians matured (at least in this one direction) in their understanding of the identity of Jesus, the impossibility of putting new wine in old wineskins became more and more apparent.

In Christian faith all human language about God (and in the 1st century that happened to be *Jewish* theological language) was and is inadequate to do justice to what God has done in Christ. That insight should allow constructive reformulation in face of new and deeper perceptions about Christ. Yet not only in the 1st century but ever since there have been Christians who could not accept reformulation and correspondingly have tended to reject new perceptions of the christological identity of Jesus. In a real sense that was true in the history of Arius: He was unwilling to go beyond what was affirmed in the older formulations, and paradoxically his questioning provoked in the church new insights about Jesus' divinity. Nor do we need think the process is finished. "Moment" christology (even that of Nicaea) has the drawback of using time categories to phrase what

lies outside time. Preexistence is a more exalted category than thinking of Jesus becoming God's Son in time but from another viewpoint there is no "pre" in the timeless realm of God. No human
language has expressed Jesus' identity perfectly, and the best that
Christians have been able to do is to reject restrictions as they became obvious. Nicaea ended the quest to limit God's presence in
Jesus by having the Son *become*. But a "time" approach is only one
form of restriction, and questions from other points of view will continue to cause Christians to probe who Jesus is. They must take care
not to think that past formulations, whether found in the Bible or in
tradition, solve all problems, lest they blind themselves to the need
of rethinking prompted by questions never previously posed. For
example, it does not take much reflection to understand that later
Christians could not consider adequate the NT proclamation that at
a future moment Jesus will be the Messiah. But in the instance of a
formula accepted as traditional by the church, such as "Jesus is true
God and true man," there is a tendency to think that this solves
all issues in christology. In particular, many Roman Catholics are
shocked to learn that their church, although insisting that its dogmas
articulate revealed truth, has recognized the historical conditioning
and, hence, the limitation of dogmatic *formulations*.[211]

I have attempted to show that the christological statement of
Nicaea is faithful to a major direction in NT christology. Yet even if
the Nicene proclamation offered a more complete answer to the issue of Jesus' divine identity than did any single formulation in the
NT, it did not take the place of the less ample NT proclamations or
render them otiose. On pp. 143–44 above, as I reviewed the various
NT christologies, I used almost as a refrain that each formulation
"was and remains true." That refrain was meant to do justice to
the fact that the development of later and more ample formulations
within the NT itself did not involve the erasing of earlier and simpler

---

[211] *Mysterium Ecclesiae*, the Roman Doctrinal Congregation's response to
Hans Küng, recognized that faith pronouncements depend "partly on the power of
language used at a certain . . . time" and usually have a limited intention "of solving
certain questions or removing certain errors." Consequently, given the fact that they
may be phrased in the changeable conceptions of a given epoch, they may need reformulation, to be done by the church's teaching authority profiting from theological
debate. (*Acta apostolicae sedis* 65 [1973], 394–408; BBRC 116–17; NJBC 72, §36.)

christological formulas. For instance, Luke in the infancy narrative describes Jesus as Son of God from the time of his conception, and at the opening of the public ministry Luke has God proclaim that Jesus is "My beloved Son." Yet Luke does not hesitate to attribute to Peter a statement that God raised up Jesus and "made" him Lord and Messiah or that at a designated future time God would send the Messiah Jesus (Acts 2:32,36; 3:19–21). It is noteworthy that he did not feel obliged to correct or change what presumably were earlier ways of phrasing the identity of Jesus. I have explained that Luke could do this because he saw the resurrection and parousia as moments of revealing an identity that was already there rather than as moments of Jesus becoming what he had not been.

This retention of the past is a very important attitude on several scores, and one that Christians should learn from. Catechisms and confessions of faith tend to prefer the most adequate formulations produced at the end of a long development, e.g., that Jesus is "true God and true man." That preference for polished formulas is pedagogically understandable, but offering answers without an effort to outline the development and issues that led to them can produce problems in several ways. In our times Christians are going to have to reach answers to new dilemmas in fidelity to God's revelation in Christ; they can be helped in that if they have seen some examples of how their ancestors in the faith had to struggle to emerge with the answers now taken for granted. Otherwise they tend to think that the answers were all revealed by God, and wonder why there has not been a similar divine answer revealed for contemporary issues.

The most important reason for paying attention to the obviously limited christological formulations of an earlier era is the fact that they contain truth which would be overlooked if we settled only for the chronologically later and more polished formulas. Nicaea proclaimed that the Son of God existed from all eternity (eternal preexistence christology), but that formulation in isolation might cause us to overlook the truth affirmed by John who relates the Word to creation. Only because God began to be self-expressive in creation was there a possibility to know much about God.[212] That

---

[212] Ignatius of Antioch (*Magnesians* 8:2) goes beyond the biblical data when he says that Jesus is God's Word proceeding from silence, for the scriptural tendency had been not to speculate about the precreational silence.

the Word was with God, indeed was God, and that through him all things were made (preexistence-before-creation christology) may have constituted the highest christological formulation in the NT; but what can be known of God through creation pales in comparison to what was revealed when, through the Holy Spirit and divine power, the Son of God was conceived in Mary's womb (conception christology). And yet we could know little of the Son of God until he began a public life and translated into words that were heard and deeds that were seen the divine presence inherent in his own being (ministry christology). Those words and deeds led him to the cross, and without the crucifixion followed by divine vindication and victory over death (resurrection christology) we would not have understood the total generosity of God who was in Christ reconciling the world (II Cor 5:18–19). Nevertheless, only those who have been given the gift of faith have perceived this face of God manifested in Jesus, a manifestation that God intends the whole human race to know ultimately when Jesus comes again (parousia christology). How impoverished would be our understanding of the revelation in Christ had the earlier ways of speaking about the identity of Jesus been erased in favor of the Nicene formulation!

My final observations are pertinent to a few modern reactions to christology. Some would complain that although Jesus spoke about God's kingdom, the early church erroneously spoke about Jesus; but that complaint is superficial. In speaking about Jesus the church was speaking about how God made the kingdom present. E. Schillebeeckx[213] would make the distinction that in the earlier stages there was only a "theology of Jesus of Nazareth" (a first-order assertion that in Jesus the man, God saves human beings) while in the later stages there was a "christology" (a second-order assertion about the identity of Jesus). Even though Schillebeeckx confirms that the first-order assertion leads necessarily to the second-order assertion, he is content with the notion that one was already a Christian in embracing the former. Chapters 5 and 6 above, however, indicate that already in Jesus' lifetime there were many indications that God was not only acting through Jesus but was present in him, so that even in that period the issue of the identity of Jesus had been

---

[213] *Jesus: An Experiment in Christology* (New York: Seabury, 1979), 545–50.

raised. Accordingly "christology" remains in my judgment a more appropriate (even if inadequate) first-order term than a "theology of Jesus of Nazareth." Another issue raised by theologians has been the functional vs. the ontological in christology. NT christology was primarily functional, indicating what role Jesus played in effecting God's salvation of human beings (*pro nobis*); but in so doing, it reflects much about what Jesus was in himself (*in se*). The Pauline affirmation that God was in Christ reconciling the world to himself (II Cor 5:19), John's affirmation that the Word was God (1:1), and Nicaea's confession of true God of true God and Chalcedon's true God and true man may show an increasing movement from the functional to the ontological, but the earliest affirmation was not without its ontological implications, and the latest had a very functional origin and goal.

Let me comment on how the statements of Nicaea and Chalcedon (which I have analyzed as loyal to NT lines of development) are functional and, in popular parlance, "relevant." Once, after a lecture I gave on Jesus as God in the NT, a student asked me why the issue of full divinity raised at Nicaea was so important. What difference does it make whether Jesus was God or the most perfect creature, so long as one has accepted him as Savior? Behind such a question there is often the suspicion that Nicaea and Chalcedon and indeed all the christological controversies of the 4th and 5th centuries were matters of diphthongs (for those who know the history, Homoousians vs. Homoiousians) and of bygone metaphysics that have no relevance today. I could not disagree more; for I think that the issue of the full identity of Jesus, which is related to the insights of Nicaea and Chalcedon, is ultimately a question of the love of God for human beings.

If Jesus is not "true God of true God," then we do not know God in human terms. Even if Jesus were the most perfect creature far above all others, he could tell us only at second hand about a God who really remains almost as distant as the Unmoved Mover of Aristotle. Only if Jesus is truly of God do we know what God is like, for in Jesus we see God translated into terms that we can understand. A God who sent a marvelous creature as our Savior could be described as loving, but that love would have cost God nothing in a personal way. Only if Jesus is truly of God do we know that God's love was so real that it reached the point of personal self-giving. This is why the proclamation of Nicaea was and is so important—not only because it tells us about Jesus, but because it tells us about God.[214] Indeed were it otherwise, the Nicene proclamation would scarcely be faithful to a Jesus who preached the kingship of God.

So also do I think that the proclamation of Chalcedon about Jesus as true man (as well as true God) has enduring value, even for those who cannot pronounce Monophysitism.[215] Again unless we understand that Jesus was truly human with no exception but sin, we cannot comprehend the depth of God's love. If Jesus' knowledge was limited, as indicated prima facie in the biblical evidence (see Chapters 3 and 4 above), then one understands that God loved us to the point of self-subjection to our most agonizing infirmities. A Jesus who walked through the world with unlimited knowledge, knowing exactly what the morrow would bring, knowing with certainty that three days after his death his Father would raise him up, would be a Jesus who could arouse our admiration, but a Jesus still far from us. He would be a Jesus far from a humankind that can only hope in the future and believe in God's goodness, far from a humankind that must face the supreme uncertainty of death with faith but without knowledge of what is beyond. On the other hand, a Jesus for whom the detailed future had elements of mystery, dread, and hope as it has for us and yet, at the same time, a Jesus who would say, "Not my will but yours"—this would be a Jesus who could effectively teach us how to live, for this Jesus would have gone through life's real trials. Then his saying, "No one can have greater love than this: to lay down his life for those he loves" (John 15:13), would be truly persuasive, for we would know that he laid down his life with all the agony with which we lay ours down. We would know that for him the loss of life was, as it is for us, the loss of a great possession, a possession that is outranked only by love.

---

[214] On this point see the excellent treatment by D. M. Baillie, *God Was in Christ* (London: Faber & Faber, 1961), 70–71.

[215] This is the thesis (condemned as heresy) that Jesus had only one nature (divine) not two (human and divine).

In the 4th and 5th centuries the question of Jesus as God and man was not an abstract question debated in the scholars' chambers; it was a question of what God and Christianity were all about. I submit that, if we take the trouble to understand, it remains all of that even in our century.

APPENDIXES

APPENDIX I.
A BRIEF HISTORY
OF THE DEVELOPMENT
OF THE ROYAL MESSIANIC HOPE
IN ISRAEL

The figure of the Messiah ultimately came to have an important place in Israel's understanding of God's plans for its future. This discussion, necessarily brief, is dependent implicitly on the exegesis of important but disputed OT texts; for details one would need to consult commentaries on the respective biblical books, or works on messianism.[216] All that is claimed is that the interpretation presented is reasonable and represents widely held views.

The English word "messiah" is from Aramaic *mešîḥāʾ*, related to Hebrew *māšiaḥ*, "anointed"; the Greek word is *christos*, whence "Christ." In this discussion a distinction will be made between "Messiah" (capitalized) and "messiahs" or salvific figures. Judaism knew of a gallery of figures who were expected to appear at the time of God's definitive intervention on behalf of Israel, e.g., Elijah, the Prophet-like-Moses, the Anointed Priest, and perhaps the Son of Man. These figures can loosely be called messianic. But the capitalized term "Messiah" is best confined to a precisely delineated concept, viz., the anointed king of the Davidic dynasty who would establish in the world the definitive kingdom intended by God for Israel. That God had sent leaders and prophets to deliver the chosen people (Moses, the Judges, Nehemiah, Ezra) is a commonplace in Israel's theological understanding of its history. But messianism, as we shall discuss it, is involved with deliverance supplied in the framework of an institution, the monarchy.

---

[216] This APPENDIX reshapes material from NJBC 77, §§152–63 where a bibliography is supplied.

Such a notion of the Messiah is the product of a long development traceable in three stages.

(A) First Stage: Before the 8th Century BC

In the early days of the Davidic monarchy (10th century BC) in Judah every anointed king (messiah) was looked on as a leader and deliverer sent by God to the people. There is no clear record in the OT of a similar sublimation of the kingship in northern Israel. Probably the first literary record of the messianic character of the dynasty of David is found in the oracle of Nathan, preserved in three forms (II Sam 7; Ps 89; I Chron 17). Scholars do not agree on which is the most primitive; and none of them appears to preserve the original oracle unmodified.[217] The most famous is II Sam 7:11–16 which has been referred to on p. 130 above as background for the annunciation to Mary about Jesus' Davidic status (Luke 1:32–33). In Ps 89:20–38 the following elements may be distinguished: the election of David by God; promises of victory and wide dominion; adoption of David and his successors as sons; covenant of God with David and his house; and the promise of an eternal dynasty, not conditioned on the fidelity of the successors of David to God. This oracle is also echoed in Ps 132:11–12. The oracle does not speak of any individual successor, nor does it look into the eschatological future. It is a simple assurance that the dynasty will endure as the chosen human agent of God's deliverance wrought in history. What is to be accomplished by David and his house does not here go beyond the political victory to be achieved by the king.

The Blessing of Judah by Jacob (Gen 49:9–12) probably comes from the early monarchy and alludes implicitly to the reign of David. However this blessing is construed, it seems to assure the permanence of the dynasty of David.

The "Royal Psalms" (in particular Pss 2; 72; 110) should also be considered in this first stage of messianism. Even though some of them may be of 10th-century origin, scholars have abandoned the traditional interpretation that these psalms were composed by David himself who was singing of the one future Messiah. Such an expectation is not attested at this period and presumably did not yet exist. Rather, these psalms were compositions applicable to any Davidic monarch, and they may have been recited on important occasions in the life of the monarch, like the coronation. The references to a divine begetting of the king (110:3) and divine sonship (2:7)—once thought to be literal references to Jesus—were part of the sym-

---

[217] A basic discussion is supplied by J. L. McKenzie, TS 8 (1947), 187–218.

bolic court language (*Hofstil*) used to describe the king as God's representative. The eternal priesthood "according to the order of Melchizedek"
(110:4) promised to the king was probably part of the hereditary titulature
of the Canaanite kings of Jerusalem, exemplified in the priest-king Melchizedek of Gen 14:17-24. The eternal and universal reign of the king—
formerly thought to be a literal reference to Jesus—was partly an exuberant
wish for long life and many victories, and partly a reflection of the perma-
nent greatness promised to the Davidic dynasty.

The prayerful wishes in Ps 72 may be the clearest expression of the idea
of the king savior. The ideal king governs with the justice that befits a ruler
and is the savior of the poor and the needy. He is victorious over his enemies,
who are also the enemies of his people; he is the deliverer of his people from
external danger. During his reign God's blessing brings fertility to the land.
Nowhere in the psalm is the king presented as a future eschatological deliverer. He is the idealized reigning successor of David and the heir to the
covenantal promises made to David.

(B) Second Stage: From the 8th Century BC to the Babylonian Exile

In the writings of the 8th cent. there is a development in royal messianism. Wicked and inept kings like Ahaz had dimmed the glory of the Davidic line and the optimistic hope that each king would be a savior of his
people. Isaiah, in particular, gives voice to a more nuanced expectation:
There would be an inbreaking of the power of God that would revive the
dynasty and ensure its permanence. God would soon raise up a successor of
David who would be worthy of the name of Davidic king; he would be an
example of charismatic power, just as David had been when the royal line
was instituted. Isaiah (7:14-17; 9:5-6) rhapsodizes in describing the heir to
the throne to be born in Isaiah's time (735 BC), perhaps the son of the wicked
Ahaz and of a well-known maiden of the court.[218] The child would be a sign

---

[218] The Greek translation of Isa 7:14 (2d century BC?) refers to this woman as
"the virgin"; the original Hebrew reference to her implies that she is not married.
Implicitly, in that culture she would most likely have been a virgin, but there is no
emphasis on that in the Hebrew text. This passage did *not* give rise to the idea of the
virginal conception of Jesus; rather Christian tradition about the virginal conception
interpreted the passage so that with hindsight God's plan for Jesus could be seen in it.
See Matt 1:22-23 and *BBM* 145-49.

that God was still with his people (Emmanuel) in the person of the Davidic king. This heir would establish justice, build a vast empire and bring peace to it, and be worthy of the traditional courtly titles of the monarch (9:5[6]): "Wonder-Counselor, God-Hero, Father-Forever, Prince of Peace." Although Isaiah may have believed that his expectations were fulfilled in the good king Hezekiah, the successor to Ahaz, the Isaian passages are describing an ideal for restoration rather than a reality; and this permitted them to be used by later generations who also looked forward to a divine renewal of the monarchy.

The passage in 11:1ff. may come from a period later than Isaiah's lifetime; scholars are divided. It looks into a more remote future than the passages we have just discussed. The charismatic power of the expected model ruler is clearly affirmed, for the spirit will rest upon him and bestow the qualities of an ideal ruler. He will save the kingdom from internal injustice and external threat. In comparison with the undisputed writings of Isaiah, the novel element in Isa 11:1ff. is the return of the conditions of paradise that the reign of this king will bring to pass. Universal peace under his reign is cosmic, for it flows from the "knowledge of God [Yahweh]" by all (i.e., the experience of the personal reality of God through revelation). Such knowledge can be communicated to the world only through Israel. These two ideas, the restoration of the dynasty of David and the universal and religious scope of the salvation of which the dynasty of David is the medium, probably appear here combined for the first time in the OT.

That the hope for a resurgence of the dynasty under a new and ideal ruler was not confined to Isaiah is seen from Micah 5:1-6. A contemporary of Isaiah, Micah sees a new David coming from Bethlehem to give his people security against the Assyrian threat. Other and later allusions to the restoration of the dynasty of David echo these earlier motifs with little modification. The "branch" or "shoot" of which Jeremiah speaks (23:5) will be the king-savior whose name will affirm the righteousness (i.e., saving will) of God. The restoration of the dynasty appears also in Jer 30:9,21. The dynasty of David is the sprig of cedar that Ezekiel sees planted by God (17:22), and in the new Israel David will once more be king (34:23; 37:24). Ezekiel does not, however, emphasize the function of the king as savior; this hesitancy may reflect the historical events of which he was a contemporary, viz., the fall of the nation and the exile of the Davidic king. The monarchy appears in Ezekiel simply because the monarchy is an Israelite institution without which the prophet cannot conceive Israel. Several interpreters have asked whether a return of David in person is not implied in these passages of Ezekiel; but such an implication is not immediately obvious, for the name may designate the dynasty.

(C) Third Stage: From the Exile to NT Times

The postexilic development of messianism is difficult to trace because of the lack of clearly dated written evidence through which we might plot a trajectory. We have to fill in the period between the detectable expectation at the time of the exile (587–539 BC) and that attested in the NT (1st century AD) by drawing upon a medley of works, namely, the last books of the OT, those Jewish works called Apocrypha that were not accepted into the canon, and the Dead Sea Scrolls.

The fact that, to the best of our knowledge, the Davidic line no longer ruled after the exile (or at least after the governorship of Zerubbabel) made a profound difference in messianism. Before the exile the ideal king who would restore the vigor of the Davidic line could always be thought of in terms of the next generation of a reigning dynasty. But now there could be no ideal king until the Davidic throne would be restored. Thus the expectations began to move toward the indefinite future; and rather than centering on one monarch in a continuing line of rulers, these expectations came to center on one supreme king who would represent God's definitive intervention to save his people. It is in this period that we may begin to speak of "the Messiah" in the strict sense (although, in fact, the title is not encountered with great frequency outside the NT[219]). Earlier Scriptures (Royal Psalms; Isaiah) were now reread with this new messianic understanding in mind.

If the definitive character of the Messiah's action is clear, the eschatological character is only partially discernible. There is no clear evidence that the Messiah was thought of as a transcendental figure whose mission would go beyond the realities of history. True, his work would be a terminating manifestation of the power of God that would make any further saving act of God unnecessary. This saving act would not be the work of ordinary historical forces, but the kind of visible inbreaking of God's power into history that had been seen in the Exodus. So far as we know, however, the inbreaking and deliverance was expected to be accomplished in historical

---

[219] From reading histories of NT times one might get the impression that many figures claimed to be the Messiah, and indeed Mark 13:21–22 warns of false Messiahs arising. Certainly from Josephus' *Antiquities*, a 20-volume history of the Jews and Israel written in Greek *ca.* AD 94, we can learn of would-be kings, prophets, deceivers who worked or promised signs, and bandit leaders in the 1st century BC and AD. Nevertheless, before the Jewish revolutionary leader Simon bar Cochba (ben Kosibah) in AD 130, who *may* have been identified as the Messiah by Rabbi Aqiba, we know of no historical Jew who ever claimed to be the Messiah or was called the Messiah except Jesus of Nazareth. In Josephus *christos* occurs twice, both in reference to Jesus (*Ant.* 18.3.3##63–64; 20.9.1#200).

circumstances, even if at times the anticipation of the Messiah may have taken on some of the trappings of apocalyptic.

In certain late OT passages the concept of the king-savior has undergone an interesting transformation. In the latter part of Zechariah (9:9ff.: written in the 4th century?) warlike traits disappear and his reign brings universal peace. He is the instrument of God's salvation, but the salvation is the work of God himself. The king has even lost the trappings of royalty. Yet this is not a universally accepted view of the Messiah, for in the much later (1st century BC) apocryphal work, *The Psalms of Solomon*, there is a strong mixture of the political and the spiritual in picturing a Messiah who would bring the Gentiles under his yoke.

From the frequency and spontaneity with which the question of the Messiah appears in the NT (Mark 8:29; 14:61; John 1:20; 4:25; etc.) and also from the evidence of early Jewish writings, we are safe in assuming that the expectation of the Messiah would have been known to most Jews in the intertestamental period whether or not they shared it. The last clause is necessary, for by the 1st century AD many had lost faith in the Davidic dynasty, which had not ruled for 500 years. Indeed, there are Jewish books that treat of eschatological questions without ever mentioning the Messiah. Moreover, often the expectation of the Messiah was accompanied by some of the other expectations mentioned above. For instance, at Qumran the sectarians awaited the coming of the Prophet, of the Davidic Messiah ("the Messiah of Israel") and of the Anointed Priest ("the Messiah of Aaron"; see NJBC 67, §§116–17). Indeed there may have been an amalgamation of the Messiah with other salvific figures, e.g., the Son of Man, into one composite figure. Certainly this happened in the Christian description of Jesus, but the evidence is quite uncertain for determining whether this happened in preChristian Judaism. The combination of Messiah, Son of Man, and Isaian Chosen or Elect One did happen in the "Parables" section of *I Enoch*; but that section of the Enoch literature, as I explained on p. 93 above, is maddeningly difficult to date, and there is much debate whether it was composed or just edited by Christians. Thus far we have no clear evidence of a pre-Christian description of a suffering Messiah. (Later Judaism presents a Messiah descended from Joseph who is a victim.) The Christian reader must beware of an instinctive tendency to interpret the Jewish expectation of the Messiah in the light of Jesus' career and person. Actually, the Jewish concept of the Messiah had to undergo considerable modification before it could be applied to Jesus,[220] whence Jesus' reluctance to accept the title without qualification (pp. 73–80 above).

---

[220] In particular, although the Jewish hope of the Messiah was highly idealized, there was no expectation of a divine Messiah in the sense in which Jesus is professed

The manner of the advent of the Messiah was a cause of speculation in early Judaism. How would people know him? In some NT passages (Matt 2:4–6; John 7:42) we can see the popular expectation that he would be born at Bethlehem, David's city, and that his birth would be known to all Israel. But in other passages (John 7:27; 1:31; Mark 8:29) we see the thought that the Messiah would be hidden; for people would not know where he would come from, and he could stand in their midst without their knowing it—an attitude toward the Messiah attributed also to the Jewish antagonist in Justin's 2d-century AD *Dialogue with Trypho* (8.4; 110.1).

*   *   *

In summary, in the course of 1,000 years Israelite messianism developed to the point where the expectation of the Messiah embodied one of the principal hopes for God's intervention to save his people. While this king-savior almost by definition would offer political deliverance, he would do so by virtue of the charisma and power of God; and so his saving acts would never be merely political. In his reign, the Messiah would bring to Israel the ideal rule of God himself. That the salvation mediated by the Messiah would have a scope outside Israel is less frequently mentioned and is often viewed chauvinistically.

---

as Son of God. Moreover, a nationalistic coloring was never absent from any stage of the preChristian development of messianic thought, any more than the OT concept of salvation itself was devoid of earthly and nationalistic aspects. It is inaccurate and unjust to say that the Jews of Jesus' time had corrupted the idea of the Messiah as a spiritual savior by making it secular and nationalistic and that Jesus restored the concept to its pristine meaning. The Christian understanding of a spiritual Messiah with a kingdom not of this world represented a change rather than a restoration—a change that Christians believe brought the development of the messianic expectation to a rich fruition, but a change nevertheless.

APPENDIX II.
THE REALITY OF THE
RESURRECTION OF JESUS

The raising of Jesus from the dead was unlike all the other restorations to life mentioned in the Bible. In the NT Lazarus, Jairus' daughter, and the son of the widow of Nain are described as miraculously resuscitated or revived, returning to ordinary human existence; but there is no suggestion that they were glorified or that they would not have to die again. Jesus, to the contrary, is portrayed as conquering death, rising to a different form of life (eternal life), and as returning immortal in glory and power. The resurrection of Jesus, then, was the supreme intervention of God in human existence, the supreme miracle. No wonder that, on the one hand, the resurrection has become a principal apologetic argument for the truth of Christianity and that, on the other hand, the reality of the resurrection has been questioned.

One would need a book to do justice to all aspects of the NT presentation of the resurrection.[221] Here, as explained on p. 106 above, I have a restricted interest. The christological presentation of Jesus by NT authors that goes beyond his self-presentation during his public ministry flows to a

---

[221] The primary import of the resurrection is, of course, theological. The passion, death, resurrection, and ascension of Jesus constitute one indissoluble action for human salvation, as Paul implicitly recognized in Rom 4:25 when he said that Jesus "was put to death for our sins and raised for our justification." The life to which Jesus was restored through the resurrection is eternal life that he now can share with those who believe in him. It was with this theological understanding, and not primarily with apologetic intent, that Paul exclaimed, "If Christ has not been raised, then our preaching is in vain, and your faith is in vain" (I Cor 15:14). I make no effort to present the theology of the resurrection here or even all the biblical aspects; for the latter and for bibliography, see NJBC 81, §§118–34.

large extent from their belief that he was raised from the dead. The resurrection is a presupposition of NT christology, and so books on christology usually do not discuss the factuality of the resurrection. Yet those who read an introductory book such as this have often heard doubts raised about the reality of the resurrection and may well wonder whether NT christology is a house built without foundations. To the contrary, in my judgment, the evidence for the bodily resurrection of Jesus is strong; and a brief treatment of it may help to remove misconceptions.

The NT does not claim that anyone saw the resurrection and makes no attempt to describe it, as does the apocryphal 2d-century *Gospel of Peter* 10:39–42. Therefore, the reality of the bodily resurrection hinges on the missing body or the empty tomb and, above all, on the validity of the experiences of those who claimed they saw the risen Jesus. Objections to either or both of those two factors have been raised both on general grounds (resurrection from the dead does not happen; it is scientifically impossible; etc.) and on the recognition of difficulties in the biblical narratives.

(A) General Objections to the Reality of the Resurrection

The rationalistic or liberal criticism of the last century tried to discredit the resurrection stories as demonstrative either of apostolic *fraud* (the apostles invented the stories; they stole the body and thus fabricated the emptiness of the tomb) or of apostolic *credulity* (he was not dead but in a coma; the tombs were confused; hallucinations were mistaken for real appearances). Christian apologists pointed out quite correctly that there is nothing in the NT to support such gratuitous charges.[222] It is of interest here to point out that some of these attacks were already current in the 1st century and have left their mark on the later layers of the NT resurrection accounts that sought to offset them. The assertion that the apostles were lying in claiming to have seen the risen Jesus when others did not see him is implicitly challenged in Peter's explanation in Acts 10:41. The charge that the apostles stole the body is attributed to the priests and Pharisees in Matt 28:13 (cf. 27: 62), and Matthew refutes it with the story of the guards at the tomb. Seemingly, although the empty tomb is the background for the Easter morning stories, it played little direct role in NT apologetics; and according to John (20:2) the brute fact of the empty tomb suggests to Mary Magdalene only that the body has been stolen. Thus the notion of apostolic fabrication of

---

[222] F. Morison, *Who Moved the Stone?* (London: Faber and Faber, 1930) is an apologetic classic.

the empty tomb for apologetic purposes is not really plausible. Furthermore, the contention that the narratives centered on the empty tomb developed only at a later time does not make a necessary distinction between the fact of the empty tomb and the use of that fact in a narrative as a vehicle for expounding revelation (as will become apparent on pp. 169–70 below). The fact was most likely accepted from the beginning. Even the Jews who sought to refute the followers of Jesus never suggested that the tomb was not empty; and there are indications that the idea of the empty tomb may have been implicit in the early preaching, e.g., in the mention of burial in I Cor 15:4, and in the comparison hinted at in Acts 2:29–31.[223] The suggestion that the apostles were credulous probably prompted the constant reminder that at first they did not believe that Jesus was truly risen (Matt 28:17; Luke 24: 11,37; Mark 16:11,14; John 20:25). An apologetic stress on the corporeal and tangible qualities of the risen Jesus underlies the insistence that he ate food (Luke 24:41–43; Acts 10:41) and that his wounds could be verified by the apostles (Luke 24:39; John 20:24–28).

In the early part of the 20th century, a new assault was mounted on the reality of the resurrection through the comparative study of religions. It was proposed that the early followers of Jesus, either consciously or unconsciously, had conformed the story of Jesus to the pagan legends and mystery cults surrounding the dying and rising gods (Attis, Adonis, Osiris, Dionysus)—usually gods of nature whose death came with winter and rising with the spring and the renewed life of plants. But Christian apologists were quick to point out that while Jesus may have risen in the spring, his death which was followed shortly by evidence of resurrection was quite unlike the annual natural cycle of winter dormancy and spring flowering.

Another attempt to explain the resurrection in terms other than real bodily restoration is centered on the theory that the genuine faith of the Jewish Christians in Jesus' victory over death could be expressed by a Hebrew mind only in terms of corporeal resurrection, for the resurrection of the body was the only form of immortality known to the disciples. Truly Jesus was glorified; and since spiritual happiness was inconceivable without one's body, Jesus' glorification was described as a resurrection. Thus the resurrection of the body becomes a symbol of a spiritual truth. In fact, however, bodily resurrection was not the only way in Judaism to express victory over death; as indicated in footnote 50 above, there were also ideas of the

---

[223] For a defense of the antiquity and importance of the memory of the empty tomb, see H. F. von Campenhausen, *Tradition and Life in the Church* (Philadelphia: Fortress, 1968), 42–89; W. L. Craig, NTS 31 (1985), 39–67.

survival of a spiritual principle and of eternal life that did not require resurrection.[224] Moreover, the great subtlety supposed on the part of the disciples in the theory just mentioned and the difficulty of reconciling this theory with the very early insistence that people did see the risen Jesus[225] challenge a purely symbolic approach to the resurrection.

Still another objection against the resurrection of Jesus has been derived from medical science, namely, the physical fact that immediately after death irreversible processes of dissolution begin. That argument might present a challenge to the revivifying or resuscitation of a corpse, but it is not applicable to the resurrection of Jesus properly understood. One must recognize that there are two elements in the NT understanding of the resurrection of Jesus. (a) The various NT writers clearly speak about a *bodily* resurrection of *Jesus*. Both underlined elements are important. The one who is raised and is seen in appearances by named eyewitnesses (e.g., I Cor 15:5–7) is the Jesus who had walked with many of these same people during the public ministry and who was crucified and buried. Specifically, the resurrection involves Jesus' body which is no longer in the grave;[226] that is supported by the tradition of the empty tomb, by Paul's terminology involving a raised body (I Cor 15:44), and by the fact that no disbeliever ever claims the ability to point out the body of Jesus still in the grave. This aspect of the resurrection might be confused with revivification. (b) Nevertheless, the same NT writers make it clear that they are thinking of transformation that is quite different from revivification. Paul, who draws a close analogy between the resurrection of Jesus and the future resurrection of the dead (I Cor 15:12), characterizes the transformation that takes place thus: What died was perishable, weak, and mortal; what rises is imperishable, glorious, and immor-

---

[224] G.W.E. Nickelsburg, *Resurrection, Immortality, and Eternal Life in Intertestamental Judaism* (Harvard Theological Studies Monograph 26; Cambridge MA, 1972); P. Perkins, *Resurrection* (Garden City, NY: Doubleday, 1984), 37–56.

[225] It is obvious that Paul believed not only that he himself had seen the risen Jesus (Gal 1:12,16) but that many others had seen Jesus (I Cor 15:5–8). The attempt to get around this by distinguishing between the experience of "seeing" Jesus and the interpretation of that experience as the resurrection of Jesus is not really successful, for what would have caused Paul to think of resurrection unless what he saw had some element of the bodily?

[226] In this light, I judge it biblically irresponsible to claim that Christian faith in the resurrection is independent of the question of whether or not Jesus still lies buried in Palestine. Christian faith in the resurrection is in continuity with apostolic faith in the resurrection, and there is no evidence that the first witnesses took such a stance of indifference toward the body in the tomb.

tal (15:42–43,52–54). In short, "It is sown a physical [*psychikos*] body; it is raised a spiritual body" (15:44).[227] The evangelists imply the fact and character of the transformation by having people who knew Jesus well not recognize him (Luke 24:16; John 20:14; 21:4; Mark 16:12 ["he appeared in another form"]) and by picturing a Jesus who could ignore the laws of physics (pass through locked doors, suddenly appear and disappear). The distinguished Lutheran theologian, W. Pannenberg[228] writes:

> Something happened in which the disciples in these appearances were confronted with a reality which also in our language cannot be expressed in any other way than by that symbolic and metaphorical expression of the hope beyond death, the resurrection from the dead. Please understand me correctly: Only the name we give to this event is symbolic, metaphorical, but not the reality of the event itself. The latter is so absolutely unique that we have no other name for this than the metaphorical expression of the apocalyptic expectation. In this sense, the resurrection of Jesus is an historical event, an event that really happened at that time.

One must leave to theologians the task of evaluating what is analogical and what is literal in the general concepts of "life" after death and the resurrection of a body.[229]

(B) Difficulties Arising from the Biblical Narratives of the Resurrection

I have been citing what the biblical narratives actually report, so that it may be clear that most of the objections listed above are not based on NT passages but on getting around or avoiding the import of those passages. Yet one must also recognize that some difficulties about the resurrection stem from what is reported in the NT accounts themselves. One may divide the principal difficulties under two headings: differences among the narratives

---

[227] See M. E. Dahl, *The Resurrection of the Body* (SBT 36; London: SCM, 1962).

[228] "Did Jesus Really Rise from the Dead?" *Dialog* 4 (1965), 128–35, specifically 135.

[229] For examples, see W. Pannenberg, *Jesus—God and Man* (Philadelphia: Westminster, 1968), 66–114; F. S. Fiorenza, *Foundational Theology* (New York: Crossroad, 1984), 5–55; J. P. Galvin, TS 49 (1988), 25–44; Perkins, *Resurrection* 391–452.

of the appearances of the risen Jesus; differences among the narratives of the empty tomb. What follows will discuss these differences and whether they call into question the reality of the bodily resurrection.[230]

DIFFERENCES AMONG THE NARRATIVES OF THE APPEARANCES

Each of the Gospels presents a continuous passion narrative, the general sequence of which is unusually parallel in all four. (This has been a reason for assuming that the passion narrative was one of the earliest portions of Gospel tradition to take shape.) But the resurrection tradition consists of isolated appearances with little agreement among the various Gospels on circumstances and details. A close study of the reports in the individual Gospels[231] shows how numerous the variations are.

To whom? Matt 28:9–10; John 20:14–18; and Mark 16:9–11 report an early-Sunday-morning appearance to Mary Magdalene, sometimes with other women, in the area of the tomb. Mark 16:1–8 and Luke 24:1–11,22–23 do not and leave little or no room for it. The narratives are much more in agreement, explicitly or implicitly, that the risen Jesus appeared to Peter and other members of the Twelve.

Where? If we concentrate on the appearance(s) to the Twelve, there are traditions attached to two different localities. Appearances in Jerusalem are attested by Luke, John 20, and the Marcan Appendix; appearances in Galilee are attested by Matt, John 21, and implied by Mark.[232] Neither of the two traditions shows any awareness of a tradition of appearances in the

---

[230] I dealt with these matters at greater length in *The Virginal Conception and Bodily Resurrection* (New York: Paulist, 1973), 69–129; see also W. L. Craig, *Assessing the New Testament Evidence for the Historicity of the Resurrection of Jesus* (Lewiston, NY: Mellen, 1989).

[231] Readers should be alerted that scholars tend to think of six different Gospel testimonies to the appearances: Mark 16:1–8; Matt 28; Luke 24 (plus Acts 1:1–11); John 20; John 21; and Mark 16:9–20. In that arrangement there are two assumptions. First, that Mark 16:9–20 was not written by Mark but was a later compilation (partly from material similar to Luke) added to the Gospel—the "Marcan Appendix" (see NJBC 41, §109). Second, that John 21, although composed within the Johannine school, was not by the same writer as the rest of John, so that, despite a redactional attempt to make John 20 and 21 consecutive, John 21 contains an independent tradition about the appearances of Jesus.

[232] Although seemingly Mark originally ended in 16:8 without describing an appearance of the risen Jesus, 14:28 and 16:7 point to such an appearance occurring in Galilee. Scholars who would argue that Mark had no tradition of postresurrectional verses have to excise these verses or explain them away as references to the parousia— two dubious expedients. See BDM 1.130–33.

other locale. Indeed, the Jerusalem accounts leave little or no room for subsequent appearances in Galilee. Luke 24:50–51 portrays the heavenly departure of Jesus from his disciples as taking place at Bethany, just outside Jerusalem, on Easter night; and the Marcan Appendix by implication has much the same picture. A study of how Luke 24:6 changes the import of Mark 16:7 would seem to indicate a desire on Luke's part to avoid mention of appearances in Galilee. True, in Acts 1:3 there is evidence of Lucan awareness of a longer period of postresurrectional appearances; but there is no mention of Galilee, and the ascension takes place in the Jerusalem area (1:12). In John we have postresurrectional appearances over an eight-day period (20:19,26), and then the Gospel comes to an end (20:30–31). On the other side, the Galilean accounts seem to rule out prior Jerusalem appearances to the Twelve. The angel's directive in Mark 16:7 and Matt 28:7 bids the disciples to go to Galilee to see Jesus—a command that would make little sense were they to see him first in Jerusalem. When Jesus does appear to the disciples on the mountain in Galilee (Matt 28:16–17), they express doubt;[233] and there would be little reason for doubt if they had already seen him in Jerusalem. The editor who added John 21 made it seem that the Galilean appearances followed the Jerusalem ones by inserting verses that sew the two accounts together (21:1,14). But it is quite apparent from the story itself of the Galilean appearance (21:4,7) that the disciples are seeing Jesus for the first time.

Writers of harmonizing lives of Jesus have imposed their own sequence on the Gospel evidence: Jesus first appeared to the Twelve in Jerusalem for a week; then, for some inexplicable reason, they went to Galilee where he appeared to them at the seashore and on the mountain; and finally they returned to Jerusalem where Jesus appeared to them before ascending. Such a sequence does violence to the Gospel evidence. If one must venture beyond the evidence to establish a sequence, then (after the discovery of the empty tomb in Jerusalem and perhaps after appearances of Jesus to the women in Jerusalem and to "minor" disciples on the road to Emmaus) one might place the appearances to the Twelve in Galilee before the appearances to them in Jerusalem—a sequence that is not ruled out in the Galilean accounts. The Lucan and Johannine attempt to have the main appearance to the Twelve take place on Easter day is probably a construction dictated by theological rather than historical interests.

But the more biblical answer is to recognize that the evidence does not permit us to establish a sequence with any assurance. Each Gospel tradition

---

[233] The other Gospels associate this hesitancy with *initial* appearances (Luke 24:37; John 20:25; Mark 16:13–14).

centers on an all-important appearance to the Twelve in which they are commissioned for their future task (Matt 28:19–20; Luke 24:47–49; Mark 16:15; John 20:21–23; and 21:15–17 following the symbolism of the catch of fish). Each tradition gives the impression that Jesus is appearing to the Twelve for the first time, whence the doubt and reassurance. Thus, in a certain way, as far as substance is concerned, all the Gospels are narrating the same appearance to the Twelve.

How did it arise that an evangelist recorded appearances only in Jerusalem or in Galilee and that there was no attempt to make a sequence of all the postresurrectional appearances of Jesus? V. Taylor[234] makes an interesting suggestion. In preaching the resurrection, what was essential was a testimony that a well-known apostolic witness had seen Jesus. There was no chain of related events in the resurrection as there was in the passion. Thus, in Paul's primitive kerygma of the resurrection (1 Cor 15:5–7) only the names of those to whom Jesus appeared are listed, and no locale is mentioned. Each community would preserve the memory of an appearance of Jesus to figures known to that community. The important Palestinian Christian communities of Jerusalem and of Galilee would retain the memory of appearances with local associations, or perhaps would have adapted to the respective local settings the tradition of a basic appearance to the Twelve. The individual evangelists drew on one or the other of these local traditions available to them, perhaps in ignorance of the existence of other traditions. Thus if one understands the function of the appearance narratives, the diversity in the accounts of the appearances constitutes no argument against their historicity.

DIFFERENCES AMONG THE NARRATIVES OF THE EMPTY TOMB

Here we must distinguish between the underlying occurrence (the fact that the tomb was empty of the body of Jesus) and the supplied interpretation of that occurrence. All the Gospel witnesses that refer to the tomb agree that after the Sabbath Mary Magdalene (mentioned alone in John 20 and the Marcan Appendix; and with other women in Mark 16:1–8; Matt; and Luke) went to the tomb either later Saturday night or very early Sunday morning and did not find the body of Jesus there. They also agree that the reason why it was not there was that he had been raised from the dead. All agree that this understanding of why the tomb was empty came from revelation.

---

[234] *The Formation of the Gospel Tradition* (2d ed.; London: Macmillan, 1953), 59–62.

The Gospel witnesses disagree widely in how they describe the circumstances of the revelation. For example, did Mary Magdalene (alone or with the other women) encounter one angel or angelic man (Mark 16:5–7; Matt) or two (Luke; John 20:12)? Was the angel (or angels) sitting (Mark 16:5; Matt; John 20:12) or standing (Luke)? Was he (or they) outside (Matt) or inside (Mark 16:5; Luke; John)? The wording of the angel's (or angels') message also varies. The simplest explanation is that in the oldest tradition the discovery of the empty tomb in itself did not enlighten those who found it as to the resurrection.[235] Only later when the risen Jesus appeared did it become clear why the tomb was empty. When the discovery of the empty tomb was made part of a narrative, that revealed explanation was incorporated so that readers could understand the import of the tomb. An interpreting angel of the Lord was a standard OT way of describing revelation and that was employed by the Synoptics, while John 20:14 and Mark 16:9 retain, whether intentionally or not, the original idea that the revelation came from the appearance of Jesus himself. Understood properly, then, the differences among the tomb narratives really do not call into question the facticity of the emptiness of the tomb and what that contributes to the bodily character of the resurrection.

---

[235] John 20:2 tells us that Mary Magdalene thought the body had been stolen; by implication John 20:8–9 indicates that sight of the tomb and the garments did not bring Peter to faith.

APPENDIX III.
DID NEW TESTAMENT CHRISTIANS CALL JESUS GOD?

Part III of this book surveyed how NT Christians made an association between particular moments in Jesus' career and designations/titles that helped to express his identity or role in God's plan. Some of those designations represent high christology (pp. 4–5 above), especially "Son of God" and "Lord." Because of Christian history, however, one designation or title deserves particular discussion, for in postNT times the debate came to settle on whether Jesus was "God." At the Council of Nicaea in AD 325 it was confessed that the Son was God and not a creature; he was "true God of true God." The recognition that such a belief is still the hallmark of the Christian is found in the Amsterdam Confession of the World Council of Churches, which stated that the World Council is composed of "Churches which acknowledge Jesus Christ as God and Savior." Yet, when we accept in faith that Jesus was God as confessed at Nicaea, there still remains a question: *To what extent and in what manner is this confession contained in the NT?* A development from the Scriptures to Nicaea, at least in formulation and thought patterns, must be recognized by all. Indeed, the council Fathers at Nicaea were troubled over the fact that they could not answer Arius in purely biblical categories.[236] Moreover, by the time of Nicaea there had been a definite progression from a more functional approach to Jesus to an ontological approach.[237] Before this development what was the attitude of the NT authors toward calling Jesus "God"? The investigation will involve a survey of select NT passages, the interpretation of which in some instances

---

[236] Athanasius, "Letters" (footnote 209 above) 5.18–21; NPNF series 2, 4.161–164.

[237] See J. C. Murray, *The Problem of God* (New Haven: Yale University Press, 1964), 40–41.

is highly disputed. Although I shall make every effort to make intelligible to readers who do not know Greek the defensible interpretations of such passages, at times the discussion will be more complex than has hitherto been true in this book. For that reason I chose to place this material in an APPENDIX.[238]

From what has preceded in this book it should be obvious that the NT attitude toward the divinity of Jesus is much broader than the scope of this chapter, both in terms of what Jesus thought of himself and of what his followers thought of him. Even were we to discover that the NT never calls Jesus God, this would not necessarily mean that the NT authors did not think of Jesus as divine. There is much truth to Athanasius's contention that the Nicene definition that Jesus was God and not a creature collects the sense of the Scriptures, and thus, as we may deduce, is not dependent on any one statement of Scripture.[239] Nevertheless, the issue of whether passages in the NT had reached the development of using "God" for Jesus is important for several reasons.

First, there are scholars who are not liberal or seeking to disprove Jesus' divinity but who are uneasy about the Nicene confession of Jesus as God because they are uncertain that this is biblical language. The above-mentioned confession of the World Council of Churches provoked considerable criticism precisely on that score.[240]

Second, it has been contended that this formula does not do justice to

---

[238] I mentioned above (p. 107) that an approach to christology involving the study of individual titles in all the NT passages that use each of them would be too complicated for an introductory book; perusing here this instance of that approach may convince readers that my judgment was correct. I have revised in this APPENDIX and greatly simplified material I published in TS 26 (1965), 545–73 and BJGM 1–38. Those desiring more detail and bibliography should consult that treatment; also M. J. Harris, *Jesus as God: The New Testament Use of* Theos *in Reference to Jesus* (Grand Rapids: Baker, 1992).

[239] "Letters" (footnote 209 above) 5.21: "If the expressions are not in so many words in the Scriptures, yet they contain the sense of the Scriptures." Also 5.20: "The Bishops . . . were compelled to collect the sense of the Scriptures."

[240] Among those who conclude that the NT exercises great restraint in describing Jesus as God and do not favor the designation are R. Bultmann, "The Christological Confession of the World Council of Churches," in his *Essays Philosophical and Theological* (New York: Scribners, 1955), 273–90; and V. Taylor, "Does the NT Call Jesus God?" *Expository Times* 73 (1961–62), 116–18. More positive in their evaluation of the NT evidence are O. Cullmann, *The Christology of the New Testament* (London: SCM, 1959), 306–14; A. W. Wainwright, "The Confession 'Jesus is God' in the New Testament," *Scottish Journal of Theology* 10 (1957), 274–99; and Harris, *Jesus*.

the fullness of Christ: "To describe Christ as God is to neglect the sense in which He is both less and more, man as well as God within the glory and limitations of His Incarnation."[241] This fear that an exclusive emphasis on the divinity of Christ may lead to a failure to appreciate his humanity is quite realistic. Throughout this book, especially as I discussed limitations in Jesus, I have reminded readers of the danger of a semidocetic understanding of Jesus that would exclude from his life such human factors as testing, fear, lack of knowledge, and hesitation.[242] However, the answer to the exaggeration of divinity would seem to lie in properly emphasizing the humanity of Jesus, rather than in rejecting the validity of the formula "Jesus is God."

Third, it has been contended that this formula objectivizes Jesus: "The formula 'Christ is God' is false in every sense in which God is understood as an entity which can be objectivized, whether it is understood in an Arian or Nicene, an Orthodox or a Liberal sense. It is correct, if 'God' is understood as the event of God's acting." Bultmann, who raises that objection ("Christological" 287), would avoid the danger by referring to Christ not as "God" but as "the Word of God." This approach may to some extent reflect an exaggerated stress on the functional; after all, it is meaningful and necessary to ask what Jesus is in himself and not only what he is as far as we are concerned or for me personally. Yet Bultmann's remarks do warn us against neglecting the soteriological implications of the formula "Jesus is God"— only God can give us God's life, and that is why the issue of Jesus as God is of major importance for Christian existence. Once again the answer to the danger would seem to lie in properly explaining the formula, rather than in rejecting it. Nicaea certainly did not ignore the soteriological aspect, for in the one breath it described Jesus as "true God of true God . . . who for us and our salvation . . . became man, suffered and rose."

Thus, it seems that the last two challenges are centered primarily on the objectionable meaning that one can give to the formula "Jesus is God" and can be answered in terms of a corrective emphasis. I shall concentrate now on the first objection and the scriptural justification for the formula. The important, relevant texts will be discussed under three headings: (A) Passages that seem to imply that the title "God" was not used for Jesus; (B)

---

[241] Taylor, "Does" 118.

[242] Another aspect of the fear that "Jesus is God" distorts the full picture of Jesus is the contention that the formula is open to a Sabellian interpretation that would reduce the Son to an aspect of God the Father. That 3d-century error seems less dangerous in our times than the danger of semidocetism. If anything, the current tendency may be to emphasize the Son at the expense of the Father and of the Holy Spirit.

Passages where, by reason of textual variants or syntax, the use of "God" for Jesus is dubious; (C) Passages where Jesus is clearly called God. I shall then evaluate the information that these texts give us about the frequency, antiquity, and origin of the use of "God" for Jesus.

(A) Passages that Seem to Imply that the Title "God" Was Not Used for Jesus

It seems best to begin with negative evidence that otherwise might be neglected, especially by exegetes who believe strongly in the divinity of Jesus. It is quite obvious that in the NT the term "God" is applied with overwhelming frequency to the One whom Jesus calls Father, i.e., to the God revealed in the Scriptures of Israel. The attitude toward Jesus in the sermons of Acts, which may retain early formulations (p. 108 above), is that he was a man attested by God (2:22) and that God preached to Israel through him (10:36). Throughout most of the NT there tends to be a distinction between God (= the Father) and Jesus. We may illustrate this by several passages:

#1. Mark 10:18. In response to the man who addresses him as "good teacher," Jesus says: "Why do you call me good? No one is good but God alone."[243] Luke 18:19 agrees with Mark but omits the article before *theos.* Matt 19:17 seems to reflect embarrassment at the thrust of the Marcan saying, for it reads: "Why do you ask me about what is good?" There are a number of interpretations of this Marcan verse. A frequent patristic understanding is that Jesus was trying to lead the man to a perception of his divinity, i.e., showing the man what he unconsciously (but correctly) implied when he addressed Jesus as good. It is difficult not to think that such an exegesis is motivated by an apologetic concern for protecting the divinity of Jesus. Other interpreters stress that Jesus was trying to direct attention away from himself to his Father. This is undoubtedly true, but it should not disguise the fact that the text strongly distinguishes between Jesus and God, and that a description of himself to which Jesus objected was applicable to God. From this text one would never suspect that the evangelist referred to Jesus as God.[244]

#2. Mark 15:34; Matt 27:46. As Jesus hangs on the cross, he cries out:

---

[243] The crucial phrase (*ei mē heis ho theos*) may also be translated: ". . . but the one God."

[244] I shall treat all the passages on the level of what they reflect of the NT authors' attitude toward using "God" for Jesus. I am not concerned at the moment with whether these are the *ipsissima verba* of Jesus, or with whether Jesus could have used the term "God" for himself.

"My God, my God, why have you forsaken me?" If either evangelist was accustomed to speak of Jesus as God, it is indeed strange that he would report a saying where Jesus is portrayed as addressing another as "my God." Of course, this argument is weakened by the fact that Jesus is citing Ps 22:1 and thus is using a conventional form of address. However, no such explanation is possible for the similar use of "my God" by Jesus in John 20: 17: "I am ascending to my Father and your Father, to my God and your God."[245]

#3. Eph 1:17: "The God of our Lord Jesus Christ, the Father of glory" (see also II Cor 1:3; I Pet 1:3). In Eph 1:3 we hear of the "God and Father of our Lord Jesus Christ," but the abruptness of 1:17 makes an even stronger impression. Just as in the preceding examples from the Gospels wherein Jesus speaks of "my God," these examples from the Epistles make it difficult to think that the author designated Jesus as God.

#4. There are several passages that by means of immediate juxtaposition seem to distinguish between the one God and Jesus Christ. Here is a sampling:

- John 17:3: "This is eternal life: that they know you, the only true [or real: *alēthinos*] God and him you sent, Jesus Christ."
- I Cor 8:6: "For us there is one God, the Father, from whom are all things and for whom we exist, and one Lord, Jesus Christ, through whom are all things and through whom we exist."
- Eph 4:4–6 distinguishes between ". . . one Spirit . . . one Lord . . . one God and Father of us all." In I Cor 12:4–6 a similar distinction is made: ". . . the same Spirit . . . the same Lord . . . the same God"; see also II Cor 13:14.
- I Tim 2:5: "For there is one God, and there is one mediator between God and men [*anthrōpoi*], the man [*anthrōpos*] Christ Jesus."

Such passages closely associate Jesus the Lord with God the Father (and sometimes with the Spirit as well); therefore, they are useful in discussing the NT attitude toward the divinity of Jesus and the NT roots of the later

---

[245] I reject the contention that in this passage Jesus is making a careful (and theological) distinction between his own relationship to the Father and the relationship of his disciples to the Father, i.e., between his natural sonship and their broader sonship/childhood gained through baptism. This passage must be interpreted against the background of Johannine theology: The ascension of which Jesus is speaking in 20:17 will lead to that giving of the Spirit (20:22; also 7:38–39) which will beget the disciples anew from above (3:3) and make them God's children (1:12). Thus Jesus' Father will now become the disciples' Father and they will become Jesus' brothers (and sisters). Note that the message in 20:17 is to be relayed to his "brothers." As in Ruth 1:16, the meaning is "My God who is now your God" (BGJ 2.1016–17).

doctrine of the Trinity. However, for our purposes they show that while Jesus was associated with God and was called the Lord or the mediator, there was a strong tendency to reserve the title "God" to the Father who is the one true God.

#5. Tangentially related to our discussion are a number of passages that seem to state that Jesus is less than God or the Father.[246] Exegesis of these passages was germane to previous chapters in this book where we discussed Jesus' attitude and that of NT Christians toward his divinity; but they do not directly involve the use of the title "God." Nevertheless, it is well at least to list them by way of reminder:

- John 14:28: "The Father is greater than I." This is the third Johannine text we have mentioned in this APPENDIX. Noting that there are Johannine passages that do not favor the application of the term "God" to Jesus will serve as a balance to the emphasis below that the Fourth Gospel supplies us with clear examples of such an application.
- Mark 13:32: "Of that day or that hour no one knows, not even the angels in heaven, nor the Son, but only the Father." (See pp. 56–57 above.)
- Philip 2:5–10: "Christ Jesus, who, though he was in the form/image [*morphē*] of God, did not count being equal with God a thing to be clung to/grasped at, but emptied himself, taking the form of a servant. . . . Therefore God has highly exalted him and bestowed on him the name which is above every name . . . that every tongue should confess that Jesus is Lord, to the glory of God the Father."[247]
- I Cor 15:24 speaks of the triumphant Christ of the Second Coming, who is to deliver the kingdom to God the Father. In 15:28 Paul continues: "Then the Son himself will also be subjected to Him who put all things

---

[246] Needless to say, for those who believe in Nicaea and Chalcedon, these passages will be explained in a way that will not deny the truths that from all eternity the Son is equal to the Father and that from the first moment of his incarnation Jesus was true God and true man. The NT authors would not have phrased their affirmations with a sensitivity to future conciliar debates and formulas.

[247] As we saw on pp. 134–35 above, for some this language suggests a parallelism between Adam and Jesus: Both are in the image of God, but neither is yet equal to God; and while one grasps possessively but unsuccessfully at equality, the other accepts the lower, servant status with the result that he is elevated and given the divine name. For more scholars the language suggests that Jesus, having started equal to God, did not consider that state one to be clung to but emptied himself (a kenosis = emptying) by taking on the form of a servant. Also, it should be noted that in the exaltation described at the end of this hymnic passage the name bestowed on Jesus is not "God" but "Lord." The "God" who exalted Jesus and bestowed the name upon him is God the Father.

under him, that God may be everything to everyone." Some have suggested that Paul is speaking of the Son in his role as head of the church; in any case "God" is reserved as the title for the One to whom the Son is subjected.

(B) Passages where the Use of the Title "God" for Jesus Is Dubious

The doubts about these texts arise on two scores: the presence of textual variants and problems of syntax.

PASSAGES INVOLVING TEXTUAL VARIANTS:[248]

#6. Gal 2:20: "It is no longer I who live, but Christ who lives in me; and what I now live in the flesh, I live in faith in *the Son of God* who loved me and gave himself for me." I have italicized the crucial words, where some important witnesses to the Greek NT read "the God and Christ."[249] There are two ways to translate this variant: "faith in God and in Christ who loved me and gave himself for me," or "faith in the God and Christ," etc. Only in the second translation of this variant is "God" used as a title for Jesus. In general, critical editions of the Greek NT prefer the reading "Son of God" to the variant; but, in part, this may be because the editors consider "Son of God" to be the less developed reading from a theological viewpoint and thus more original. The phrase "the God and Christ" is never found elsewhere in the Pauline writings, and so is suspect; nor is it clear why, were it original, a scribe would change it to "the Son of God." Thus, this text should not be counted among those passages that call Jesus God.

#7. Acts 20:28: "The Holy Spirit has made you overseers to feed *the church of God which he obtained with his own blood.*" There are two problems about the italicized words: One concerns a variant reading ("the church of the Lord"); the other concerns grammatical understanding. As for the variant reading, "the church of God" is slightly better attested than

---

[248] I shall discuss only those that I think have some merit, ignoring, for instance, I Timothy 3:16, where some later witnesses have a reference to *God* being manifested in the flesh instead of a pronominal reference to Jesus. The attestation for such a reading is not strong enough to warrant serious consideration.

[249] P[45], Codices Vaticanus and (the original hand of) Bezae. MTC 593 explains how this and other variants could have arisen by scribal misreading of "the Son of God."

"the church of the Lord."[250] Moreover, the reasoning why later copyists might have changed an original "the church of God" to "the church of the Lord" is somewhat stronger than that for a change in the opposite direction.[251] Overall, then, the weight of the arguments favors "the church of God" as more original.

Grammatically that reading raises the possibility that the passage is referring to Jesus as God who obtained the church "with his own blood." However, there is another possibility: Perhaps "God" refers to the Father and "his own" refers to the Son; thus, "the church of God (the Father) which He obtained with the blood of His own (Son)." Many favor this interpretation or an alternative: "the church of God which he (Christ) obtained with his own blood," positing an unexpressed change of subject. And so, even when we read "the church of God," we are by no means certain that this verse calls Jesus God.

#8. John 1:18: "No one has ever seen God; it is *the only God/Son/One*, ever at the Father's side, who has revealed Him." The textual witnesses do not agree on the Greek reading represented by the italicized words. There are three major readings, all referring to Jesus, but describing him in a different way:

(a) "the only God," in which the adjective "only" (*monogenēs*[252]) modifies "God" (*theos*). This has superior textual support.[253] This phrase occurs nowhere else in John, but for that very reason no copyist is likely to have introduced it in place of an original, more familiar description. Since it calls Jesus God, some exegetes suspect that it is too highly developed theo-

---

[250] The first is supported by Codices Vaticanus, Sinaiticus, and the Vulgate; the second by Codices Alexandrinus, Bezae, and some minor versions. The Byzantine reading, "the church of the Lord and God," represents a scribal conflation of the two.

[251] Although "the church of the Lord" occurs seven times in the Greek OT, it does not occur elsewhere in the NT, while "the church of God" occurs eleven times in the epistles attributed to Paul; thus here copyists of the NT might have changed an original but highly unusual "the church of the Lord" to the more customary expression. On the other hand "the church of God" could have struck copyists of the NT as objectionable because the sequence would then seem to be speaking of God's blood; accordingly they might have changed the phrase to refer to "the Lord (Jesus)."

[252] This adjective literally means "one of a kind, unique" (Latin *unicus*). Jerome translated it as *unigenitus*, "only-begotten," probably with an apologetic thrust against Arian christology. See D. Moody, *Journal of Biblical Literature* 72 (1953), 213–19.

[253] This reading is supported by the evidence of the best Greek manuscripts (including both the Bodmer papyri from *ca.* AD 200), by the Syriac, by Irenaeus, Clement of Alexandria, and Origen.

logically to be early; but we shall see that elsewhere in John Jesus is clearly called God. Perhaps the only real objection to the reading is the strangeness of the affirmation that God reveals God, and that only God has seen God; but this strangeness disappears when one understands that for John Jesus is the divine Son revealing or seeing the divine Father.

(b) "the only Son" where the word for "Son" (*huios*) appears instead of the word for "God."[254] Three of the other four uses of "only" (*monogenēs*) in the Johannine writings (John 3:16,18; I John 4:9) are combined with "Son"; and so the appearance of the combination here may be the reflection of a copyist's tendency to conform.

(c) "the only One" (*monogenēs* without an accompanying noun), a reading dependent on patristic support.[255] Because of the context it has to refer to the Son. Some scholars have favored it as the original reading, of which the above two readings would represent an expansion and clarification. However, the complete lack of attestation in the Greek copies of the Gospel makes it very suspect. When one is dealing with patristic citations of the Gospel, one is never certain when, for the sake of brevity, the Fathers are citing only the essential words of a passage.

Overall there is good reason to accept the first reading (a) as original; and according to Harris, *Jesus* 83, that is the view of the majority of scholars. That reading calls Jesus God.[256]

PASSAGES WHERE OBSCURITY ARISES FROM SYNTAX:

#9. Col 2:2–3: ". . . the fullness of understanding for the knowledge of the mystery *of the God, Christ*, in whom are hidden all the treasures of wisdom and knowledge." There are several possible interpretations of the italicized phrase,[257] which in Greek has three words in the genitive (the definite article, "God," and "Christ"):

(a) "Christ" is in apposition to "God," or at least dependent on

---

[254] This reading is supported by some early versions (Latin, Curetonian Syriac), by Codex Alexandrinus and sundry later Greek manuscripts, by Athanasius, Chrysostom, and many of the Latin Fathers.

[255] M.-E. Boismard, *St. John's Prologue* (Westminster: Newman, 1957), 66, favored this, citing in support Tatian, Origen (once), Epiphanius, and Cyril of Jerusalem. His more recent French writing, however, seems to indicate support for reading (b) above.

[256] There are different ways of phrasing the English translation of *monogenēs theos*, depending on whether one construes the word as adjective + substartive ("only[-begotten] God"), or substantive + substantive ("God the only Son" or "the Only-begotten who is God").

[257] In addition there are textual variants as copyists tried to clarify it.

"God"; and since there is no article before "Christ," the two nouns are united: "the knowledge of the mystery of the God Christ." This interpretation calls Jesus God. However, in the NT there is no other instance of the formula "the God Christ."

(b) The genitive "Christ" qualifies "God" possessively: "the knowledge of the mystery of the God of Christ." Grammatically this offers no difficulty, and we saw above (#3) that Eph 1:17 speaks of "the God of our Lord Jesus Christ"; see also Col 1:3.

(c) "Christ" is the content of the mystery: "the knowledge of the mystery of God which is Christ."[258] This is an awkward way for the author to have phrased such a concept (compare the much clearer Col 1:24,27; I Cor 3:11). The grammatical difficulty is not insuperable, however; and this interpretation fits well into the Pauline concept of "the mystery."[259]

Be this as it may, the interpretations (b) and (c) are clearly preferable to (a), and therefore this text is not a good one to use in our discussion.

#10. II Thess 1:12: The concluding phrase reads literally: "according to the grace of the God of us and Lord Jesus Christ." There are two possible interpretations of the Greek genitives: (a) "the grace of our God-and-Lord Jesus Christ"; (b) "the grace of our God and of the Lord Jesus Christ."

The first interpretation, which gives Jesus the title "God," is favored by the absence in the Greek of an article before "Lord," creating the impression that the two genitives are bound together and governed by the one article that precedes "God." Yet, the exact three-word Greek combination for "God and Lord" is not found elsewhere in the Bible in reference to one person; and perhaps "Lord Jesus Christ" was so common a phrase that it would automatically be thought of as a separate entity and could be used without the article. The second interpretation is favored by the fact that pronominal "of us" (= "our") separates the two titles; but, as we shall see below in discussing II Pet 1:1, this is not a decisive argument. The most impressive argument for the second interpretation is that "our God" occurs four times in I and II Thessalonians as a title for God the Father. By analogy in the passage at hand, then, "our God" should be distinguished from "(the) Lord Jesus Christ,"[260] as most commentators acknowledge. Thus this text cannot be offered as an example of the use of the title "God" for Jesus.

---

[258] This reading is spelled out in the Greek of Codex Bezae, which is really supplying an early interpretation.

[259] See R. E. Brown, "The Semitic Background of the NT *Mystērion*," *Biblica* 40 (1959), 72.

[260] Much the same issue arises in James 1:1, where James is described as "a servant of God and (the) Lord Jesus Christ." There, however, no article appears before "God" to suggest that the two nouns should be bound together as "God-and-Lord."

#11. Titus 2:13: ". . . the appearance of the glory *of (the) great God and Savior of us Jesus Christ.*" Three interpretations of the Greek underlying the italicized words are possible:

(a) "the glory of the great God and of our Savior Jesus Christ." This interpretation that clearly separates "the great God" and "our Savior Jesus Christ" is not really favored by the Greek, which binds together the three words "God and Savior." Once again it may be argued that "our Savior Jesus Christ" was so common a creedal formula that it would automatically be thought of as a separate entity from "God." However, the argument is less convincing here than it was in #10, for in II Thess 1:12 the placing of "of us" broke up the two nouns. Moreover, the separation proposed in this interpretation of Titus 2:13 means that the author is speaking of a twofold future glorious appearance, one of God and the other of the Savior Jesus Christ. There is no real evidence in the NT for a double epiphany.

(b) "the glory of our great God-and-Savior, which (glory) is Jesus Christ." This interpretation follows the Greek in keeping together "God and Savior" but applies the compound title to the Father. Jesus Christ (grammatically in apposition to "glory") is taken to represent the personification of the glory of God the Father. The objection to this interpretation is the same as that encountered under #9 in dealing with interpretation (c) of Col 2:2–3, namely, that we would expect in the Greek an explanatory "which is." Otherwise, there is no real hindrance to applying the title "Savior" to the Father, for other passages in Titus (1:3; 2:10; 3:4) speak of "God our Savior" (as contrasted with 1:4 and 3:6 that speak of "Jesus Christ our Savior"). Nor can one object to the idea that Jesus is the glory of the Father, for other NT passages (John 1:14; 12:41; 17:24; Heb 1:3) identify Jesus as the bearer of divine glory.

c) "the glory of our great God-and-Savior Jesus Christ." Here the compound title "God-and-Savior" is given to Jesus Christ. This is the most obvious meaning of the Greek. It implies that the passage is speaking only of one glorious epiphany, namely, of Jesus Christ, in harmony with other references to the epiphany of Jesus Christ in the Pastoral Epistles (I Tim 6: 14–15; II Tim 4:1). The likelihood that "Savior" is applied to Jesus Christ rather than to God the Father is suggested by the next verse in Titus (2:14), which speaks of the redemption wrought by Jesus. Some would rule out this interpretation that gives Jesus the title "God" because elsewhere in the Pastorals (I Tim 2:5; see #4 above) a clear distinction is made between the one God (= the Father) and the man Jesus Christ. However, as we have noted, in the Fourth Gospel there are passages that call Jesus God along with passages that distinguish between Jesus and the one true God.

A decision is difficult. Some careful scholars (H. Conzelmann, J. Jeremias, J.N.D. Kelly) reject interpretation (c), while the majority[261] (including O. Cullmann, J. D. Quinn, C. Spicq) argue for it, accepting the fact that here Jesus is called God. Personally, I am inclined to recognize interpretation (c) as the probable meaning of the passage. It is unfortunate that no certainty can be attained, for it seems that this passage helped to shape the confession of the World Council of Churches in "Jesus Christ as God and Savior" (p. 171 above).

#12. Rom 9:5 joins these clauses: "Of their race [i.e., the Israelites] is the Christ according to the flesh *the one who is over all God blessed forever. Amen.*" To whom do the italicized words refer? It has been claimed that this verse has been subjected to more discussion than any other verse in the NT. The problem may be phrased in terms of various possible punctuations of which two are dominant:

(a) A full stop (period) may be put after "flesh," as in Codex Ephraemi Rescriptus, so that the following words become a separate sentence blessing the God who is over all forever—a reference to God the Father. Why Paul should stop at this point in his chain of thought and introduce a doxology to the Father is not clear; for 9:1–5 concerns Christ, and one would expect praise of Christ, not of the Father. Yet if one takes the whole context of Rom 9:1–5, Paul might be praising God for the privileges of Israel that have been listed, especially the gift of the Messiah (Christ). The word order in the Greek offers considerable difficulty for this interpretation. In independent doxologies "blessed" normally comes first in the Greek sentence (II Cor 1: 3; Eph 1:3); here it is the sixth word in the sentence. The presence of the participle translated "who is" is also awkward for this interpretation, for it is superfluous. Such a construction is normal only if there is an antecedent in the previous clause (II Cor 11:31; Rom 1:25).[262]

(b) A full stop may be put at the end, after "forever," and a comma after "flesh." All the words after "flesh," then, are a relative clause modifying "Christ," thus: ". . . the Christ according to the flesh, who is over all God blessed forever." This interpretation would mean that Paul calls Jesus

---

[261] See the listing of scholars in Harris, *Jesus* 185, who points out that this is the virtually unanimous view of grammarians and lexicographers.

[262] A variant of this interpretation in which God (the Father) is blessed is found in putting a full stop may be put after "all," with a comma after "flesh," thus: ". . . the Christ according to the flesh, who is over all. God be [is] blessed forever." This interpretation avoids the difficulty mentioned in the text above about the presence of the participle. In the independent doxology, however, "blessed" still does not have the normal first position in the Greek sentence (it is now second), and the lack of contextual justification for suddenly introducing a doxology to the Father remains a difficulty.

God. From a grammatical viewpoint this is the better reading. Also, the contextual sequence is excellent; for, having spoken of Jesus' descent according to the flesh, Paul now emphasizes his position as God. The major objection to this interpretation is that nowhere else does Paul speak of Jesus as God.[263]

Distinguished scholars are aligned on both sides of the issue.[264] Personally, I am swayed by the grammatical evidence in favor of (b) whereby the title "God" is given to Jesus. But one may claim no more than plausibility.

#13. In I John 5:20 there are two sentences: "And we know that the Son of God has come and has given us understanding to know the true One [*alēthinos*]; and we are in the true One, in His Son Jesus Christ. *This is the true God* and eternal life." In the first sentence of this passage it is quite obvious that "the true One" is God the Father; indeed, some textual witnesses[265] clarify it by adding "God," giving a combination that would be translated "the true God" (cf. John 17:3 under #4 above). This first sentence tells us that the Son has come and enabled people to know the Father, and that the Christian abides in Father and Son.

The real problem concerns the opening of the second sentence that I have italicized. To whom does the "this" refer? The most proposed possibilities are that it is a reference to either "Jesus Christ" or to "the true One" (i.e., the Father) in the preceding sentence. Grammar favors the nearest antecedent, which here is "Jesus Christ" who thus would be called "true God."

---

[263] Already in this APPENDIX under B, in treating passages from the Pauline corpus, I have rejected such texts as Gal 2:20; I Tim 3:16 (footnote 248); Col 2:2–3; II Thess 1:12; and under A above I pointed out a number of Pauline texts that would seem to indicate that Paul did *not* refer to Jesus as God. Besides Rom 9:5, the only text in the corpus that has serious plausibility as an instance of Jesus' being called God is Titus 2:13; but this is in the Pastoral Epistles, which most scholars regard as not written by Paul himself. Nevertheless, it might be argued that the Pastorals are in some areas a homogeneous development of Pauline thought, so that the usage in Titus 2:13 may be a continuation of Paul's own way of speaking already instanced in Rom 9:5. In any case, we should note that an argument based on Paul's usage or nonusage of the title "God" for Jesus is different from the claim that Paul was so imbued with Jewish monotheism that he could not have thought of Jesus as God. Such a claim assumes that Paul could find no way of reconciling two truths. Even though he may use other terminology, there is no doubt that Paul believed in the divinity of Jesus (in preexistent categories): Philip 2:5–6; II Cor 8:9.

[264] One might have the impression that the majority of recent commentaries (Kuss, Dunn) refer the passage to God the Father; but Harris, *Jesus* 154, lists authors to disprove that. In their commentaries Cranfield (1979, 1985) and Fitzmyer (1993) favor the application to Christ.

[265] Codex Alexandrinus, Vulgate, Bohairic.

Yet, since God the Father was referred to as "true" twice in the first sentence, one might suspect that "true God" is a reference to Him. Certainly in John 17:3 "the one true God" refers to God the Father and not to Jesus Christ. Can we learn something from the other predicate in this second sentence of I John 5:20, i.e., "eternal life"? Twice in the Fourth Gospel Jesus speaks of himself as "the life" (11:25; 14:6), while the Father is never so called. Yet John 6:57 speaks of "the living Father" and makes it clear that the Father is the source of the Son's life. Thus it seems probable that in Johannine terminology either the Father or the Son could be designated as "life," even as both are designated as "light" (I John 1:5; John 8:12; note that it is the Epistle that calls the Father light while the Gospel calls Jesus light). It may be, however, that the predicate "eternal life" does favor making Jesus Christ the subject of the sentence we are discussing, for only eight verses earlier (5:12) the author of the Epistle stated: "The person who has the Son has life." Moreover since the first sentence of I John 5:20 ends with Christians dwelling in God the Father, tautology is avoided if the second sentence ends by relating Christians to Jesus. When all the factors are added, probability seems to favor the thesis that I John 5:20 calls Jesus God—a usage not unusual in Johannine literature.

#14. II Pet 1:1: "To those who have obtained a faith of value equal to ours in *the righteousness of the God of us and Savior Jesus Christ*." The italicized words present the same grammatical problem that we saw in II Thess 1:12 (#10 above), where amid two possibilities, "the grace of our God-and-Lord Jesus Christ" and "the grace of our God and of the Lord Jesus Christ," I favored the latter, a reading that distinguished between God (the Father) and Jesus Christ, on the basis of usage in the rest of II Thessalonians. Here are we to prefer "the righteousness of our God-and-Savior Jesus Christ" (one person) or "the righteousness of our God and of the Savior Jesus Christ"? The presence of only one definite article favors the former; the position of "of us" (= "our") favors the latter; but neither argument is very persuasive. If one turns to usage in the rest of II Peter, the phrase in 1:2 "in the knowledge of (the) God and of Jesus the Lord of us" favors distinction of persons; notice, however, a different word order. A closer and a more frequent parallel construction with a compound title for Jesus is illustrated by 1:11: "the eternal kingdom of the Lord of us and Savior Jesus Christ" (= "Lord-and-Savior"; see also 2:20; 3:18); it suggests that the author very probably intended both titles, "God" and "Savior," to be applied to Jesus Christ. This passage could almost be classified in the next section of our article under texts that clearly call Jesus God.[266]

---

[266] Harris, *Jesus* 238, lists names showing that this is the majority view of scholars by far.

* * *

The second main subdivision (B) has treated passages where the use of the title "God" for Jesus is dubious in order to see just how dubious they are and whether any offered probable support for recognizing that the title was actually employed. Nine texts (##6–14) were considered under two headings. First, under "Passages Involving Textual Variants" Gal 2:20 and Acts 20:28 were considered very dubious, while John 1:18 was judged to be a very probable instance where Jesus is called God. Second, under "Passages where Obscurity Arises from Syntax" Col 2:2–3 and II Thess 1:12 were considered very dubious, while Titus 2:13; Rom 9:5; I John 5:20; and II Pet 1:1 were judged instances in which in ascending order there is increasing probability that Jesus is called God. Thus, five (## 8,11,12,13,14) of the nine instances must be taken seriously in our discussion. A methodological note is in order here. Sometimes these five examples are rejected by scholars, despite the grammatical arguments in their favor, on the grounds that the use of "God" for Jesus is rare in the NT and therefore always to be considered improbable.[267] However, is not the rarity of the usage to some extent dependent on the rejection of these examples? If these five instances are joined to the three we shall cite in the next section, then the usage is not so rare.

(C) Passages where Jesus Is Clearly Called God

With the reminder that there are more passages in the NT that imply that Jesus is divine,[268] we shall confine our attention to three passages that explicitly use "God" (*theos*) of Jesus.

#15. Heb 1:8–9: Employing the words of Ps 45:7–8, the author says that God has addressed Jesus His Son: [8]"Your throne, O God, is forever and ever, and the scepter of uprightness is the scepter of your [his] kingdom. [9]You have loved righteousness and hated iniquity; therefore (O) God, your

---

[267] Wainwright, "Confession" 277, makes two points worth repeating. First, "Many critics have chosen a less natural translation of the Greek because they believe it was psychologically impossible for the writer to have said that Christ was God." Second, the argument from inconsistency in usage (i.e., elsewhere the writer does not call Jesus God) must be used with care, for we are not certain that the writer saw an inconsistency in only occasionally using a title.

[268] Besides those cited in footnote 276 below, we may mention John 10:30, "I and the Father are one"; John 14:9, "He who has seen me has seen the Father"; and the absolute use of "I AM" (*egō eimi*) in John 8:24,28,58; 13:19.

God has anointed you with the oil of gladness. . . ." The psalm is cited by Hebrews according to the Septuagint, the Greek translation of the OT.[269] The first question we must ask is whether "God" (*ho theos*) in v. 8 is to be rendered as a vocative (as I have translated it) or as a nominative. A few scholars, including B. F. Westcott, J. Moffatt, and E. J. Goodspeed, have opted for the latter, suggesting the interpretation: "God is your throne for ever and ever." This is rejected by the vast majority of scholars for various reasons. Were a nominative rendering intended, one would expect a different word order placing "God" before "throne." In the preceding verse of the psalm in the Septuagint we read: "Your weapons, O Mighty One, are sharpened"; the law of parallelism would indicate that the next verse should read: "Your throne, O God, is for ever and ever." Moreover, the parallelism from the very next line in the psalm cited by Hebrews in v. 8 ("and the scepter of uprightness is . . .") suggests that in the line under consideration the subject is not "God" but "throne" ("Your throne is"). There can be little doubt, then, that the translation of v. 8 that I have offered is the correct one. Cullmann (*Christology* 310) states that "Hebrews unequivocally applies the title 'God' to Jesus," and that is a true estimate of the evidence of v. 8.[270]

V. Taylor admits that in v. 8 the expression "O God" is a vocative spoken of Jesus, but he says that the author of Hebrews was merely citing the psalm and using its terminology without any deliberate intention of suggesting that Jesus is God.[271] It is true that the main point of citing the psalm was to contrast the Son with the angels and to show that the Son enjoys eternal dominion, while the angels are but servants. Therefore, in the citation no major point was being made of the fact that the Son can be addressed as God. Yet we cannot presume that the author did not notice that his citation had this effect and surely, at least, he saw nothing wrong in this address.

---

[269] Actually, the Septuagint reading is a misunderstanding of the Hebrew (Masoretic) text of the psalm, but that is a problem in psalm exegesis and does not affect the meaning of the citation in Hebrews.

[270] Perhaps Heb 1:9 also refers to Jesus as God. Yet there scholars are more evenly divided on whether the first "God" that precedes "your God" is to be rendered as a vocative, thus: "O God [= Jesus], your God [= the Father] has anointed you"; or as a nominative in apposition, thus: "God, your God has anointed you." In the latter interpretation "God, your God" is the Father.

[271] "Does" 117. The type of argument advanced by Taylor is not implausible. For instance, Matt 1:23 cites Isa 7:14 in relation to the birth of Jesus: ". . . his name shall be called Emmanuel (which means 'God with us')." We cannot be certain that, because he used this citation, the evangelist took "God with us" literally and meant to call Jesus God.

Indeed, calling Jesus "God" reinforces his greatness over that of the angels. The picture is complemented by the similar situation in Heb 1:10, where the application to the Son of Ps 102:26–28 has the effect of addressing Jesus as Lord. Of course, we cannot be certain what the "O God" of the psalm meant to the author of Hebrews when he applied it to Jesus. Ps 45 is a royal psalm; and on the analogy of the "Mighty God" of Isa 9:5(6),[272] "God" may have been looked on simply as a royal title and hence applicable to Jesus as the Davidic Messiah king. More likely, however, the OT address has been focused and specified in its NT usage to identify Jesus as divine.

#16. John 1:1: "In the beginning was the Word;
and the Word was with (toward) God,
and the Word was God."

This is the first verse of the Johannine Prologue, the interpretation of which is extremely complicated. Here, even more than elsewhere, I refer readers to commentaries for the complexities of interpretation, and attempt only a basic explanation. In the Greek word order the second line has as its last word "God" (= the Father) with the definite article (*ho theos*), while the third line has as its first word "God" (which is the predicate) without an article (*theos*). The positioning of the word *theos* is to a certain extent explained by the "staircase parallelism" in the Greek lines where the last word in one line is the first word in the next line. The lack of the article before *theos* in the third line is more difficult. Some would explain it by the simple grammatical rule that definite predicate nouns that precede the verb generally lack the article. However, the absoluteness of the rule is debatable (see Harris, *Jesus* 301–13), and it is not a total solution.

Part of the explanation of why the author of the Prologue chose to use "God" without the article to refer to the Word while he used "God" with the article to refer to the Father is that he desired to keep the Word distinct from the Father. Even if the Word shares something with the Father that deserves to be called *theos*, the Word (Jesus) is not the Father, as will be patently clear throughout the Gospel.

Does this difference, hinted at by having the predicate "God" without the article in the third line and "God" with the article in the second line, lie

---

[272] This is a literal translation of '*Ēl gibbōr*. Many think that the list of titles in Isa 9:5(6) was borrowed from the traditional titles of the monarchs of other countries, especially of the Egyptian pharaoh. As used outside Israel the title may have identified the king as a god; when brought within the monotheism of Israel, however, the title applied to the king of Judah portrays him as one specially favored by God, e.g., "the divine mighty one" or "divine warrior." Nevertheless, the NT could use such language more literally of Jesus. In John 10:34 we have an instance where the OT reference to the judges as "gods" is interpreted as a reference to divinity.

in the fact that the Word is somewhat less than the Father (see John 14:28)? Some would answer affirmatively and translate: "The Word was divine." But that is too weak. After all, there is in Greek an adjective for "divine" (*theios*) which the author did not choose to use. *The New English Bible* paraphrases: "What God was, the Word was." That is certainly better than "divine," but loses the terseness of the Prologue's style. Moreover, several factors suggest that we should not attach the note of being less to the lack of the article. This first verse of the Prologue forms an inclusion[273] with the last line of the Prologue, and there (1:18; see #8 above) in the best attested reading we hear of the Word as "the only God." Moreover, as the beginning of the Gospel, the first verse of the Prologue also forms an inclusion with the (original) end of the Gospel,[274] where in 20:28 Thomas calls Jesus "My Lord and my God." Neither concluding passage in those inclusions (1:18; 20:28) would suggest that in Johannine thought the Word in 1:1 was being presented as less than God in the full sense.[275] To a certain extent, calling Jesus God represents for the Fourth Gospel a positive answer to the charges made against Jesus that he was arrogantly making himself God (John 10:33; 5: 18). The Roman author Pliny the Younger (*Epistle* 10.96.7) describes the Christians of Asia Minor as singing hymns to Christ as to a God. The Prologue, a hymn of the Johannine community at Ephesus, fits this description.

#17. John 20:28: On the Sunday evening one week after Easter Jesus appears to Thomas and the other disciples, causing Thomas to confess him as "My Lord and my God." This is the clearest example in the NT of the use of "God" for Jesus.[276] Here Jesus is addressed as "God" (a nominative

---

[273] An inclusion "packages" a section by repeating at the end of a section an idea or phrase from the beginning.

[274] Along with most scholars I think that when the Fourth Gospel was first written, it ended with chapter 20; then in a final stage of editing chapter 21 was added.

[275] It may be well, however, to reemphasize what has been stated earlier, namely, that not even the Johannine Prologue's exalted hymnic confession "The Word was God" has the same ideological content found in Nicaea's confession that the Son was "true God of true God." A different problematic and a long philosophical development separate the two.

[276] The contention of Theodore of Mopsuestia that Thomas was uttering an exclamation of thanks *to the Father* finds few proponents today. Bultmann ("Christological" 276) calls it: "The only passage in which Jesus is undoubtedly designated or, more exactly, addressed as God." That statement is exaggerated, however, for it does not give proper emphasis to the probabilities or, indeed certainties that Heb 1:8; I John 5:20; and II Pet 1:1 refer to Jesus as God. Moreover, it draws more attention than is warranted to the fact that "God" is used with an article in John 20:28 and without an article in John 1:1. As I noted above, the two passages form an inclusion and thus say the same thing. C. K. Barrett, *The Gospel According to John* (2d ed.;

form with definite article, which functions as a vocative). The scene is designed to serve as a climax to the Gospel: As the resurrected Jesus stands before the disciples, one of their number at last gives expression to an adequate faith in Jesus. He does this by applying to Jesus the Greek (Septuagint) equivalent of two terms applied to the God of the OT (*kyrios*, "Lord," rendering *YHWH*; and *theos*, "God," rendering *'Elōhîm*). The best example of the OT usage is in Ps 35:23, where the psalmist cries out: "My God and my Lord." It may well be that the Christian use of such a confessional formula was catalyzed by the Roman emperor Domitian's claim to the title "Lord and God" (*dominus et deus noster*).

(D) Evaluation of the Evidence

The question that forms the title of this APPENDIX must be answered in the affirmative. In three reasonably clear instances in the NT and in five instances that have probability[277] Jesus is called God. The use of "God" for Jesus that is attested in the early 2d century was a continuation of a usage that had begun in NT times. There is no reason to be surprised at this. "Jesus is Lord" was evidently a popular confessional formula in NT times, and in this formula Christians gave Jesus the title *kyrios* which was the Septuagint translation for *YHWH*.[278] If Jesus could be given this title, why could he not be called "God" (*theos*), which the Septuagint often used to translate *'Elōhîm*? The two Hebrew terms had become relatively interchangeable, and indeed *YHWH* was the more sacred term.

This does not mean that we can take a naive view about the development that took place in the NT usage of "God" for Jesus (nor, for that

---

Philadelphia: Westminster, 1978), 573, warns apropos of John 20:28: "The difference between the present verse and 1:1 (where *theos* is anarthrous) cannot be pressed."

[277] The neglect of these five instances is what, in my opinion, makes Taylor's and Bultmann's treatment of the question too pessimistic: e.g., Bultmann, "Christology," 276: "It is only with the Apostolic Fathers that free, unambiguous reference to Jesus Christ as 'our God' begins."

[278] The earliest major preserved copies of the Septuagint were copied by Christians in the 4th and 5th centuries AD. We are not certain about how consistently earlier copies and other Greek translations circulating in NT times used *kyrios* for *YHWH*. I make no claim that all "high christology" appearances of *kyrios* for Jesus in the NT consciously reflected a translation of YHWH. Yet in general the NT authors were aware that Jesus was being given a title which in Greek was used to refer to the God of Israel.

matter, in the gradual growth in the understanding of Jesus' divinity[279]). The eight instances with which we are concerned are found in these NT writings: Romans, Hebrews, Titus, John, I John, and II Peter. Let us see what this means in terms of the antiquity of the usage of the title.

Jesus is never called God in the Synoptic Gospels, and a passage like Mark 10:18 would seem to exclude a preserved memory that Jesus used the title of himself. Even the Fourth Gospel never portrays Jesus as saying specifically that he is God.[280] The sermons that Acts attributes to the beginning of the Christian mission do not speak of Jesus as God. Thus, there is no reason to think that Jesus was called God in the earliest layers of NT tradition. This negative conclusion is substantiated by the fact that Paul does not use the title in any epistle written before AD 58. The first likely occurrence of the usage of "God" for Jesus is in Rom 9:5; if we could be certain of the grammar of this passage, we could thus date the usage by Paul to the late 50s; but even then we would not know if it was widespread.

Chronologically, Heb 1:8–9 and Titus 2:13 would be the next examples (and if Rom 9:5 is not interpreted to refer to Jesus, they would be the first examples). The uncertainty of the date of composition of these epistles creates a problem. Hebrews cannot be dated much before the fall of Jerusalem, and probably should be dated after it, perhaps in the 80s. The date of Titus depends on the acceptance or rejection of the Pauline authorship of the

---

[279] The 1964 Instruction of the Pontifical Biblical Commission, "The Historical Truth of the Gospels," section VIII, recognizes that only after Jesus rose from the dead was his divinity clearly perceived. That need not mean that this perception was instantaneous; it took a long time to come to understand the mystery of Jesus and to give it formulation. The Arian dispute shows this clearly; see Chapter 10 above.

[280] More than the other Gospels, John brings the "God problem" to the fore in the ministry of Jesus (5:18; 8:58–59; 10:30–33). This is part of the Johannine technique of spelling out the challenge that Jesus brings to the "Jews," and of making explicit what was implicit in Jesus' ministry. Yet John does show a certain caution about anachronism; and so, even in 10:33–37, Jesus does not give a clear affirmation to the charge of the Jews that he is making himself God. These disputes must be understood against the background of the evangelist's own time and the debates in certain synagogues of the 60s through the 90s about what Christians were claiming in reference to Jesus. John 20:28 portrays Jesus being confessed as God one week after the resurrection. Without necessarily questioning the Johannine tradition of an appearance to Thomas, a critical evaluation of the scene would suspect that a confessional formula of the evangelist's own time has been used to vocalize that disciple's belief in the resurrected Jesus. Were the title "God" used for Jesus so soon after the resurrection, one could not easily explain the absence of this title in documented Christian confessions before the 60s.

Pastorals; a high percentage of scholarship treats them as postPauline, written between 80 and 120. The Johannine writings offer us the most frequent examples of the use of the title (three in John; one in I John), and they are generally dated from 90 to 110. The common opinion of recent exegetes is that II Peter is one of the latest NT works.

If we date NT times from 30 to 130, quite clearly the use of "God" for Jesus becomes *frequently* attested only in the second half of the period.[281] This chronological context is confirmed by the evidence of the earliest extrabiblical Christian works.[282] At the beginning of the 2d century Ignatius freely speaks of Jesus as God. In *Ephesians* 18:2 he says: "Our God, Jesus the Christ, was carried in Mary's womb"; in 19:3 he says: "God was manifest as man." In *Smyrnaeans* 1:1 Ignatius begins by giving glory to "Jesus Christ, the God who has thus made you wise."[283] We have already cited Pliny's testimony that just after the turn of the century the Christians of Asia Minor sang hymns to Christ as to a God. By mid-2d century (?) *II Clement* 1:1 can state: "We must think of Jesus Christ as of God."

The geographical spread of the usage is also worth noting. If Rom 9:5 is accepted, then Paul, writing from Greece, betrays no hesitation about the acceptability of the usage to his Roman audience. (Yet Mark, traditionally accepted as the Gospel of Rome, written in the 60s [?], does not hesitate to report a saying of Jesus in which he distinguishes himself from God: see #1 above.) Titus (purportedly written from Macedonia) is addressed to Crete. The place of the composition of Hebrews is not known: Rome is thought to be the destination. Most often the Johannine works are associated with

---

[281] Of course, there is a danger in judging usage from occurrence, for NT occurrence does not create a usage but testifies to a usage already extant. None of the passages we have cited gives any evidence of innovating, and indeed a passage like Heb 1:8–9 seems to call on an already traditional use of the psalm. Yet frequency of NT occurrence in a question such as we are dealing with is plausibly a good index of actual usage, for the passages cited under (A) above show that Jesus was not spoken of as God in many NT works. The facts are not adequately explained by a theory which holds that from the very beginning Jesus was called God, but by accident this usage is not attested till late in the NT.

[282] Some authors cite *Didache* 10.6, where "Hosanna to the God of David" is addressed to Jesus. However, J.-P. Audet, in his exhaustive commentary on the *Didache* (Paris: Gabalda, 1958), 62–67, argues strongly for the originality of the reading "Hosanna to the house of David."

[283] See also the problematic *Trallians* 7:1; *Romans* 7:3. The reference in *Ephesians* 1:1 to "God's blood" is reminiscent of one of the above-cited interpretations (#7) of Acts 20:28: "the church of God which he obtained with his own blood."

Ephesus in Asia Minor, although some think of Syria. Ignatius, from Antioch in Syria,[284] seems free to use "God" of Jesus when writing both to Asia Minor and to Rome. Pliny's statement reflects the Christian practice in Bithynia in Asia Minor. Thus, the usage seems to be attested in well-known Christian centers or areas of the NT world (Syria, Asia Minor, Greece, and Rome), and there is no evidence to support a claim that in the late 1st century the custom of calling Jesus God was confined to a small area or faction within the Christian world.

Is this usage a Hellenistic contribution to the theological vocabulary of Christianity? Since we have no evidence that Jesus was called God in the Jerusalem or Palestinian communities of the first two decades of Christianity, the prima-facie evidence might suggest Hellenistic origins.[285] This is supported by the fact that in two NT passages "God" is closely joined to "Savior" as a title for Jesus (Titus 2:13; II Pet 1:1), and "Savior" is to some extent a Hellenistic title. However, there is other evidence to suggest that the usage had its roots in the OT and is most likely Jewish. As we saw, Heb 1:8–9 is a citation of Ps 45. The confession of Thomas in John 20:28 echoes an OT formula (although one cannot exclude the possibility of an anti-Domitian apologetic). The background for John 1:1 is the opening of Genesis, and the concept of the Word reflects OT themes of the creative word of God and personified Wisdom. Perhaps the best we can do from the state of the evidence is to leave open the question of background for the custom of calling Jesus God.

The slow development of the usage of the title "God" for Jesus requires explanation. Not only is there the factor that Jesus is not called God in the earlier strata of NT material; but also there are passages, cited under A above, that by implication reserve the title "God" for the Father (even in the Pastorals and the Johannine literature). The most plausible explanation is that in the earliest stage of Christianity, the OT heritage dominated the use of "God"; hence "God" was a title too narrow to be applied to Jesus. It referred strictly to the One in heaven whom Jesus addressed as Father and to whom he prayed. Gradually (in the 50s and 60s?), in the development of

---

[284] The Gospel of Matthew is often associated with the church of Antioch. The fact that Matt 19:17 modifies Mark 10:18 (where Jesus avoids an adjective proper to God alone: #1 above) may be evidence that the custom of calling Jesus God was alive in that church several decades before Ignatius' time.

[285] I remind readers that I am speaking about the origin of the use of this *title* for Jesus, not about the origins of understanding Jesus as divine. That understanding was very early and expressed in various ways.

Christian thought, "God" was understood to be a broader term.[286] God had been so revealed in Jesus that the designation "God" had to be able to include both Father and Son.[287] The late Pauline literature seems to fall precisely in this stage of development. If Rom 9:5 calls Jesus God, it is an isolated instance within the larger corpus of the main Pauline works, which present Jesus as Lord and the Father as God. By the time of the Pastorals, however, Jesus is well known as God-and-Savior. The Johannine works come from the final years of the century, when the usage of "God" for Jesus has become common. Yet the Fourth Gospel preserves some traditional material about Jesus that has been handed down from a much earlier period before such usage; see 14:28; 17:3; and 20:17 which, prima facie, would not favor equating Jesus with God or putting him on the same level as the Father.

Can we, perhaps, go farther and suggest the ambiance of this development? Calling Jesus God could have been a liturgical usage that had its origin in the worship and prayers of the Christian community. Bultmann ("Christological" 277) has maintained that the title "Lord" was given to Jesus in the Hellenistic communities as they recognized him as the deity present in the act of worship. Without committing ourselves to this theory with its inaccuracies about Hellenistic setting (footnote 17 above), we can easily recognize the liturgical setting of some instances of confessing Jesus as Lord; and therefore we might anticipate a similar setting for the confession of Jesus as God.

Of the eight instances of the latter confession, the majority are clearly to be situated in a background of worship and liturgy. Four are doxologies (Titus 2:13; I John 5:20; Rom 9:5; II Pet 1:1), and it is well accepted that many of the doxologies in the epistolary literature of the NT echo doxologies known and used by the respective communities in their public prayer. Heb 1: 8–9 cites a psalm that was applied to Jesus, and we know the custom of singing psalms in Christian celebrations (I Cor 14:26; Eph 5:19). Certainly this could include OT psalms that were thought to be particularly adaptable to Jesus. Thus, it is not too adventurous of Wainwright to suggest that the

---

[286] Was there a similar development in the use of "Lord" (*kyrios*) *wherever it was thought of as a translation of* YHWH? Yet *kyrios* was applied to Jesus much more quickly than *theos*. Was the more obvious danger of a polytheistic conception in the use of *theos* a retarding factor?

[287] I omit from our discussion the problem of the Holy Spirit, a problem complicated by uncertainty as to when the NT authors began to think of the Spirit (Greek *pneuma*, neuter) as a personal agent. For some reflections see my *Biblical Exegesis and Church Doctrine* (New York: Paulist, 1985), 101–13.

author of Hebrews was calling on psalms that his readers sang in their liturgy and was reminding them of how these psalms voiced the glory of Jesus. The Prologue of John that twice calls Jesus God was originally a hymn; and we have already recalled Pliny's dictum about the Christians singing hymns to Christ as to a God.

Perhaps, at first glance, John 20:28 seems an exception to the rule, for the confession of Thomas is given a historical rather than a liturgical setting. Yet even here the scene is carefully placed on a Sunday, when the disciples of Jesus are gathered together. Moreover, it is a very plausible suggestion that the words in which Thomas confesses Jesus, "My Lord and my God," represent a confessional formula known in the church of the evangelist's time.[288] In this case it is not unlikely that the confession was a baptismal or liturgical formula along the lines of "Jesus is Lord."

This theory of the liturgical origins of the usage of the title "God" for Jesus in NT times has some very important implications concerning the meaning of this title, and, indeed, goes a long way toward answering some of the objections against calling Jesus God that were mentioned at the beginning of the APPENDIX. For instance, it was objected that calling Jesus God neglects the limits of the incarnation. But this objection is not applicable to the NT usage, for there the title "God" is not directly given to the Jesus of the ministry. In the Johannine writings it is the preexistent Word (John 1:1) or the Son in the Father's presence (1:18) or the resurrected Jesus (20:28) who is hailed as God. The doxologies confess as God the triumphant Jesus; Heb 1:8–9 is directed to Jesus whose throne is forever. Thus, in the NT there is no obvious conflict between the passages that call Jesus God and the passages that seem to picture the incarnate Jesus as less than God or the Father.[289] The problem of how during his lifetime Jesus could be both God and man is presented in the NT, not by the use of the title "God," but by some of the later strata of Gospel material that bring Jesus' divinity to the fore even before the resurrection.[290] Ignatius of Antioch does use the title "God" of Jesus during his human career. This may be the inevitable devel-

---

[288] Barrett, *John* 573, concurs on the liturgical coloring of the passage under discussion.

[289] See the passages cited under ##1 and 5 above. The only passage that really offers a difficulty in this connection is I Cor 15:24, for here Paul speaks of the triumphant Christ as subject to the Father. This text needs more study in the light of Nicene christology.

[290] For instance, the infancy narratives, which show the child of Bethlehem to have been conceived by no human father; and the Fourth Gospel, in which the Jesus of the ministry makes patently divine claims. See the discussion of ministry christology in Chapter 8 above.

opment (doctrinally logical and justifiable) of the NT usage of calling the preincarnational and the resurrected Jesus God; but from the evidence we have, it is a postNT development.

The liturgical ambiance of the NT usage of "God" for Jesus also answers the objection that this title is too much of a metaphysical definition that objectifies Jesus and is untrue to the soteriological interest of the NT. As far as I can see, none of the eight instances we have discussed attempts to define Jesus metaphysically.[291] The acclamation of Jesus as God is a response of prayer and worship to the God revealed in Jesus. John 1:18, in speaking of the Son as God, says that he has revealed the Father; John 1:1 tells us that God's Word is God. The confession of Jesus as God is a recognition by believing subjects of the sovereignty and lordship of divine rule in, through, and by Jesus, e.g.: Thomas' "My Lord and my God" (John 20:28); and Romans' "God who is over all" (9:5); and Hebrews' "Your throne, O God, is for ever and ever" (1:8). How could the confession of Jesus as God be more soteriological than when Jesus is called "our God-and-Savior" (II Pet 1:1; Titus 2:13)? If there is validity in Bultmann's concern that belief in Jesus must have reference "for me," then he can have no objection to what I John 5:20 says of Jesus Christ: "This is the true God and eternal life."

Thus, even though we have seen that there is a solid biblical precedent for calling Jesus God, we must be cautious to evaluate this usage in terms of the NT ambiance. Firm adherence to the later theological and ontological developments that led to the confession of Jesus Christ as "true God of true God" must not cause believers to overvalue or undervalue the less developed NT confession.

---

[291] Even in John 1:1 the approach is largely functional. There are no speculations about how the Word is related to God the Father; and the very designation "the Word" implies the function of speaking to an audience. The fact that 1:1 is set "in the beginning" relates the Word to creation. Nevertheless, it is true to say that passages like John 1:1 would be destined soon and inevitably to raise questions of more than a functional nature. See APPENDIX IV A, under Käsemann.

APPENDIX IV.
FEATURES IN THE CHRISTOLOGY OF THE GOSPEL ACCORDING TO JOHN

One way of studying NT christology is to concentrate on the christology of each writer. In such an approach the christologies of the Pauline and of the Johannine writings often receive the greatest attention because the issues of "high" christology come to the fore there.[292] In this book I have not chosen to adopt that approach; and the present APPENDIX is only a partial exception to the policy, for it is not an overall description of Johannine christology. The reason for the partial exception is that most Christians, even if unconsciously, have had their views of Christ massively shaped by John; often they assume John's high christology to be that of the whole NT. In my judgment the uniqueness of John among the Gospels does not receive sufficient attention either in preaching or religious education.[293] On the other hand scholars are very aware of Johannine uniqueness and peculiarities, even if they do not agree on the underlying reasons. Accordingly the APPENDIX has two goals: (A) to introduce readers to some specific scholarly approaches to Johannine christology; (B) to explain the possible origins of what is peculiar to John among the Gospel christologies. This emphasis on Johannine uniqueness, however, needs to be cautiously phrased lest John appear a maverick in the NT, as has sometimes occurred in modern theories about its christology.

---

[292] There are articles on Pauline Theology and Johannine Theology in the NJBC, and in each christology is a major concern (respectively 82, §§24–80; 83, §§24–54). See also R. Scroggs, *Christology in Paul and John* (Philadelphia: Fortress, 1988).

[293] I called attention to some of the peculiarities in Chapters 8 and 9 above, but that treatment does not focus enough attention on the specificity of Johannine christology.

(A) Some Approaches to Johannine Christology in Contemporary Writing

Here I must be extremely selective, but I think it would help readers if I presented briefly the very different approaches to Johannine christology represented by R. Bultmann, O. Cullmann, E. Käsemann,[294] and F. Dreyfus.

R. BULTMANN. As in many other NT discussions of the 20th century, it is Bultmann who by the consistency of his existential approach has brought the problem of the Johannine understanding of Jesus into clear perspective. Bultmann acknowledges that John describes Jesus as the pre-existent Son of God who has appeared as man, but he thinks that such a mythological notion is not to be taken literally. "Jesus is not presented in literal seriousness as a pre-existent divine being who came in human form to reveal unprecedented secrets."[295] Rather, according to Bultmann, John uses preexistence to stress that Jesus' words did not arise from human experience but came from beyond. In John there is no christological instruction nor any teaching about the metaphysical quality of Jesus' person—what is important is that Jesus brings the words of God. The Johannine Jesus reveals nothing but that he is the Revealer; and even that must be understood in existential terms: It is he who in his own person brings that for which human beings yearn. Thus, by faith in Jesus, Christians receive the affirmation and fulfillment of their longing for life; yet they come to know nothing of Jesus other than the fact that Jesus makes salvation from God possible: only the *Dass* ("that"), not the *Was* ("what").

Such demythologizing of the Johannine picture of Jesus has encountered opposition. We can well understand this if we remember that Bultmann is not claiming that he himself has demythologized the Johannine Jesus but that this was the evangelist's idea! Although below I shall give two opposing views that supply necessary correctives, I wish to emphasize that in the starkness of his position Bultmann has captured one aspect of the Johannine Gospel, namely, the decision to which John calls the believer. The Johannine portrait of Jesus depicts more about Jesus himself than Bultmann can see, but it truly does depict Jesus as the fulfillment of human

---

[294] For my discussion of these three men I reuse with major adaptation material from my article "The Kerygma of the Gospel According to John," *Interpretation* 21 (1967), 387–400, esp. 392–98. M. Meye, *The Humanity of Jesus in the Fourth Gospel* (Philadelphia: Fortress, 1988), compares Bultmann and Käsemann and weaves her own way between the two.

[295] *Theology of the New Testament* (New York: Scribners, 1955), 2.33–69, specifically 2.62.

desire to whom people cannot remain indifferent. (Thus in the light of an issue discussed in Chapter 10 above, it remains highly functional.) Because Jesus is the light, people must either open their eyes and see or turn away into darkness (John 3:19–21). Thus Bultmann has offered a healthy corrective to purely mystical and speculative approaches to the Johannine Jesus.

Yet while doing justice to the challenge in the Johannine discourses and to the element of decision demanded by the words of Jesus, Bultmann does not do justice to the theological implications of the context in which John has set these words.[296] In an overall outline of the Gospel John 1–4 presents Jesus as the new Tabernacle and the new Temple, as the one who replaces the waters of Jewish purifications and the locus of Jewish worship. Systematically John 5–10 has Jesus acting on the occasion of great Jewish feasts and replacing the significance of themes that were prominent in these feasts.[297] All this is meant to tell the reader something about Jesus himself in relation to Israel: He embodies all the salvific significance that those OT institutions and feasts once conveyed. Moreover, if one reads between the lines of John, one learns much about the way Jesus was understood by members of the Johannine community, much to the discomfort of the Jewish synagogue with which they were in contact. (One of Bultmann's weaknesses is his translation of opposition to "the Jews" largely as opposition to the world, thus divorcing John from the historical context in which it was written.) "The Jews" in rejecting a Jesus who makes himself equal to God are not simply rejecting a Revealer without a revelation. They are rejecting a figure who has been given the highest christological evaluation by the Johannine Christians.

O. CULLMANN has insisted most strenuously on this broader aspect of the Johannine picture of Jesus.[298] He agrees with Bultmann that John situ-

---

[296] Bultmann's source theory of the composition of John has profoundly influenced his understanding of Johannine theology. Precisely because he thinks the speeches of Jesus come from a source consisting of discourses, while the actions (miracles) come from another source consisting of "signs," and the narrative framework comes from the evangelist, he does not give sufficient emphasis to the way in which the various parts modify each other in the existing Gospel. His picture of the Revealer without revelation is the distillate of the thought of his hypothetical discourse source, but is it faithful to the thought of the whole Gospel? It is interesting that Cullmann centers his opposition to Bultmann's interpretation precisely on the fact that John has written in the format of a Gospel account of Jesus' life.

[297] For details on this, see BGJ 1.CXLIV, 201–4, 206. Or in simpler form see my small book *The Gospel and Epistles of John* (Collegeville: Liturgical Press, 1988), 15–16.

[298] *Salvation in History* (New York: Harper & Row, 1967), esp. 268–91.

ates the Christian before Jesus in a position of decision but stresses that the decision is founded on and related to salvation history. By the fact that he has written in the format of a Gospel that professes to recall the historical life of Jesus, the evangelist makes the career of Jesus the center of God's salvific process.[299] According to Cullmann's interpretation of John's thought, in accepting Jesus one accepts both the before and the after of the salvific process, that is, what God has done in Israel and what God has done in the church. John's picturing Jesus as preexistent is not simply a mythological way of describing the origin of his teaching. It is a necessary part of the portrait, for if Jesus unifies salvation history, he must have existed from its beginning. Nor is the Johannine interest in a futuristic eschatology (which Bultmann denies) accidental; for if Jesus unifies salvation history, then through the Paraclete he must be at work in the era of the church that followed his career.

Cullmann does justice to elements in the Fourth Gospel that Bultmann's existential approach neglects; nevertheless, one may wonder whether the picture Cullmann paints of the Johannine Jesus as "the center of time" is not more Lucan than Johannine. John does present Jesus as related to Israel and to the subsequent Christian life, but he reinterprets this relationship in both directions. *In reference to the past*, the institutions of Israel are not so much fulfilled as they are replaced. John would not deny that these institutions had significance before Jesus came, but only Jesus is from above.[300] Abraham, Moses, and Isaiah were important, not primarily because they advanced God's plan of salvation in their own times, but because they saw Jesus and spoke of him (John 5:46; 8:56; 12:41). A sense of the continuity of OT history leading to Jesus is not prominent in John. *In reference to the future*, the uniqueness of Jesus and the importance of the individual's relation to him dominate in John over any emphasis on continuity from Jesus to the church. The Paraclete is the most important bond of union between Jesus and later Christians. By describing the origins and

---

[299] Even though he has thoroughly reinterpreted the tradition of the words and deeds of Jesus' public ministry, the evangelist would insist that in and through that reinterpretation Jesus continues to speak. The Fourth Gospel is an example of the Paraclete taking what he has received from Jesus and proclaiming it anew; the Paraclete adds nothing of his own (16:13–15). Thus the Johannine portrait of Jesus is self-consciously presented as faithful to Jesus as he was.

[300] We find the statement "Salvation is from the Jews" (4:22); also 1:16–17 can be taken to mean that there was grace (*charis*) in the Law given to Moses even if this has been replaced by the fullness of grace in Jesus Christ. Yet in Johannine terminology the things of the OT were not "real, true" (*alēthinos*). The manna was not the real bread from heaven (6:32); Israel was not the real vine of the Father (15:1).

work of the Paraclete in the same language used to describe the origins and work of Jesus, the evangelist makes it clear that under this peculiar title he is thinking of the Spirit in a special way, namely, as the invisible presence of Jesus in the period when Jesus has returned to his Father. In and through the Paraclete (14:15,16,21) Jesus has come back to those who love him and keep his commandments. Remaining within them (and thus not dying out with the apostolic generation), the Paraclete functions as the basic teacher of all Christians. The Paraclete's special function is to take what belongs to Jesus and to proclaim it anew in each generation (16:13–14). But this concentration on the internal presence of the Paraclete to each believer means that in Johannine thought the Paraclete is not really an ecclesiastical figure. Thus John's approach to the Holy Spirit under the title of the Paraclete is quite different from Luke's more ecclesiastical portrayal of the Spirit in Acts.

Cullmann insists that salvation history implies discontinuity as well as continuity. Perhaps, if sufficient emphasis is placed on discontinuity, one could say that John presents Jesus in the context of salvation history. But personally I would wonder whether use of this terminology in reference to the Johannine view of Jesus brings out sufficiently the uniqueness of John's approach. There is, moreover, as we shall see immediately below, an element of Johannine christology that is not accounted for in terms of salvation history.

E. KÄSEMANN, while also reacting to Bultmann, is almost at the opposite extreme from Cullmann in highlighting the uniqueness of John, even to the point where it has little in common with other NT thought.[301] From a

---

[301] *The Testament of Jesus* (Philadelphia: Fortress, 1968). Käsemann's strength is his use of dialectic; by his sharp contrasts he makes scholars think. Yet his very method means that the resultant picture is often more sharply delineated than was true of the original situation. What Käsemann sometimes gives us is what a NT author should have thought if he had been perfectly logical and had followed his ideas to the conclusions toward which they were directed. I do not question either the novelty or the uniqueness of Johannine thought, but I do question whether it is a radical break with traditional Christian thought. Käsemann maintains that the Fourth Gospel came out of a naively docetist circle of Christian enthusiasm and that in bringing John into the canon the church did not recognize that she was preserving the voice of those enthusiasts whom she would later condemn as heretical. In my opinion, he reaches this judgment only by isolating certain tendencies in Johannine thought and by making John responsible for a development of these tendencies that did not demonstrably come until later. The tendencies that Käsemann sees in John are, for the most part, really there, e.g., a one-sided insistence on divinity leading to an insufficient presentation of Jesus' humanity (closer to monophysitism than to docetism, however). Yet considerable exaggeration and exclusivity were required before they would

study of the Last Discourse and the prayer of chapter 17 he maintains that John was proposing a real christology. In portraying Jesus as the preexistent, John has reinterpreted the historical career of Jesus to mean that God actually walked upon this earth. The faith that John demands of the Christian is not simply a commitment to Jesus but an incipient faith in certain aspects of Jesus' identity (*fides quae creditur*); it is a faith that involves an acceptance of the one basic christological dogma of the unity of Jesus with the Father. Käsemann's words (*Testament* 23) are like a gauntlet thrown down before the whole Bultmannian position:

> The mythology used in the Fourth Gospel, in distinction from the other New Testament writings, no longer merely has the purpose of proclaiming the world-wide and salvation-history dimension of the christological event. The Johannine mythology is at the same time an expression of the beginning of dogmatic reflection in the strictest possible sense and thus opens the door for patristic christology. The problem of the nature of Christ is discussed thematically in John, to be sure still within the frame of his soteriology, but now with an emphasis and a force which can no longer be explained on the basis of a purely soteriological interest. The internal divine relationship of the Revealer as the Son is just as strong as his relation to the world.

Although I might like to modify the absoluteness of Käsemann's affirmations, I believe that he is right in insisting that Johannine faith has a "dogmatic" content and that John was very much interested not only in the *Dass* ("that") but also in the *Was* ("what"). How can Bultmann's contention that John is not really interested in who Jesus is do justice to 20:31 which insists explicitly that people must believe in who Jesus is (the Messiah, the Son of God) so that they "*may have life in his name*"?[302] The inclusion of the italicized clause shows that John's outlook on the question of Jesus' identity is not purely ontological; nevertheless John insists that

---

become heretical. In BCBD 145–64 I contend that this came with the group that broke away from the Johannine community as described in I John 2:18–19.

[302] I John is not distorting John when it continues the demand for christological content in faith; however the content is now oriented against misinterpretations of John by those who seceded from the community, in part because they do not sufficiently appreciate the humanity of Jesus, e.g., "Every spirit that acknowledges Jesus come in the flesh belongs to God" (I John 4:2; also 5:6).

faith, in order to be saving faith, must involve the affirmation that Jesus is the Son of God (because otherwise he cannot give God's life).

Käsemann is also right in insisting that John does not simply portray Jesus in the context of salvation history. That an element of Johannine faith touches on the relation of Jesus to salvation history is implied in the demand for belief in Jesus as the Messiah, who, after all, is descended from David. But the Johannine portrait of Jesus as the Son of God moves out of the realm of history and has incipiently ontological implications about the inner life of God: "I have life because of the Father" (John 6:57).

While one cannot reconcile Bultmann, Cullmann, and Käsemann in their views of the Johannine portrait of Jesus, each scholar has brought out important elements in that portrait. None of their three positions is totally satisfactory; but by using one to tone down the other, we can come to a rather good appreciation of the Jesus that John presents to his readers for their belief. If we return to the Gospel's own statement of its purpose in 20: 31, we find (admittedly by way of oversimplification) that Cullmann does the most justice to John's demand for belief in Jesus as the Messiah. Käse- mann does the most justice to John's demand for belief in Jesus as the Son of God. Bultmann does the most justice to the quality of the Johannine Jesus that calls forth a decision, "that believing you may have life in his name."

F. DREYFUS presents a view of Johannine christology that is totally the opposite of the three described above in the sense that he would remove virtually all distance between Jesus as he was in the ministry and the Jesus presented in John. In itself his book[303] is not significant and has caused little discussion among Johannine scholars. Yet it is worthy of at least a brief comment in this introduction to NT christology because it represents a scholar's attempt to defend the very assumption with which most beginners approach the Gospels. My overall judgment is that Dreyfus laudably wants to protect John from a minimalist approach, but sees literalism as the only way to do this. Consequently I shall present his views and with each suggest a more subtle way of preserving the truth that he affirms.

Dreyfus spends a chapter seeking to show that "The author of the

---

[303] *Jésus savait-il qu'il était Dieu?* (2d ed.; Paris: Cerf, 1984); English translation: *Did Jesus Know He Was God?* (Chicago: Franciscan Herald, 1988). My page refer- ences are to the French, and my translations are made from that edition. For a de- tailed discussion see my review article "Did Jesus Know He Was God?" *Biblical Theology Bulletin* 15 (#2, April 1985), 74–79. There are also perceptive critical re- views in French by M.-É. Boismard, *Revue Biblique* 91 (1984), 591–601; and G. Rochais, *Studies in Religion* 14 (1985), 85–106. Despite the simplicity (almost na- iveté) of his approach, Dreyfus cannot be classified as a fundamentalist; and, unlike

Fourth Gospel was convinced that the portrait he traced of Jesus of Nazareth both in act and in word substantially conformed to the historical reality: Jesus was God and he knew it" (p. 21). A distinction would help. Certainly the evangelist was convinced that the portrait conformed to historical reality. But how is that conformity expressed in John? Is it a conformity of substantially exact words, or a conformity of correct insight? While I agree with Dreyfus that not only was Jesus God but also that he knew his identity, I disagree with the suggestion that Jesus would have phrased it almost exactly as John phrased it. That does not take into account the limitation of the theological language available to an early-1st-century Jew, nor the development in clarity of expression gained by the Johannine community in its struggles to defend Jesus' divinity against synagogue rejection. In part what motivates Dreyfus, a Dominican priest, is revealed in a final chapter of Part One of his book where he argues that the Roman Catholic Church has consistently taught, even against opposition, that Jesus knew he was God. Again he needs to make a distinction: Church teaching that Jesus knew his divine identity does not necessarily include a teaching that he would have been able to phrase this identity.

Dreyfus asks would Jesus agree with the Gospel of John if he read it. My first reaction to that way of positing the issue would be a question that Dreyfus apparently never asked himself. Since there is no evidence that Jesus had a reading knowledge of Greek, how could he have read the Gospel of John and understood it? Whoever would regard that as a foolish question is not taking the humanity of Jesus seriously. I do not find anything in the NT that would lead me to suspect that Jesus had a knowledge of languages that he was not taught in the same way that the rest of us are taught languages.[304]

If we go beyond the (immense) barrier of the Greek language and turn to content, Dreyfus (*Jésus* 7) appeals to "Father, in your presence glorify me with the glory that I had with you before the world began." He is convinced that modern critical scholars do not think that this statement of the Johannine Jesus in 17:5 solves the issue of Jesus' knowing that he was God

other French revisionists, he is refreshingly nonpolemic in treating the majority of Johannine scholarship.

[304] Because I believe that the Holy Spirit guided the scriptural authors in their interpretation of Jesus as the Christ, I would not object to the thesis that if Jesus reappeared about the year 100 and were taught Greek and could have read John, he would have found in that Gospel a suitable (but not an adequate) expression of his own identity. But I would add that in the course of the reading he would be learning terminology and specification that went beyond what was available to him in his lifetime. See Chapter 4 above on issues of Jesus' knowledge.

because they do not believe he was God (but only a prophet) and because they dismiss 17:5 as John's theological creation that does not embody a correct historical evaluation. I cannot answer for others, but Dreyfus's reasoning would not cover me. I believe that Jesus was/is God and that 17:5 embodies a correct evaluation, but I do not think that belief solves the question of how Jesus could express what he knew. If Dreyfus had looked at the context of 17:5, he might have been warned that the phraseology has gone beyond what Jesus would have said. In 17:3 we hear "This is eternal life, that they know you the one true God and him whom you sent, Jesus Christ." Surely Jesus never spoke of himself in the third person as "Jesus Christ"! On p. 12 Dreyfus argues that John's Gospel is best understood as involving a progressive discovery of the true dimensions of the historical person Jesus of Nazareth. I agree but would add that John develops a language for expressing the discovery which often goes beyond the phrasing of Jesus.

On p. 14 Dreyfus states what will be the conclusion of the book: "There is no serious reason to refuse to the historical Jesus the knowledge of the mystery of his own being: Son of God preexistent in glory from all eternity, true God and true man." I can agree with Dreyfus about what precedes the colon; my qualifications concern what follows the colon. There is insufficient historical evidence that Jesus was able to *express* the mystery of his own being *in such terms* as preexistence, Son of God from all eternity, true God and true man, even though these terms are valid Christian insights into the mystery. In other words Dreyfus is removing John's Gospel from the historical context of the 1st century. If one wants to study how Jesus expressed himself, one needs to look at the christology of the other Gospels and the earliest evidence from the nonGospel NT literature. If we do not find such expressions as "from all eternity" and "true God of true God" until much, much later in Christian history, how can we think Jesus articulated his identity thus? They are obviously Christian specifications, but, I would insist, specifications of a reality that was already there. Or, even more pointedly, if we do not find Johannine christological articulation in the other NT witnesses to Jesus, what right have we to claim that Jesus spoke thus? The Johannine Epistles show us much the same articulation as the Johannine Gospel without any claim that it came from Jesus. Why then should we not think that Johannine christology involves specification and interpretation that goes beyond Jesus? None of that suggests falsehood, misunderstanding, or creation from nothing on the part of the evangelist. Rather it does justice to a fundamental principle without which discussions of christology become hopelessly muddled: The language of religious belief developed between the time of Jesus and the writing of the NT.

(B) Possible Factors in the Development of Johannine Christology

There are probably many factors that led to the development of a peculiarly Johannine manner of phrasing Jesus' identity; but I would like to concentrate on factors relevant to the most significant difference between John and the Synoptics, namely that the Johannine Jesus is clearly conscious of having preexisted with God before the world began (17:5) and of having come into this world from that world of previous existence in order to say and do what he heard and saw when he was with God. Although the Synoptic Jesus can speak of having been sent, there is no clear indication that this involves preexistence—the sending is comparable to the sending or commission of a prophet (see Matt 10:40–41).[305] The notion of preexistence is apparent in different forms in other NT works (Chapter 9 above); but John alone in the NT brings this into the heart of a Gospel account of Jesus' public life, inviting readers to see in a visible, human figure functioning in this world, the stranger from above who is not of this world. Let us discuss two particular factors that may have influenced such a development in Johannine christology.[306]

INCARNATE WISDOM

From the time of the monarchy two representative figures played a major role in guiding Israel: the prophet and the wise man. They differed in many ways almost to the point of opposition. Prophets, addressing themselves to priests, kings, nobles, and even the people at large, dealt with major religious issues facing the nation: issues of justice, peace, divine worship, fidelity to the covenant. Often prophets claimed to have shared in a vision of the heavenly court from which experience they could speak God's word about the issue addressed. The advice given by prophets was frequently opposed to human calculation. For instance, when Judah or Israel was threatened by a neighboring world power, instead of counseling compromise, the

---

[305] To explain the authority with which the Synoptic Jesus speaks, it is never suggested in those Gospels that during his life on earth Jesus received revelation from God, but neither is it made clear (as it is in John) that his revelation came from a previous existence in which he was with God. One need not jump from that *fact* to conclude that the Synoptic evangelists would have denied such a previous existence; they may never even have thought of the issue.

[306] In addition to what I shall mention, one might theorize that the Johannine Christians learned this from other Christians e.g., that they were familiar with the thought of Hebrews or that of the hymns in the Pauline Epistles. A relationship between Hebrews and John is a serious possibility (BGJ 1.cxxvi).

prophet might urge the king to trust in God for protection, e.g., Isa 7:1–9. The overwhelming power of the enemy in terms of horses and chariots would be held up to ridicule by the prophet who characterized such human force as insignificant compared to the power of God. Professional OT men of wisdom did not claim to speak for God, even though they might praise fear of the Lord. Normally they were cast as old men who had been success-ful in life and who were passing on to their children their accumulated ex-perience—what had made it possible for them to succeed. During the mon-archy wise men functioned at court, advising the king.[307] Frequently their political advice would have been contrary to that of the prophets. For in-stance they would have been specialists in diplomacy, making human cal-culations about superior force and the prudence of making concessions rather than resisting. In the postmonarchical OT period (after 539 BC but more particularly after 400 BC) the prophets played a lesser role; indeed it became almost axiomatic that there were no longer prophets in the land. Men of wisdom did continue, and most OT wisdom literature stems from the postexilic period.[308] The concern was now no longer with what made the writer successful at court or in diplomacy, but what made him successful, admired, and happy in business and family relationships. Thus the wisdom writings offer us examples of practical, everyday morality and good behavior among the Jews in the centuries just before Jesus' time. Often the advice is phrased in figurative language (proverbs, similes, metaphors).

Jesus was remembered as being both prophet and wise man. In the Synoptics and in John there are echoes of Elijah and Elisha in his miracles. According to Mark 8:28 some were saying that he was Elijah or one of the prophets (Matt 16:14 adds Jeremiah); in John 6:14 he was identified by the crowd as "the prophet who is to come into the world."[309] But Jesus was also portrayed against the background of the OT wisdom literature. The first three Gospels show him always speaking in parables (Mark 4:33–34). Say-ings, similes, parables, and proverbs mark the wisdom collection of the OT

---

[307] We have evidence of wise men and wisdom literature at the Egyptian court long before the Israelite monarchy developed under David and Solomon, and early Israelite wisdom may have been derived from Egyptian wisdom, even as many fea-tures of the Israelite court were patterned on the court of the pharaoh.

[308] The OT canon used by Roman Catholics is larger than the OT canon used by most Protestants, and most of the additional books in the Catholic canon (the deuterocanonical books) are of late origin. A large proportion of them (Sirach, Wis-dom, Baruch) are wisdom literature.

[309] A. Yarbro Collins, "Jesus the Prophet," *Biblical Research* 36 (1991), 30–34, argues for the category of "popular prophet" as the most adequate *historical* descrip-tion of Jesus.

(Proverbs, Sirach, and Wisdom in particular).[310] The figurative language taken from nature that the Synoptic Jesus used (sheep and shepherds, sowing seed, lilies of the field, birds of the air, etc.) is very close in genre to the symbolism employed by the OT wise men (Prov 25:13–14; 26:2–3; 30:24–31). At times, on the principle that God would provide, Jesus showed a prophetic disdain for worldly calculations (Matt 6:32). In other sayings attributed to him, however, he exhibited the caution of an OT man of wisdom, e.g., in the advice not to start building a house unless one has the money to finish it, and not to enter a war unless one has more military strength than one's opponents (Luke 14:28–32).

Only in a minor way does John exhibit this aspect of the wisdom tradition; for, with the exception of the allegories of the good shepherd (chap. 10) and the vine (chap. 15), the Johannine Jesus does not speak in parables taken from nature. But there is a major echo of another aspect of the wisdom tradition. A custom already visible in Prov 1:20–33; 8:1–9:6 (perhaps pre-exilic) but much more common in the later OT wisdom books is the personification of divine wisdom as a female figure, sometimes called Lady Wisdom.[311] This personification is poetic, for Wisdom is not a real person. Nevertheless, her origins and career are described as if she were a real person—in much the same language as the origins and career of the Johannine Jesus,[312] the Word made flesh. Although Wisdom is never called the word of God (the Greek for "word" [*logos*] is masculine), she came forth from the mouth of the Most High (Sir 24:3);[313] and Wis 9:1–2 puts God's word and

---

[310] Thus besides being a prophet, Jesus is very much a teacher. See P. Perkins, *Jesus as Teacher* (New York: Cambridge, 1990).

[311] Both the Hebrew (*ḥokmâ*) and Greek (*sophia*) words for "wisdom" are feminine. Personification of Wisdom may be found in Sir 1:1–18; 4:11–19; 6:18–31; 14:20–15:10; 24:1–31; 51:13–30; Wis 7–9; Baruch 3:9–38. Job 28 praises wisdom but without clear personification.

[312] For an overall treatment, see M. E. Willett, *Wisdom Christology in the Fourth Gospel* (San Francisco: Mellen, 1992). When she speaks, Wisdom expresses herself in poetry. This is understandable since she is of God; and in the OT God usually speaks in poetry, not in prose. The Johannine Jesus, unlike the Synoptic Jesus (with rare exception), tends to speak quasi-poetically in rhythmic lines of approximately the same length, each constituting a clause, so that a number of modern commentators and translators (Bultmann, *New American Bible*, *Bible of Jerusalem*, myself) set up the speeches of Jesus in John in poetic format (see BGJ 1.cxxxii–cxxxv). This may reflect the influence of the wisdom literature on John or more simply that, like Wisdom, the Johannine Jesus is of God and speaks like God even as to format.

[313] I shall follow the versification of Sirach used in the *New American Bible*. That of the Revised Standard Version differs.

God's Wisdom in parallelism. Prov 8:22–23 [Septuagint] has Wisdom say, "The Lord created me at the beginning . . . before the earth was made," just as John's Word was "in the beginning" (1:1) and John's Jesus speaks of his existence "before the world came to be" (17:5). Sir 1:1 affirms that Wisdom comes from the Lord and remains with (*meta*) him, just as the Prologue of John states that the Word who was with (*pros*) God (1:1) is ever at the Father's side (1:18). If like Prov 8:22, Sir 24:9 speaks of the creation of Wisdom, the more Hellenistically patterned Wis 7:25–26 describes Wisdom as an aura of the might of God, a pure effusion of the glory of the Almighty (compare John 1:14), the effulgence of eternal light. For I John 1:5 God is light, and for John 8:12; 9:5 Jesus has come into the world as the light of the world. Wis 7:22 applies the adjective *monogenēs* to Wisdom in the sense of "unique," and John refers to Jesus as *monogenēs*.[314]

Wisdom was active in creation:[315] She was present when God made the world (Wis 9:9) as "the artificer of all" (7:22), aiding God in creation, crafting things (Prov 8:27–30). In John's Prologue we hear that through the Word "all things came into being, and apart from him not a thing came to be." In Prov 8:35 Wisdom says, "The person who finds me finds life"; Baruch 4:1 promises that all who cling to Wisdom will live. Of the Johannine Word it is said: "That which came to be in him was life and this life was the light of human beings" (1:4), and Jesus says, "I came that they may have life and have it to the full" (10:10).

Wis 9:10 records Solomon's prayer that Wisdom be sent down from heaven to be with him and work with him. Prov 8:31 says that Wisdom was delighted to be with human beings. Solomon (Wis 9:17) expresses wonder, asking God, "Who ever knew your counsel, except you had given Wisdom and sent your holy spirit from on high?" John 3:13 says of Jesus, "No one has gone up into heaven, except the one who came down from heaven—the Son of Man." There were foolish people who rejected Wisdom (Sir 15:7); the apocryphal *I Enoch* 42:2 says plaintively, "Wisdom came to make her dwelling place among the human beings and found no dwelling place"; and Baruch 3:12 is addressed to Israel: "You have rejected the fountain of wisdom." The Prologue reports of the Johannine Word: "To his own he came; yet his own people did not accept him." Sir 24:8ff. says that Wisdom set up her tent/tabernacle in Jacob (Israel); John 1:14 says that Word dwelt or set

---

[314] John 1:18; 3:16,18; I John 4:9. For a discussion of this word, see p. 178 above.

[315] A picture that may be of some service is that, in continuance with the female imagery, Wisdom is almost like a little girl helping God in making a new toy world, and eventually, as we shall see, she wants to live in the doll's house with her toys.

up his tent/tabernacle among us.[316] In particular Wisdom fixed her abode in Zion or Jerusalem, "the chosen city" (Sir 24:10–11).[317] Much more than in the Synoptics the public career of Jesus in John was largely in Jerusalem.

The role of Wisdom among human beings is to teach them the heavenly things that otherwise are too high to be known (Job 11:6–7; Wis 9:16–18), to utter truth (Prov 8:7; Wis 6:22), to give instructions as to what pleases God and the divine will (Wis 8:4; 9:9–10), and thus to lead people to life (Prov 4:13; 8:32–35; Sir 4:12; Baruch 4:1) and immortality (Wis 6:18–19). This is precisely the function of Jesus as revealer in numerous passages in John. Wisdom is not satisfied simply to offer her gifts to those who come; she roams the streets seeking people and crying out to them (Prov 1:20–21; 8:1–4; Wis 6:16). So also we find the Johannine Jesus walking along, encountering those who will follow him (1:36–38,43), searching out people (5:14; 9:35), and crying out his invitation in public places (7:28,37; 12:44). Wisdom's offering is rejected by many, causing her to warn of their destruction (Prov 1:24–32; Bar 3:10–13). Similarly to their own loss many turn away from Jesus the light and source of eternal life (John 3:18,19,36); they do not believe when he speaks the truth (8:46; 10:25). Thus the coming of Wisdom produces a division: Some seek and find (Prov 8:17; Sir 6:27–28; Wis 6:12); if they change their minds, they will seek and not find (Prov 1:28). The same "seek/find" language is used by John to describe the effect he produces (7:34; 8:21; 13:33).

Wisdom instructs those who become her children (Prov 8:32–33; Sir 4:11; 6:18). Similarly the Johannine Jesus calls his followers "little children" (13:33). In her instructions, Wisdom speaks in the first person in long discourses (Prov 8:3–36; Sir 24), sometimes comparing herself to life-giving elements in nature (vine, stream of water: Sir 24:17,28). Characteristic, too, of the discourses of the Johannine Jesus is the "I am" pattern, sometimes with a predicate like the vine (15:1,5); from within him flow rivers of living water (7:38). The instruction that Wisdom offers can be symbolized as food and drink: "Come eat of my food and drink of the wine I have mixed" (Prov 9:5); "Come to me all you who yearn for me and be filled with my fruits. . . . The one who eats of me will hunger still; the one who drinks of me will thirst for more" (Sir 24:18,20). John's Jesus offers living water that springs up to eternal life so that whoever drinks of it will never thirst (4:14); "I am

---

[316] The Greek *skēnoun*, "to dwell," is related to *skēnē*, "tent"; and the tabernacle was the tent of the presence of God during the desert wanderings.

[317] Increasingly Wisdom became identified with the Law (Sir 24:22–23; Baruch 4:1), and the tables of the Ten Commandments were supposed to be in the Ark of the Covenant in the Jerusalem Temple of Solomon.

the bread of life; no one who comes to me will ever be hungry, and no one who believes in me will ever again be thirsty" (6:35). Wisdom tests those who accept her and forms them (Sir 6:20–26) until they love her (Prov 8:17; Sir 4:12; Wis 6:17–18) and become friends of God. Likewise Jesus purifies and sanctifies his disciples with his word and truth (John 15:3; 17:17) and tests them (6:67) until he can call them his beloved friends (15:15; 16:27). The ultimate return of Wisdom to heaven (*I Enoch* 42:2) offers a parallel to Jesus' return to his Father.

Personified Wisdom language appears in the Synoptic tradition on a few occasions;[318] but there is nothing to match the massive number of echoes in John; and there can be little doubt that this background supplied a major element in the vocabulary and imagery for the Johannine presentation of Jesus as a preexistent who came into this world from another, heavenly realm where he had been with the Father.

MOSES PARALLELISM

Nevertheless, we can scarcely explain the whole Johannine picture of the preincarnate Word/Jesus from the personified Wisdom picture. Jesus, after all, was a real person, while Wisdom was not. Another factor may have entered the picture. In the Synoptic Gospels, as can be seen from the trial of Jesus before the Jewish authorities, the highest confession of Jesus is "the Messiah, the Son of God" (also Matt 16:16). In Chapter 10 above I pointed out that the fundamental confession of Jesus as the Messiah, the anointed king of the House of David, had a tendency to favor an imagery of "becoming" in christological language because at a certain moment in one's life one is crowned and becomes king. John never dispenses with the Davidic Messiah image for Jesus (10:24–25; 20:31), but Moses imagery is much stronger in the Johannine descriptions of Jesus than is Davidic imagery.[319]

---

[318] The Q saying called "the Johannine logion" (Matt 11:25–27; Luke 10:21–22; discussed on p. 88 above) presents Jesus as a revealer, as the Son who enables people to know the Father. The saying that follows in Matt 11:28–30, wherein Jesus invites people to come to him to find rest, closely echoes the appeals of Wisdom in Sir 24:18–19 and 51:23–27.

[319] I think that the presence of Samaritans in the tree of Johannine community origins (4:39–42) may have catalyzed this development. Samaritans rejected the role of David and his kingdom, as well as worship at Jerusalem, his city. The central figure of their salvific history was Moses, and so Samaritans who came to believe in Jesus may have brought a greater emphasis on the parallelism between Moses and Jesus. Among the Gospels only Matt approaches John in this Moses factor. Implicitly Matt compares the Moses birth story (the wicked Pharaoh killing the male Hebrew chil-

In some of Jesus' dialogues a comparison between the actions and claims of Jesus and the actions and claims of Moses are very important.[320]

The key issue for our purposes is the source of Moses' authority. His importance does not stem from his *becoming* king, as in the instance of David, but in his having contact with God from whom he received his authority to command Israel. What he heard with God he transmitted by way of statutes and ordinances that make up the Law, and his design of the Tabernacle as a place of worship stemmed from what he was shown by God. In Num 16:28 Moses says, "The Lord has sent me to do all these works, and it has not been of myself." Similarly the authority that Jesus invokes is not from his having been made Messiah but from his contact with God. We hear in John 5:19: "Amen, amen, I say to you, the Son cannot do a thing by himself" (also 8:28); rather the Father has given him all the power he has, e.g., the power to raise the dead, pass judgment, and give life (5:21–27). The Son does only what he sees the Father doing (5:19), and he reports what he has seen in the Father's presence (8:38). "My teaching is not my own but comes from the One who sent me" (7:16); "I say only those things that the Father has taught me" (8:28); "I am someone who told you the truth I heard from God" (8:40). In almost the last public words he addresses to the Jewish crowds to whom he has spoken so many times, the Johannine Jesus says: "It was not on my own that I spoke. No, the Father who sent me has Himself commanded me what to say and how to speak" (10:49).

If we reflect on the pictures of Moses and Jesus, we have two revelatory figures, each claiming that contact with God is the source of his whole mission and authority, of all that he says and does. The Johannine Christians did not deal with this similarity by discounting Moses. Rather they proclaimed that Moses prepared for Jesus, so that rejection of Jesus was a rejection of Moses. "If you believed Moses, you would believe me, since it is about me that he wrote" (5:46). Eventually, however, their proclamation brought hostility on the part of those who thought they were being loyal to Moses, as we see from what the synagogue authorities say to a man who was coming to believe in Jesus: "You are that fellow's [= Jesus'] disciple; we are

---

dren) and the Jesus birth story (Herod killing the male children at Bethlehem), and *perhaps* imitates the five books of Moses (the Pentateuch) with five sermons of Jesus, carefully marked off in the Gospel. Many think that Matt's presentation of Jesus' Sermon on the Mount containing the Beatitudes is meant to remind readers of Moses on Mt. Sinai and the Ten Commandments. Yet Matt does not carry over the subtle Moses parallelism into the issue of christology as John does.

[320] 1:17; 3:14; 5:45–47; 6:31–32,49–50; 7:19,22–23; 9:28–29. The language of these dialogues reflects debates over belief in Jesus within the synagogue in the course of Johannine history.

disciples of Moses. We know that God has spoken to Moses, but we don't even know where this fellow comes from" (9:28–29). In part the hostility was produced by the Christian claim that Jesus brought something greater from God than Moses had brought: "For while the Law was a gift through Moses, this enduring love came through Jesus Christ" (1:17).[321] Moses may have given manna to the ancestors in the desert, but they died; Jesus has come to give a heavenly bread "that a person may eat it and never die" (6:50).

However, already in that claim we come to the deeper root of the problem, for Jesus *himself* is the true bread from heaven.[322] The basic issue is not what Jesus brought but who he is. This is apparent in two points of contrast between Jesus and Moses. First, the OT evidence is somewhat ambiguous on whether Moses saw God. Some passages are clear that he did not: In Exod 33:18–20 Moses asks to see God's glory, but the Lord says, "You cannot see my face and live." Other passages, however, can be read to imply that Moses did see God (Exod 24:9–11), and Deut 34:10 says that there never has been another prophet like Moses who knew God face to face. (Later rabbinic interpreters reconciled the traditions: The prophets saw God through many panes of glass, but Moses saw him through only one.) John's attitude is clear: "No one has ever seen God; it is the only (Son of) God, ever at the Father's side, who has revealed Him" (1:18); "Not that anyone has seen the Father— only the one who is from God has seen the Father" (6:46). Thus Jesus, because he is the only one to have seen God, has a greater intimacy with God than had Moses, and indeed an intimacy related to his origin ("from God"). The latter point is even more apparent in the second element of contrast between Jesus and Moses. Whatever Moses saw and heard in God's presence took place after he went up (the mountain) to encounter God; Jesus did not have to go up to meet God but was already there with God. "No one has gone up to heaven, except the one who came down from heaven, the Son

---

[321] This contrast is made all the sharper when we realize that the two great characteristics of the covenant made by God through Moses were *ḥesed* and *'ĕmet*: God's *gracious love or kindness* in choosing Israel who did not deserve to play the special role of being God's people; and God's *truthfulness or enduring fidelity* to the covenant even when Israel sinned. John's *charis* ("grace") and *alētheia* ("truth") in 1:17 are renderings respectively of *ḥesed* and *'ĕmet*, as I have tried to indicate by the translation "enduring love."

[322] The bite of the Johannine words is sharper than it first seems when we give full value to Jesus' claim in 6:32 to be the "true/real" (*alēthinos*) bread from heaven when compared with the bread that Moses gave. The connotation is "genuine," so that by contrast the OT manna was not real bread from heaven (see footnote 300 above).

of Man" (3:13). Here we have the point of contact between the reflection on the personified Wisdom figure who was with God before creation and came down to share her nourishment with human beings and the reflection on Moses who came down from the mountain as the authoritative teacher of what he heard and saw when he was with God. The divine Word is very much like Wisdom, existing with God in the beginning before the world was created and coming down into the world. Yet unlike Wisdom and like Moses, the Word become flesh in Jesus is a real human being authoritatively revealing and teaching what he heard and saw with God.

I set out in this subsection to explore two factors that might help to explain why the Johannine Jesus is portrayed as clearly conscious of having preexisted with God before the world began (17:5) and of having come into this world from that previous existence in order to say and do what he heard and saw when he was with God. As I conclude this APPENDIX, a few words on the impact of such a portrayal are in order. Traditional Christianity since the 4th century has affirmed the preexistence of the divine Son who became man as Jesus of Nazareth; and on several occasions in this book we have discussed the language of the Council of Nicaea, "There never was a time when he was not." Sometimes there is a tendency to think of the Johannine proclamation of preexistence as the earliest expression of the future dogma. For John, however, Jesus' previous existence with God is more than a creedal dogma; it is the linchpin in understanding the whole Christian life. Moses and the Prophets could tell us how to live; but only Jesus who is truly of God and comes down from being with God can give us God's life. A human child gets life from a father and mother and has the same kind of life they have. The divine Son has the same kind of life the heavenly Father has, and so Jesus not only brings a word to be believed but embodies a life to be shared. We may sum up Johannine christology in these words of Jesus (6:57):

> "Just as the Father who has life sent me,
>   and I have life because of the Father,
>   so the person who feeds on me
>   will have life because of me."

AN EVALUATIVE LIST
OF SELECT BOOKS
ON NEW TESTAMENT CHRISTOLOGY

As I stressed in the Foreword, this is an introductory book in which a long bibliography would be out of place. Nevertheless, it may help readers to know some of the classics or most famous books in the field. The list that follows is confined to works in English written in the twentieth century. Obviously the personal judgment of the author of this book is represented in the choice (although I have not necessarily chosen books I agree with), and other scholars and teachers may wish to supplement or substitute their choices for books in the list.

Bousset, W., *Kyrios Christos* (Nashville: Abingdon, 1970). Originally written in German in 1913, this work is seriously out of date in details of its attribution of titles to different phases of early Christianity. Nevertheless it is a classic of liberal christology; and its basic picture of a totally human Jesus who was divinized by early Christians remains a standard liberal approach.

Cullmann, O., *The Christology of the New Testament* (London: SCM, 1959). In the 1950s and early 1960s the Protestant scholars most widely read in "middle-of-the-road" English-speaking NT courses (including Roman Catholic circles) were probably Oscar Cullmann, C. H. Dodd, Joachim Jeremias, and Vincent Taylor. After that the trend turned toward a sharper, less conservative criticism. This book is a classical study of the titles of Christ supplying an optimistic evaluation of the antiquity of their use by Jesus and the early Christians.

de Jonge, M., *Christology in Context. The Earliest Christian Response to Jesus* (Philadelphia: Westminster, 1988); *Jesus, the Servant-Messiah* (New Haven: Yale, 1991): good studies of christology by a judicious scholar; the second is the simpler of the two.

Dunn, J.D.G., *Christology in the Making* (Philadelphia: Westminster, 1980). In a series of works, including *The Evidence for Jesus* (Philadelphia: Westminster, 1985) and sections of *Unity and Diversity in the New Testament* (2d ed.; Philadelphia: Trinity, 1990), James Dunn has made some truly important contributions to the study of Jesus and of NT christology. As readers make progress in the field, he is an author who absolutely must be read.

Evans, C.A., *Jesus* (Grand Rapids: Baker, 1991): a very useful, annotated bibliography of books and articles on Jesus.

Fitzmyer, J. A., *A Christological Catechism* (new ed.; New York: Paulist, 1991). This Jesuit scholar is almost unrivaled in his application of a knowledge of the Aramaic of NT times and the Dead Sea Scrolls to christological issues. This knowledge combined with very balanced judgment makes this little book of twenty-five questions and answers about Jesus invaluable. Useful too is his *Scripture and Christology: A Statement of the Biblical Commission with a Commentary* (New York: Paulist, 1986).

Fuller, R. H., *The Foundations of New Testament Christology* (New York: Scribners, 1965). In the 1960s detailed NT christology study began to move beyond the conservatism of Cullmann, Dodd, Jeremias, and Taylor. This movement can be seen in the 1963 German work of Ferdinand Hahn translated into English as *The Titles of Jesus in Christology* (London: Lutterworth, 1969). Reginald Fuller's book may be an easier entry into the complicated, detailed exegesis that undergirds the conclusions. In subsequent articles Fuller has continued to deepen his reflection on christology in debate with other writers, and a more recent work was done in cooperation with Pheme Perkins, *Who Is This Christ?* (Philadelphia: Fortress, 1983). An Episcopalian with deep ecumenical interests, Fuller is one of the most important figures in the field in the last third of the 20th century.

Jeremias, J., *New Testament Theology: The Proclamation of Jesus* (New York: Scribners, 1971). A lifetime of careful, detailed work on the language and historical circumstances of Jesus' times (including studies of Jerusalem, the parables, and the Last Supper) fed into Joachim Jeremias's view of Jesus. (For the importance of Jeremias, see above under Cullmann.) The results he reached were conservative and optimistic; subsequent studies would challenge some of his claims, but his writings are still a most interesting entree into the period of Jesus' lifetime.

Kasper, W., *Jesus the Christ* (New York: Paulist, 1976). Written by a German Roman Catholic systematic theologian, this is a concise blend of biblical exegesis, patristic christology, and modern philosophical approaches. It is a good example of how current biblical thought can be brought into the service of traditional theology. For a wide view of the approaches of different theologians to christology, see W. M. Thompson, *The Jesus Debate* (New York: Paulist, 1985); B. Hill, *Jesus the Christ: Contemporary Perspectives* (Mystic, CT: Twenty-Third, 1991); E. A. Johnson, *Considering Jesus: Waves of Renewal in Christology* (New York: Crossroad, 1990); J. Macquarrie, *Jesus Christ in Modern Thought* (Philadelphia: Trinity, 1990).

Meier, J. P., *A Marginal Jew* (New York: Doubleday, 1991-). Historical Jesus study is *not* the same as the study of NT christology; yet the validity of christology (the evaluation of Jesus) is necessarily related to the realities of Jesus' own life. When John Meier's work (at least three volumes) is finished it will be the best historical Jesus study produced in the twentieth century— a necessary antidote to the unwarrantedly speculative (and historically minimizing) character of the work of "The Jesus Seminar" (footnote 24 above) and of books like J. D. Crossan's *The Historical Jesus: The Life of a Mediterranean Jewish Peasant* (San Francisco: Harper Collins, 1991); *Jesus, A Revolutionary Biography* (San Francisco: Harper Collins, 1994); and B. Mack *The Lost Gospel. The Book of Q & Christian Origins* (San Francisco: Harper Collins, 1993). For an anticipation of Meier's results, see his article (78) on Jesus in NJBC.

Perrin, N., *Rediscovering the Teaching of Jesus* (New York: Harper & Row, 1967). A British scholar who studied in Germany and taught in Chicago, Norman Perrin was a major figure in christological study on the American scene. His views gradually became more radical, and some of the change is visible in *A Modern Pilgrimage in New Testament Christology* (Philadelphia: Fortress, 1974). Perhaps by the end of his life he had moved beyond *Rediscovering*, but in many ways it remains his best contribution.

Sanders, E. P., *Jesus and Judaism* (Philadelphia: Fortress, 1985). In a series of books, including *Jewish Law from Jesus to the Mishnah* (London: SCM, 1990) and *Judaism: Practice and Belief, 63 BCE – 66 CE* (Philadelphia: Trinity, 1992), Sanders has taken Jeremias's place as a major Christian guide to the Jewish mindset in Jesus' time. His view of Jesus has little of the supernatural, but he offers a healthy corrective to prejudiced contrasts between superior Christianity and inferior Judaism.

Schillebeeckx, E., *Jesus: An Experiment in Christology* (New York: Seabury, 1979); *Christ: The Experience of Jesus as Lord* (New York: Seabury, 1980). This prestigious Dutch Roman Catholic systematic theologian immersed himself in biblical studies for three years to produce these two large volumes totalling over 1600 pages. Unfortunately the end product is marred by his tilt toward very radical exegesis. The much shorter work of Kasper is a more solid effort.

Taylor, V., *The Names of Jesus* (London: Macmillan, 1954). This is a classic of the "titles" approach to christology by one of the most respected British scholars of the century (see under Cullmann above), famous for his commentary on Mark. The scope of his intelligently conservative approach can be seen when the book is added to his *The Life and Ministry of Jesus* (Nashville: Abingdon, 1955) and *The Person of Christ in New Testament Teaching* (London: Macmillan, 1959).

INDEXES

BIBLIOGRAPHICAL INDEX OF AUTHORS

TOPICAL INDEX

BIBLIOGRAPHICAL INDEX
OF AUTHORS

This is not an index of all the places where authors are mentioned or their views discussed; rather it lists the page on which readers can find bibliographical information about a book or article of an author who has been cited. Family names beginning in *de*, *di*, *du* and in *van*, *von* are listed under *d* and *v* respectively. Those beginning in *Mc* are treated as if the prefix were *Mac*.

TOPICAL INDEX

Some authors are listed here, not for bibliographical purposes (see preceding index), but because there is a discussion of their views.

BOOKS by RAYMOND E. BROWN

Paulist Press
New Testament Essays (out of print)
Priest and Bishop
The Virginal Conception and Bodily Resurrection of Jesus
Peter in the New Testament (coeditor) out of print
Biblical Reflections on Crises Facing the Church
Mary in the New Testament (coeditor)
The Community of the Beloved Disciple
The Critical Meaning of the Bible
Antioch and Rome (with J. P. Meier)
The Churches the Apostles Left Behind
Biblical Exegesis and Church Doctrine
Responses to 101 Questions on the Bible
An Introduction to New Testament Christology

Doubleday
* *THE GOSPEL ACCORDING TO JOHN* (2 vols.; Anchor Bible Commentary)
* *THE EPISTLES OF JOHN* (Anchor Bible Commentary)
* *THE BIRTH OF THE MESSIAH* (*New Updated Edition* 1993; Anchor Bible Reference Library)
* *THE DEATH OF THE MESSIAH* (2 vols.; 1994; Anchor Bible Reference Library)

The Liturgical Press (Collegeville, MN)
A Coming Christ in Advent (Matthew 1 and Luke 1)
An Adult Christ at Christmas (Matthew 2 and Luke 2)
A Crucified Christ in Holy Week (Passion Narratives)
A Risen Christ in Eastertime (Resurrection Narratives)
A Once-and-Coming Spirit at Pentecost (Acts and John)
The Gospels and Epistles of John—A Concise Commentary
Recent Discoveries and the Biblical World (A Michael Glazier Book)
* *The New Jerome Bible Handbook* (coeditor)

Prentice-Hall
* *THE NEW JEROME BIBLICAL COMMENTARY* (coeditor)

Books marked with an asterisk are hard back
Many of the above have been published in England
by Geoffrey Chapman